Essays on Indian Religion

History and Culture Series

ESSAYS ON INDIAN RELIGION

Edited by
Dr. Raj Kumar

2003

DISCOVERY PUBLISHING HOUSE
NEW DELHI-110002

First Published-2003
Reprint : 2012

ISBN 81-7141-693-4

Published by
DISCOVERY PUBLISHING HOUSE
4831/24, Ansari Road, Prahlad Street,
Darya Ganj, New Delhi-110002 (India)
Phone: 23279245 • Fax: 91-11-23253475
E-mail:dphtemp@indiatimes.com

Printed at: Dynamic Printers

Preface

Religion should unite and not divide the peoples of the world. There is no doubt that each religion has its own mission in the world, was suited to the nations to whom it was given, and to the type of civilization, it was to permeate, bringing it into line with the general evolution of the human family.

Unfortunately today religion has not only divided peoples and communities but has created blood baths and worst of problems. Our objective in collecting and presenting these essays to our reader is to provide them food for thought, so as to enable us to live in peace and harmony.

Raj Kumar

Acknowledgement

Religion is the name for man's total conscious attitude towards life as it is found and enlightened by rational awareness. In preparing these collection of essays I have incurred deep gratitude of prominent scholars on the subject especially Annie Besant, Radhakrishnan, G.C. Pande, Lalanji Gopal, A.L. Basham, R.K. Mookerjee, Ranganathananda and S.P. Gupta.

A number of universities, institutions, librarians and their staff members have been extremely co-operative. I am Thankful to them.

I have discussed the subject with my colleagues and friends during seminars and conferences, I am grateful to them.

My publisher Shri Tilak Wasan and his staff has worked hard for its prompt publication. They richly deserve my readers patronage.

Raj Kumar

CONTENTS

1

INTRODUCTION

Let me begin this attempt at compilation of essays on religion by my own article on Annie Besant and religion. A search for right perspective on religion has been one of the major problems confronting India and the world today. This paper aims at an examination and understanding of the growth and evolution of Annie Besant's concept of religion and studying its impact on the Indian society during the crucial period in the Indian History in the late nineteenth and the early twentieth century.

I

Due to impact of industrial revolution in the late 19th and early 20th century India in common with many other nations was faced with the problem of adopting and adjusting the ancient heritage to a set of new rapidly altering social condition brought about by the immense technological changes.[1]

The special characteristics of 19th and 20th century social reform movement was that, that much of it originated from secular motives based on rationalistic critiques of society which lead to secular as well as religious movements of social reform.[2]

History is an integral part of social consciousness. Every individual and group inherit history as constructed and disseminated by society. The presence of history and social consciousness enables its appropriation by those who are sensitive to its force.

Therefore appropriation of history is a common occurrence in any society particularly by social and political movements. Indian society is no exception to this. Rewriting and reconstructing the history of a society is an continuing process.[3]

Colonial domination induced some scholars to inquire into the social formation. Efforts made European and the Indian scholars mainly emphasis on theorising of Eurocentric ideologies.

There is no denying that while western world started realising the drawbacks of their material existence and started examining religious and social aspects of human existence, India started looking seriously towards the western ideas to bring about social change and modernization.[4]

The contemporary social reformers considered the prevailing social evils in the Indian society to be the root cause of the Indian religion.[5] They held the hyponotic control over society of corrupt Brahmins as the cause of India's down fall. Indian society as it existed during the period was considered to be a race degenerated, paralysed in all their energies.[6]

The Hindu civilization based on the ancient Aryan institutions was heading for a doom.[7] It was realised that Christian missionaries had brought much social wisdom to India.[8]

II

Annie Besant was born in victoria England to a secptical London doctor and a very religious Irish mother. She was no doubt physically English emotionally and ideologically Irish, but culturally and spiritually Indian. Young Annie, appears to me, devoted to the Christ as Meera was to Lord Krishna.

Passionate love of religion made her wish to die a martyr for truth as Jesus Christ did. Her marriage at the age of twenty to an orthodox Christian priest was due mainly to her love of religion.

But when her infant girl fell seriously ill with whooping cough and watching her suffering child in agony and finding no answer to her anguished prayers, she began to question the ways of providence. Her faith in God was snapped and she became an agnostic like the Buddha.

This led to her leaving the church and to her being expelled from her home, and even to her being deprived of the custody of her too little children. This was the price which she had to pay to assert the integrity of her soul. She wrote.

"I went out into the darkness alone, not because religion was too good for me, but because it was not good enough; it was too meagre, too commonplace, too little exacting, too bound up with earthly interests, too calculating in its accommodations to social conventionalities."

Forsaken and forelone, her love for them everflowed as love for every child, for everyone who was weak and helpless, for even animals, birds, trees and plants. Having lost her faith in a beneficent diety, she sought man's salvation from himself.

Annie Besant saw her three dearest one's die. Two in her tender age when she was just 5 years old, her father and her little brother, and now her dearest mother, who was a friend, philosopher and guide to her and with whose apron string she wanted to be tied for ever.

But she was a warrior soul. She studied at the British Museum, wrote articles, lectured and became a close associate of charles Bradlaugh, the formost freethinker of those times. In her search for truth she became closely associated with Fabian socialism led by Bernard Shaw.

Inspite of the way she sought to forget herself in work for others, she always felt a certain spiritual emptiness. She had written extensively on agnosticism and socialism. Now she carried out thorough research on spiritualism, hypnotism and various other fields in order to find solutions to the mystery of life and death in her quest for understanding the nature of Ultimate Reality.

It was in this state of mind when she was asked to review the too bulky volumes of Madame H.P. Balavatsky's 'The Secret Doctrine'. She later wrote:

'Home I carried my burden and sat me down to read. As I turned over page after page the interest became absorbing; but how familiar it seemed; how my mind leapt forward to presage the conclusion; how natural it was, how coherent, how subtle, and yet how intelligible. I was dazzed, blinded by the light in which disjointed facts were seen as parts of a mighty whole, and my puzzles, riddles, problems, seemed to disappear. The effect was partially illusory in one sense, in that they all had to be slowly unravelled later, the brain gradually assimilating that which the swift intuition had grasped as a truth. But the light had been seen and in that flash of illumination I knew that the weary search was over and the very Truth was found.

What brought Annie Besant to India? Why she read professedly of the Veda, the Upanishads, the Puranas, the Gita and all the religions and philosophies of India? Why and how did she so meticulously write commentaries and translated so clearly on the Indian religions? All this should give us clues to the growth and evolutions of her concept of religion and society.'

III

Let us take some illustrations from her voluminous writings, on our topic.

1. I should define religion as that inner urge that we find in the human being to realise that life which is the life of God in man, the God within the man, cramped, cabinet by his material surroundings, reaching out, as it were, to the God outside him, Universally enveloping him as well as entering him, Called often in Philosophy, God immanent in the first cause, Transcendent in the second case.[10]

2. Modern life is becoming petty because we are not strong enough to reverence. Modern life is becoming base, sordid, and vulgar, because men fear that they will sink if they bow their heads to that which is greater then they are themselves.[11]

3. To Know Him everywhere is the true wisdom;
To Love Him everywhere is the true desire;
To Serve Him everywhere is the true action.[12]

4. Brotherhood means holding everything for all, so that others may share in what we have, and rise to where we are today. It means sharing all willingly, not by compulsion of law, but by the most imperious compulsion of the spirit within, which knows the unity of all.[13]

5. I plead for social reconstruction on the basis of the family, and that is that the weakest shall be most cared for, that the baby shall have the least toil and the most amusement. It was put into a splendid sentence by a French Socialist:

"From every man according to his ability; to every man according to his needs". That is the true rule of human society.[14]

6. A great word was spoken by the Christ. "Let him that is the greatest among you be as your servant". Such preaching of the Law of Brotherhood means social justice.[15]

7. Important as economies may be and are, behind economies lies men and women and unless those men and women are trained into a noble humanity, economic schemes will fail as hopelessly as any political schemes can possibly do.[16]

8. I suggest that the moral training which should make men and women understand that growing knowledge and power is duty, is one of the most vital lessons for these modern days.[17]

9. We must change our estimate of the relative value of things, and substitute intellectual and spiritual wealth for material riches as a standard of social consideration.[18]

IV

On Annie Besant, it appears, fell the responsibility of giving right orientation and necessary strength and stability to its degenerating society. On her arrival in India in 1893 Annie Besant made up her mind to rouse self-respect of Indians.

To a people imprisoned in alien ideals and bewitched by western standards and modes of life, to awake them from dungens of their own musings and imaginations and inferiority complex.

The Adyar headquarters over which she presided was the centre of cultural activity which had led to a wider appreciation of India's ancient culture. It also worked for peace in the broadest sense of world by studying the essential features of the great religions of the world.

Thus she not only made a scientific study of the Indian religions but also paved the way for the world religion. Through her service to India and revival of its culture she worked through out her life to bring about a healthy social change in India.

Annie Besant reply to the glowing tribunes at the Queen's Hall, London, on the occasion of her golden jubilee of public work further explains her concept of religion when she said that there was no joy like the joy of sacrifice for a great cause. She believed all men and women were simply carrying out the will of the creator. She made the point from a discussion with his socialist friend:

"Herbert, I wonder why on earth we go on doing this," and his answer was: "We can't help it".

And in that there was a great truth, for the God, she added who unfolds within us pushes us onwards even when our eyes are blinded to his glory. She concluded by saying:-

And—If I may finish with words which I believed to be intensely true, and that are so often left only half said—when Kipling spoke about the East and the West and "never the twain shall meet," he went on to say:

"But there is neither East nor West,

Border, nor Breed nor Birth,

When two strong men stand face to face,

Though they come from the ends of the earth.

And that is true, whether they be from Britain or from India. Whether it be from one side of the world or the other, there is only one life, and we are one in him, and we shall bring the outer lands together because the inner life is ever one.

V

I would like to conclude that inspite of the fact that the great scientific inventions had liberated the mankind from servitude to nature, people seemed to suffer from a type of neurosis from cultural disintegration. Science had relieved individuals of grinding poverty, mitigated the tortures of physical pain, yet they suffered from an inward loneliness. All growth was marked by pain. All transition belonged to the realm of tragedy. The transition that they had to effect, to survive, was a moral and spiritual revolution.

The enemy to fight was not capitalism or communism. It was folly, spiritual blindness, love of power and lust for domination.

—Raj Kumar

REFERENCES

1. Works of Arnold Toynbee, Radha Krishnan and A.L. Basham have been Referred for Developing Basic Understanding on the Topic.
2. *Ibid.*
3. K.N. Pannikkar, Appropriation of History and Historian's Rôle, Presidential Address, South Indian History Congress, March 1-3, 1991, Calicut.
4. Raj Kumar, Theosophy and Social Change in India, Sansthan.
5. M.G. Ranade and Iswar Chandra Vidyasagar Quoted, *Ibid.*
6. K.T. Telang, *Ibid.*
7. The Indian Social Reformer, 8 March, 1903.
8. Freed B. Fisher India's Silent Revolution, p. 85.
9. Section Two of this Paper has Mainly been Deveioped From Annie Besant's Autobiography and other Biographies Besides My Book on Annie Besant's Rise to Power in Indian Politics 1914-1917, New Delhi, 1989.
10. Annie Besant, the Religion of the New Civilisation.

11. Annie Besant, The Spiritual Life.
12. Annie Besant, Esoteric Christianity.
13. Annie Besant, Evolution of Man's Destiny.
14. Annie Besant, The Problems of Reconstruction.
15. Annie Besant, *Ibid.*
16. Annie Besant, The Future of Socialism.
17. Annie Besant, *Ibid.*
18. Annie Besant, Some Problems of Life.
19. The Fourth Section is Based Upon My Study of:
    (a) Annie Besant, *Four Great Religion,* Adyar, 1978 (Reprint)
    (b) Annie Besant, *The Indian Ideals,* Adyar, Madras, 1965.
    (c) *A Woman World Honoured.*
    (d) Annie Besant, *Hints on the Study of the Bhagvad Gita,* Adyar, 1973 (Reprint)
    (e) Annie Besant, *The Wisdom of the Upanishads,* Adyar, 1974 (Reprint)
    (f) Annie Besant, *Theosophy,* Adyar, 1961 (Reprint).

2

THE UNITY OF INDIAN RELIGION

Indian religion placed four necessities before human life. First it imposed upon the mind a belief in a highest consciousness or state of existence universal and transcendent of the universe, from which all comes, in which all lives and moves without knowing it and of which all must one day grow aware, returning towards that which is perfect, eternal and infinite. Next, it laid upon the individual life the need of self-preparation by development and experience till man is ready for an effort to grow consciously into the truth of this greater existence. Thirdly, it provided it with a well-founded, well-explored, many branching and always enlarging way of knowledge and of spiritual or religious discipline. Lastly for those not yet ready for these higher steps it provided an organisation of the individual and collective life, a framework of personal and social discipline and conduct, of mental and moral and vital development by which they could move each in his own limits and according to his own nature in such a way as to become eventually ready for the greater existence.

The first three of these elements are the most essential to any religion, but Hinduism has always attached to the last also a great importance; it has left out no part of life as a thing secular and foreign to the religious and spiritual life. Still the Indian religious tradition is not merely the form of a religio-social system, as the ignorant critic vainly imagines. However greatly that may count at the moment of a social departure, however stubbornly the conservative religious mind may oppose all pronounced or drastic change, still the core of Hinduism is a spiritual, not a social discipline. Actually we find religions like Sikhism counted in the Vedic family although they broke down the old social tradition and invented a novel form, while the Jain and Buddhists were traditionally considered to be outside the religious fold although they observed Hindu social custom and intermarried with Hindus, because their spiritual system and teaching figured in its origin as a denial of the truth of the Veda and a departure from the continuity of the Vedic line. In all these four elements that constitute Hinduism there are major and minor differences between Hindus of various sects, schools communities and races; but nevertheless there is also a general unity of spirit, of fundamental type and form and of spiritual temperament which creates in this vast fluidity an immense force of cohesion and a strong principle of oneness.

The fundamental idea of all Indian religion is one common to the highest human thinking everywhere. The supreme truth of all that is a being or an existence beyond the mental and physical appearances we contact here. Beyond mind, life and body there is a spirit and self containing all that is finite and infinite, surpassing all that is relative, a supreme absolute, originating and supporting all that is transient, a one eternal. A one transcendent, universal, original and sempiternal divinity or divine essence, Consciousness Force and Bliss is the fount and continent and inhabitant of things. Soul, nature, life are only a manifestation or partial phenomenon of this self-aware eternity and this conscious eternal. But this truth of being was not seized by the Indian mind only as a philosophical speculation, a theological dogma, an abstraction contemplated by the intelligence. It was not an idea to be indulged by the thinker in his study, but otherwise void of practical bearing on life. It was not a mystic sublimation which could be ignored in the dealings of man with the world and Nature. It was a living spiritual Truth, an Entity, a Power, a Presence that could be sought by all according to their degree of capacity and seized in a thousand ways through life and beyond life. This Truth was to be lived and even to be made the governing idea of thought and life and action. This recognition and pursuit of something or someone supreme behind all forms is the one universal eredo of Indian religion, and if it has taken a hundred shapes, it was precisely because it was so much alive. The Infinite alone justifies the existence of the finite and the finite by itself has no entirely separate value or independent existence. Life, if it is not an illusion, is a divine play, a manifestation of the glory of the infinite. Or it is a means by which the soul growing in nature through countless forms and many lives can approach, touch, feel and unite itself through love and knowledge and faith and adòration and a Godward will in works with this transcendent. Being and this infinite existence. This self or this self-existence Being is the one supreme reality, and all things else are either only appearances or only true by dependence upon it. It follows that self-realisation and God-realisation are the great business of the living and thinking human being. All life and thought are in the end a means of progress towards self-realisation and God-realisation.

Indian religion never considered intellectual or theological conceptions about the supreme Truth to be the one thing of central importance. To pursue that Truth under whatever conception or whatever form, to attain to it by inner experience, to live in it in consciousness, this it held to be the sole thing needful. One school or sect might consider the read self of man to be indivisibly one with the universal self or the supreme spirit. Another might regard man as one with the Divine in essence but different from him in nature. A third might hold God, Nature and the individual soul in man to be three eternally different powers of being. But for all the truth of Self held with equal force; for even to the Indian dualist, God is the supreme self and reality in whom and by whom nature and man live, move and have their being and, if you eliminate God from his view of things, Nature and man would lose for him all their meaning and importance. The spirit, universal nature (whether called *Maya, Prakriti* or *Shakti*) and the soul in living beings, *Jiva,* are the three truths which are universally admitted by all the many religious sects and conflicting religious philosophies of India. Universal also is the admission that the discovery of the inner spiritual self in man, the divine soul in him, and some kind of living and uniting contact or absolute unity of the soul in man with God or supreme Self or eternal Brahman is the condition of spiritual perfection. It is open to us to conceive and have experience of the Divine as an impersonal absolute and infinite or to approach and know and feel him as a transcendent and universal semipiternal person: but whatever be our way of reaching him, the one important truth of spiritual experience is that he is in the heart and centre of all existence and all existence is in him and to find him is the great self-finding. Differences of credal belief are to the Indian mind nothing more than various ways of receding the one self and God-head in all. Self-realisation is the one thing needful; to open to the inner spirit, to live in the infinite, to seek after and discover the eternal, to be in union with God, that is the common idea and aim of religion, that is the sense of spiritual salvation, that is the living truth that fulfils and releases. This dynamic following after the highest spiritual truth and the highest spiritual aim are the uniting bond of Indian religion and, behind all its thousand forms, its one common essence.

If there were nothing else to be said in favour of the spiritual genius of the Indian people or the claim of Indian civilisation to stand in the front rank as a spiritual culture, it would be sufficiently substantiated by this single fact that not only was this greatest and widest spiritual truth seen in India with the boldest largeness, felt and expressed with a unique intensity, and approached from all possible sides, but it was made consciously the grand up-lifting idea of life, the core of all thinking, the foundation of all religion, the secret sense and declared ultimate aim of human existence. The truth announced is not peculiar to Indian thinking; it has been seen and followed by the highest minds and souls everywhere. But elsewhere it has been the living guide only of a few thinkers or of some care mystics or exceptionally gifted spiritual natures. The mass of men have had no understanding, no distinct perception, not even a reflected glimpse of this something beyond; they have lived only in the lower sectarian side of religion, is inferior ideas of the deity or in the outward mundane aspects of life. But Indian culture did succeed by the strenuousness of its vision, the universality of its approach, the intensity of its seeking, in doing what has been done by no other culture. It succeeded in stamping religion with the essential ideal of a real spirituality; it brought some living reflection of the very highest spiritual truth and some breath of its influence into every part of the religious field. Nothing can be more untrue than to pretend that the general religious mind of India has not at all grasped the higher spiritual or metaphysical truths of Indian religion. It is a sheer falsehood or a wilful misunderstanding to say that it has lived always in the externals only of rite and creed and shibboleth. On the contrary the main metaphysical truths of Indian religious philosophy in their broad idea aspects or in an intensely poetic and dynamic representation have been stamped on the general mind of the people. The ideas *Maya, Lila,* divine Immanence are as familiar to the man in the street and the worshipper in the temple as to the philosopher in his seclusion, the monk in his monastery and the saint in his hermitage. The spiritual reality which they reflect, the profound experience to which they point has permeated the religion, the literature, the art even the popular religious songs of a whole people.

It is true that these things are realised by the mass of men more readily through the farvour of devotion than by a strenuous effort of thinking, but that is as it must and should be, since the heart of man is nearer to the Truth than his intelligence. It is true too, that the tendency it put too much stress on externals has always been there and worked to overcloud the deeper spiritual motives; but that is not peculiar to India, it is a common filling of human nature, not less but rather more evident in Europe than in Asia. It has needed a constant stream of saints and religious thinkers and the teaching of illuminated Sanyasis to keep the reality vivid and resist the deadening weight of form and ceremony and ritual. But the fact remains that these messengers of the spirit have never been wanting. And the still more significant fact remains that these have never been wanting either a happy readiness in the common mind to listen to the message. The ordinary materialised souls, the external minds are the majority in India as everywhere. How easy it is for the superior European critic to forget this common fact of our humanity and treat this turn as a peculiar sign of the Indian mentality! But at least the people of India, even the "ignorant masses" have this distinction that they are by centuries of training nearer to the inner realities, are divided from them by a less thick veil of the universal ignorance and are more easily led back to a vital glimpse of God and Spirit, self and eternity than the mass of men or even the cultured elite anywhere else. Where else could the lofty, austere and difficult teaching of a Buddha have seized so rapidly on the popular mind? Where else could the songs of a Tukaram, a Ramprasad, a Kabir, the Sikh gurus and the chants of the Tamil saints with their fervid devotion but also their profound spiritual thinking have found so speedy an echo and formed a popular religious literature? This strong permeation or close nearness of the spiritual turn, this readiness of the mind of a whole nation to turn to the highest realities is the sign and fruit of an age-long, a real and a still living and supremely spiritual culture.

The endless variety of Indian philosophy and religion seems to the European mind interminable, bewildering, wearisome, useless; it is unable to see the forest because of the richness and luxuriance of its vegetation; it misses the common spiritual life in the multitude of its forms. But this infinite variety is itself, as Vivekananda pertinently pointed out, a sign of superior religious culture. The Indian mind has always realised that Supreme is the Infinite; it has perceived, right from its Vedic beginnings, that to the soul in Nature the Infinite must always present itself in an endless variety of aspects. The mentality of the West has long cherished the aggressive and quite illogical idea of a single religion for all mankind, a religion universal by the very force its narrowness, one set of dogmas, one cult, one system of ceremonies, one array of prohibitions and injunctions, one ecclesiastical ordinance. That narrow absurdity prances about as the one true religion which all must accept on peril of persecution by men here and spiritual rejection or fierce eternal punishment by God in other worlds. This grotesque creation of human unreason, the parent of so much intolerance, cruelty, obscurantism and aggressive, fanaticism, has never been able to take firm hold of the free and supple mind of India. Men everywhere have common human failings, and intolerance and narrowness especially in the matter of observances there has been and is in India. There has been much violence of theological disputation, there have been querulous bickerings of sects with their pretensions to spiritual superiority and greater knowledge, and sometimes, at one time especially in southern India in a period of acute religious differences, there have been brief local outbreaks of active mutual tyranny and persecution even unto death. But these things have never taken the proportions which they assumed in Europe. Intolerance has been confined for the most part to the minor forms of polemical attack or to social obstruction or ostracism; very seldom have they transgressed across the line to the major forms of barbaric persecution which draw a long, red and hideous stain across the religious history of Europe. There has played ever in India the saving perception of a higher and purer spiritual intelligence, which has had its effect on the mass mentality. Indian religion has always felt that since the minds, the temperaments, the intellectual affinities of men are unlimited in their variety, a perfect liberty of thought and of worship must be allowed to the individual in his approach to the Infinite.

India recognised the authority of spiritual experience and knowledge, but she recognised still more the need of variety of spiritual experience and knowledge. Even in the days of decline when the claim of authority became in too many directions rigorous and excessive, she still kept the saving perception that there could not be one but must be many authorities. An alert readiness to acknowledge new light capable of enlarging the old tradition has always been characteristic of the religious mind in India. Indian civilisation did not develop to a last logical conclusion its earlier political and social liberties,—that greatness of freedom or boldness of experiment belongs to the West; but liberty of religious practice and a complete freedom of thought in religion as in every other matter have always counted among its constant traditions. The atheist and the agnostic were free from persecution in India. Buddhism and Jainism might be disparaged as unorthodox religions, but they were allowed to live freely side by side with the orthodox creeds and philosophies; in her eager thirst for truth she gave them their full chance, tested all their values, and as much of their truth as was assimilable was taken into the stock of the common and always enlarging continuity of her spiritual experience. That ageless continuity was carefully conserved, but it admitted light from all quarters. In later times the saints who reached some fusion of the Hindu and the Islamic teaching were freely and immediately recognised as leaders of Hindu religion,—even, in some cases, when they started with a Mussulman birth and from the Mussalman standpoint. The Yogi who developed a new path of Yoga, the religious teacher who founded a new order, the thinker who built up a novel statement of the many-sided truth of spiritual existence found no serious obstacle to their practice of their propaganda. At most they had to meet the opposition of the priest and Pandit instinctively adverse to any change; but this had only to be lived down for the new element to be received into the free and pliant body of the national religion and its ever plastic order.

The necessity of a firm spiritual order as well as an untrammelled spiritual freedom was always perceived, but it was provided for in various ways and not in any one formal, external or artificial manner. It was founded in the first place on the recognition of an ever enlarging number of authorised scriptures. Of these scriptures some like the *Gita* possessed a common and widespread authority, others were peculiar to sects or schools: some like the Vedas were supposed to have an absolute, others a relative binding force. But the very largest freedom of interpretation was allowed, and this prevented any of these authoritative books from being turned into an instrument of ecclesiastical tyranny or a denial of freedom to the human mind and spirit. Another instrument of order was the power of family and communal tradition, *kuladharma,* persistent but not immutable. A third was the religious authority of the Brahmans; as priests they officiated as the custodians of observance, as scholars acting in a much more important and respected role than the officiating priesthood could claim,—for to the priesthood no great consideration was given in India,—They stood as the exponents of religious tradition and were a strong conservative power. Finally, and most characteristically, most powerfully, order was secured by the succession of gurus or spiritual teachers, *parampara,* who preserved the continuity of each spiritual system and handed it down from generation to generation but were empowered also, unlike the priest and the Pandit, to enrich freely its significance and develop its practice. A living and moving, not a rigid continuity, was the characteristic turn of the inner religious mind of India. The evolution of the vaishnava religion from very early times, its succession of saints and teachers, the striking developments given to it successively by Ramanuja, Madhya, Chaitanya, Vallabhacharya and its recent stirrings of survival after a period of langour and of some fossilisation form one notable example of this firm combination of age long continuity and fixed tradition with latitude of powerful and vivid change. A more striking instance was the founding of the Sikh religion, its long line of Gurus and the novel direction and form given to it by Guru Govind Singh in the democratic institution of the Khalsa. The Buddhist Sangha and its councils, the creation of a sort of divided pontifical authority by Shankaracharya, an authority transmitted from generation to generation for more than a thousand years and even now not altogether effect, the Sikh Khalsa, the adoption of the congregational form called Samaj by the modern reforming sects indicate an attempt towards a compact and stringent order. But it is noteworthy that even in these attempts the freedom and plastivity and living sincerity of the religious mind of India always prevented it from initiating anything like the over blown ecclesiastical orders and despotic hierarchies which in the West have striven to impose the tyranny of their obscurantist yoke on the spiritual liberty of the human race.

3

SHANKARACHARYA

Today those fundamentals of science and of life, space and time which were supposed to be the basic principles of the Universe—space, time, causality—all these have assumed new shapes. Space is supposed to be a function of time, space is supposed to be infinite, yet limited. The fourth dimension is mathematically proved to exist. All phenomena are relative and are functions of consciousness. Nothing is real, and it is not only the maxims of the Vedanta, but of Sir James Jeans which postulate that the teaching of modern science amounted to a realisation that all phenomena and events are a function of the mind. In other words, space does not exist by itself and time does not exit by itself. The doctrine of relativity which we owe to Einstein had been preached 2500 years ago, or even earlier, by the great Upanishad Karthas, and they affirmed that everything is imaginary but that there is one Immanent Mind of Supreme Consciousness whose maya manifestations are the physical causations and appearances. So, as a result of laboratory experiments and mathematical calculations, the earlier materialistic theories and hypotheses have vanished and we have come back to the Vedanta, according to which the only thing that exists is the Supreme Mind of which all minds, all phenomena, are a part and which is the summation, embodiment and integration of the universe and its evolution. That is the present state of modern science. In other words, modern science—European and American science—the science that we owe to people like Einstein and Niels Bohr has led to this conclusion, that those firm foundations on which life and the problems and phenomena of life were accepted to be based and understood to red are shifting, and that a new philosophy, a new conspectus, a new appraisal of those phenomena is essential, and therefore we come back to these daring speculations which characterised the ancient sages of the world.

Let me take you through some of the great religions of the world. Amdist many differences, you see the assertion of the supremacy of mind over matter and the phenomena of matter. Take Christianity which is a simple faith in a certain sense, its creed resting upon belief in the help and succour of a particularly evolved soul Jesus Christ. We know that on the basis of the direct, simple faith of the Teacher, the great Christian mystics and various thinkers who lived from the 3rd to the 11th country, built up a superstructure which, if carefully examined, is not very different from the Vedanta and is, to no small extent, derived from Plotinus and Plato who owed a great deal to Egypt and India. Take Islam. It again depends upon one or two hypotheses or doctrines of faith, namely, the universality and the oneness of God and the belief in an Apostle of God; but on the basis of that faith, simple, direct, democratic and absolutely close to the hearts and conscience of the people, there has been built up the elaborate edifice of Sufism which, if carefully examined in the works of Jalaluddin Rumi and Omar Khayyam, will be discovered to be not very different from the Vedanta. Our faith, if you read our Vedanta literally, is also a faith which recognises certain great powers, certain specific divinities, attributes or emanations of the Divine. *Bhakti,* worship, love, reverence—these things lead to salvation. That is a simple faith, but as human problems became more and more complicated and people began to delve deeper and deeper below the surface, they found that a more comprehensive synthesis was necessary.

Shankara presents to my mind a unique combination and the union, in the same person, of two qualities generally found separated. There are some who ascend to the heights of physical discipline and intellectual analysis; there are some who take difficult paths and attain the high peaks where, in a rarefied air of abstract thought, they commune with the Infinite. Others ascend the summits by boundless love and compassion and faith. Tukaram, Kabir, Ramdas were examples of persons whose affection, intense longing and personal devotion to some ideal of theirs (as in the case of St. Francis) led them to dedicate their lives and everything that they cherished to their particular ideal or Ishta Devata. That is the difference between what is called *jnana* and *bhakti*. It is not given to everybody to unit those qualities in the same existence or body. Shankara was able to do that. He was one of the rate examples of the union of the abstract and the concrete.

When we think of Shankara, with what do we mainly associate him? We associate him with the great *bhashyas* on the *Brahma-Sutras* and the Upanishads and the *Bhagavad-Gita* and various other commentaries which contain the most abstract analysis, the most meticulous and microscopic examination of the phenomena of matter and spirit, evil and good, duality and oneness, with a power of analysis and introspection, utilising dry and passionless thought. And yet the same person was responsible for the *Dakshinamurti Stotra,* the *Soundarya Lahiri,* the *Ananda Lahiri* and the other clinging fervid, passionate *stotras* and for all those manifestation of the Divine in language as impassioned, as lyrical, as full of rapture and personal devotion as the outpourings of the mystics of the Christian and Mohammedan religions, and of our great men like Tukaram, Kabir and those wandering generations of singers who even today are one of the glories and accompaniments of Northern Indian life.

That by itself is a miracle, but there is another aspect which is not always realised and recognised even by people who know the life of Shankara. Shankara is reported to have passed away when he was about thirty-two years old. We in this scientific age with aeroplanes, motor-cars and all conveniences find it very difficult to undertake a journey from Madras to Kashmir, but several centuries ago, the great sage Shankara started on an expedition when he was sixteen to twenty years of age according to tradition, went to Badrinath and founded one of his monasteries there, to Srinagar where he worshipped at the shrine and left his

ultimate truth of Vedanta that nothing exists apart from the great entity, call it Brahman or Over-Soul, that Over-Soul is yourself and myself and that all our conflicts and difficulties are due to an illusion which makes for separateness where no separateness exists. The vision that comes both to the *bhakta* and the *jnani* is the vision, not of anything outside one's self, but something within one's self—that vision may be obtained partly by physical means because the conquest of the body is necessary for the conquest of the mind, but, after the body has been conquered, the mind has to be canalised and then the spirit is merged in the supreme. Shankara attempted in many ways to tread the path which has been trodden by several philosophers and prophets, but his glory is characteristic in that he effected a synthesis, a harmonious adaptation of these various ideals and made it possible for people with different equipments, with different heredities and different life-histories to follow their own bent of mind, their own philosophy but, at the same time, to aspire beyond that individual philosophy to that supreme revelation in which the individual soul merges into the infinite and is not differentiated from that by interposed obstructions and which, however it may be termed is the one thing which exists and which has created everything is immanent in everything and is yet transcendental.

4

HINDUISM

History is not a mere sequence of events but is the activity of the Idea or Spirit struggling to be born, endeavouring to realize itself through events. The Idea, however, is never and cannot ever be perfectly realized. Goethe in his *Conversations* tells us that 'no organism corresponds completely to the idea that lies at its root: behind every one the higher idea is hidden. That is the God we all seek after and hope to find, but we can only feel him, we cannot see him'. If we look at the various and sometimes conflicting creeds we may wonder whether Hinduism is not just a name which covers a multitude of different faiths, but when we turn our attention to the spiritual life, devotion, and endeavour which lie behind the creeds, we realize the unity, the indefinable self-identity, which, however, is by no means static or absolute. Throughout the history of Hindu civilization there has been a certain inspiring ideal, a certain motive power, a certain way of looking at life, which cannot be identified with any stage or cross-section of the process. The whole movement and life of the institution, its entire history, is necessary to disclose to us this idea and it cannot therefore be expressed in a simple formula. It requires centuries for ideas to utter themselves, and at any stage the institution has always an element that is yet to be expressed. No idea is fully expressed at any one point of its historical unfolding.

What is this Idea of Hinduism, this continuous element that runs through all from the earliest to the latest, from the lowest to the highest stages, this fundamental spirit which is more fully and richly expressed in the highest through it is present in the very lowest? Life is present in very stage of a plant's growth and it is always the same life though it is more fully expressed in the developed tree than in the first push of the tender blade. In the Hindu religion there must be a common element that makes every stage and every movement an expression of the religion. The different phases and stages have proper content and meaning only in so far as this common element exists. With the perception of the unity which runs through error and failure up the long ascent towards the ideal, the whole achievement of Hinduism falls into coherent perspective. It is this essential spirit that any account of Hinduism would seek to express, the spirit that its institutions imperfectly set forth, the spirit that we need to develop more adequately and richly before a better age and civilization can be achieved.

Historical Outline

The spirit is not a dead abstraction but a living force. Because it is active and dynamic the Hindu civilization has endured so long and proved so capable of adaptation to the growing complexity of life. The great river of Hindu life, usually serene but not without its rapids, reaches back so far that only a long view can do justice to its nature. Form prehistoric times influences have been at work moulding the faith. As a result of the excavation in Harappa and Mohenjodāro we have evidence of the presence in India of a highly developed culture that 'must have had a long antecedent history on the soil of India, taking us back to an age that can only be dimly surmised'.[1] In age and achievement the Indus-valley civilization is comparable to that of Egypt or Sumeria. The noteworthy feature of this civilization is its continuity, not as a political power but as a cultural influence.[2] The religion of the Indus people is hardly distinguishable according to Sir John Marshall, from 'that aspect of Hinduism which is bound up with animism and the cults of Siva and the Mother Goddess'.[3] These latter do not seem to be indigenous to the Vedic religion. In the *Kulālikāmnāya* or *Kubjikāmala Tantra* there is a verse which reads: 'Go forth to India and assert your authority in the whole country. I will not get to you until you establish yourself there.' Though the Śakti cult was later accepted by the Vedic people, their original opposition to it is not altogether suppressed. To the sacrifice of Daksha, all the Vedic deities are said to invited except Śiva,, who soon gained authority as the successor of the Vedic Rudra. Even so late as the *Bhāgavata Purāna* the opposition to Śiva worship is present. 'Those who worship Śiva and those who follow them are the opponents of holy scriptures and may be ranked with Pāshandins. Let the feeble-minded who, with matted locks, ashes, and bones, have lost their purity, be initiated into the worship of Śiva in which wine and brewage are regarded as gods.'[4]

It is a matter for conjuncture whether the Indus people had any relation to the Dravidians, who, according to Risley, are 'the earliest inhabitants of India of whom we have any knowledge'.[5] Nor can we say whether the Dravidians were natives of the soil or came from outside. Besides the Āryans and the Dravidians there was also a flat—nosed, black-skinned people who are commonly known as *dāsas* or slaves. The religion, in the first literary records that have come down to us, is that of the Āryans, though it was much influenced by the Indus people, the Dravidians, and the aborigines. The simple hymns of the *Rig-Veda* reveal to us an age when Pan was still alive, when the trees in the forest could speak and the waters of the river could sing and man could listen and understand. The spells and the charms to be found in the tenth book of the *Rig-Veda* and the whole of the *Atharva-Veda* suggest a type of religious practice based on fear and associated with the spirits of the dark. A religious synthesis of the different views and practices on the basis of monistic idealism is set forth in the early *Upanishads.* Soon after, Hellenistic culture springing from a union of Greek with Persian and Bactrian influences dominated north-western India. Successive descents of Muslim conquerors from about A.D. 1000 affected Hindu life and thought. The Parsee fugitives who were expelled from Persia by Muslim invaders found a welcome shelter in India. St. Thomas brought the Christian faith from Syria to South India and for over a thousand years this remained the only Christian centre of influence. In the sixteenth century St. Francis Xavier introduced Latin Christianity. The modern Christian missionary movement started over a century ago. The cultural invasion of the West has been vigorous, thanks to its political superiority and industrial efficiency.

Jainism, Buddhism, and Sikhism are creations of the Indian mind and represent reform movements from within the fold of Hinduism put forth to meet the special demands of the various stages of the Hindu faith. Zoroastrianism, Islam, and Christianity have been so long in the country that they have become native to the soil and are deeply influenced by the atmosphere of Hinduism.

Indian was a through 'melting pot' long before the term was invented for America. In spite of attacks, Hellenic, Muslim, and European among others, Hindu culture has maintained its tradition unbroken to the present day from the fourth millennium B.C. The spiritual life of the Hindus at the present time has not precisely the same proportion or orientation as that of either the Indus people or the Vedic Āryans or even the great teachers, Samkara and Rāmānuja. Its changes in emphasis reflect individual temperaments, social conditions, and the changing intellectual environment, but the same persistent idea reappears in different forms. Hinduism grows in the proper sense of the world, not by accretion, but like an organism, under-going from time to time transformation as a whole. It has carried within it much of its early possessions. It has cast aside a good deal and often it has found treasures which it made its own. It took what it could whence it could though it adhered to its originals vision. The more it changes the more it remains the same thing. The history of Hinduism is chequered by tragic failures and wonderful victories, by opportunities missed and taken. New truth has been denied and persecuted occasionally. The unity of its body realized at the cost of centuries of effort and labour now and then came near being shattered by self-seeking and ignorance. Yet the religion itself is not destroyed. It is alive and vigorous and has withstood attacks from within and without. It seems to be possessed of unlimited power of renewal. Its historic vitality, the abounding energy which it reveals, would alone be evidence of its spiritual genius.

Universality

In its great days Hinduism was inspired to carry its idea across the frontiers of India and impose it on the civilized world. Its memory has become a part of the Asiatic consciousness, tinging its outlook on life. Today it is a vital element in world thought and offers the necessary corrective to the predominantly rationalistic pragmatism of the West. It has therefore universal value.

The vision of India, like that of Greece, is Indian only in the sense that it was formulated by minds belonging to the Indian soil. The value of that vision does not reside in any tribal or provincial characteristics, but in those elements of universality which appeal to the whole world. What can be recognized as peculiarly Indian is hot the universal truth which is present in it, but the elements of weakness and prejudice, which even some of the greatest of Indians have in common with their weaker brethren.

Religion as Experience

Hinduism represents a development from the beliefs and practices of the Indus-valley civilization to the complex of changing aspirations and habits, speculations and forms which are in vogue today. There are, however, certain governing conceptions, controlling ideas, deep dynamic links which bind together the different stage and movements. The unity of Hinduism is not one of an unchanging creed or a fixed deposit of doctrine, but is the unity of continuously changing life. In this essay we only deal with the general drift of the current of Hindu religion as whole, not with the many confusing cross-currents and sects.

Religion for the Hindu is experience or attitude of mind. It is not idea but a power, not an intellectual proposition but a life conviction. Religion is consciousness of ultimate reality, not a theory about God. The religious genius is not a pedant or a pandit, not a sophist or a dialectician, but a prophet, a sage, or a *rishi* who embodies in himself the spiritual vision. When the soul goes inward into itself it draws near its own divine root and becomes pervaded by the radiance of another nature. The aim of all religion is the practical realization of the highest truth. It is intuition of reality *(brahmānubhava),* insight into truth *(brahmadarśana),* contact with the supreme *(brahmasamsparśa),* direct apprehension of reality *(brahmasākshātkāra).*

In emphasizing the experiential as distinct from the dogmatic or cradle character of religion, Hinduism seems to be more adequate than other religions to the history of religion as well as to the contemporary religious situation. Buddhism in its original from did not avow any theistic belief. Confucius, like Buddha, discouraged his disciples from occupying their minds with speculations about the Divine Being or the Unseen World. There are systems of Hindu thought, like the Sāmkhya and the Pūrva Mīmāmsā, with, in some or the their characteristic phases, cultivate a spirit and attitude to which it would be difficult to deny the name of religion, even though they may not accept any belief in God or Gods superior to oneself. They adopt other methods for achieving salvation from sin and sorrow and do not look to God as the source of their saving. We cannot deny to Spinoza the religious spirit simply because he did not admit any reciprocal communion between the divine and the human spirits. We have instances of religious fervour and seriousness without a corresponding belief in any being describable as God. Again, it is possible for us to believe in God any yet be without any religious. We may regard the proofs for the existence of God as irrefutable and yet may not possess the feeling and attitude associated with religion. Religion is not so much a matter of theoretical knowledge as of life and practice. When Kant attacked the traditional proofs of God's existence, and asserted at the same time his faith in God as a postulate of moral consciousness, he brought out the essentially non-theoretical character of life in God. It follows that the reality of God is not based on abstract arguments or scholastic proofs, but is derived from the specifically religious experience which alone gives peculiar significance to the world 'God'. Man becomes aware of God through experience. Rational arguments establish religious faith only when they are interpreted in the light of that religious experience. The arguments do not reveal God to us but are helpful in removing obstacles to the acceptance by our minds of a revelation mediated by that capacity for the apprehension of the Divine which is a normal feature of our humanity.[6] Those who have developed this centre through which all the threads of the universe are drawn are the religious geniuses. The high vision of those who have penetrated into the depths of being, their sense of the Divine in all their exaltation of feeling and enrichment of personality, have been the source of all the noblest work in the world. From Moses to Isaiah, from Jesus and Paul on to Augustine, Luther, and Wesley, from Socrates and Plato to Plotinus and Philo, from Zoroaster to Buddha, from Confucius to Mahomet, the men who initiated new currents of life, the creative personalities, are those who have known God by acquaintance and not by hearsay.

The Vedas

What is final is the religious experience itself, though its expression change if they are to be relevant to the growing content of knowledge. The experience is what is felt by the individual in his deepest being, what is seen by him *(drishti)* or hear *śruti)* and this is valid for all time, The Veda is seen or heard, not made by its human authors. It is spiritual discovery, not creation. The way to wisdom is not through intellectual activity. From the beginning, India believed in the superiority of intuition of the method of direct perception of the supersensible to intellectual reasoning. The Vedic *rishis* 'were the first who ever burst into that silent sea' of ultimate being and their utterances about what they saw and heard there are found registered in the *Vedas.* Naturally they attribute the authorship of the *Vedas* to a superior spirit.

Modern psychology admits that the higher achievements of men depend in the last analysis on processes that are beyond and deeper than the limits of the normal consciousness. Socrates speaks of the 'daimōn' which acts as the censor on and speaks through him. Plato regards inspiration as an act of a goddess. Ideas are showered on Philo from above, though he is oblivious of everything around him. George Eliot tells us that she wrote her best work in a kind of frenzy almost without knowing what she was writing.

According to Emerson, all poetry is first written in the heavens. It is conceived by a self deeper than appears in normal life. The prophet, when he begins his message 'Thus Faith the Lord', is giving utterance to his consciousness that the message is not his own, that it comes from a wider and deeper level of life and from a source outside his limited self. Since we cannot compel these exceptional moments to occur, all inspiration has something of revelation in it. Instead of considering creative work to be due to processes which take place unwittingly, as some new phychologists imagine,[7] the Hindu thinkers affirm that the creative deeds, the inspiration of the poets, the vision of the artist, and the genius of the man of science are in reality the utterance of the Eternal through man. In those rare moments man is in touch with a wider world and is swayed by an oversoul that is above his own. The seers feel that their experiences are unmediated direct disclosures from the wholly other and regard them as supernatural, as not discovered by man's own activity *(akartrika, apaurusheya)*. They feel that they come to them from God,[8] though even God is said to be not their author but their formulator. In the last analysis the *Vedas* are without any personal author.[9] Since they are not due to personal activity they are not subject to unlimited revision and restatement but possess in a sense the character of finality *(nityatva)*.

While scientific knowledge soon becomes obsolete, intuitive wisdom has a permanent value. Inspired poetry and religious scriptures have a certain timelessness or universality which intellectual works do not share. While Aristotle's biology is no longer true, the drama of Euripides is still beautiful. While Vaiśeshika atomism is obsolete, Kālidāsa's *Śakuntalā* is unsurpassed in its own line.

There is a community and continuity of life between man in his deepest self and God. In ethical creativity and religious experience man draws on this source or rather the source of power is expressing itself through him. In Tennyson's fine figure the sluices are opened and the great ocean of power flows in. It is spirit in man that is responding to the spirit in the universe, the deep calling unto the deep.

The *Vedas* are more a record than an interpretation of religious experience. While their authority is final, that of the expression and the interpretations of the religious experience is by no means final. The latter are said to be *smriti* or the remembered testimonies of great souls. These interpretations are bound to change it they are to be relevant to the growing content of knowledge. Facts alone stand firm, judgements waver and change. Facts can be expressed in the dialect of the age. The relation between the vision and its expression, the fact and its interpretation, is very close. It is more like the body and the skin than the body and its clothes. When the vision is to be reinterpreted, what is needed is not mere verbal change but a readaptation to new habits of mind. We have evidence to show that the *Vedas* meant slightly different things to successive generations of believers. On the fundamental, metaphysical, and religious issues the different commentators, Samkara, Rāmānuja, and Mudhva, offer different interpretations. To ascribe finality to a spiritual movement is to bring it to a standstill. To stand still is to fall back. There is not and there cannot be any finality in interpretation.

Authority, Logic, and Life

Insight into reality which is the goal of the religious quest is earned by intellectual and moral discipline. Three stages are generally distinguished, a tradition which we have to learn *(śravana)*, an intellectual training through which we have to pass *(manana)*, and an ethical discipline we have to undergo *(nididhyāsana)*.[10]

To begin with, we are all learners. We take our views on the authority of a tradition which we have done nothing to create but which we have only to accept in the first instance. In every department, art or morality, science or social life, we are taught the first principles and are not encouraged to exercise our private judgement. Religion is not an exception to this rule Religious scriptures are said to have a right to our acceptance.

The second step is logical reflection or *manana*. To understand the sacred tradition we should use our intelligence.

'Verily, when the sages or *rishis* were passing away, men inquired of the gods, "who shall be our rishi?" They gave them the science of reasoning for constructing the sense of the hymns.[11] Criticism helps the discovery of truth and, if it destroys anything, it is only illusions that are bred by piety that are destroyed by it. Śruti and *Smriti,* experience and interpretation, scripture and logic are the two wings given to the human soul to reach the truth. While the Hindu view permits us to criticize the tradition we should do so only from within. It can be remoulded and improved only by those who accept it and use it in their lives. Our great reformers, our eminently original thinkers like Śamkara and Rāmānuja, rebels against tradition; but their convictions, as they themselves admit, are also revile their tradition and repudiate it altogether and condemn them as *avaidika* or *nāstika,* they are hospitable to all those who accept the tradition, however critical they may be of it.

The authoritativeness of the *Veda* does not preclude critical examination of matters dealt with in it. The Hindus believe that the truths of revelation are justifiable to reason. Our convictions are valuable only when they are the results of our personal efforts to understand. The accepted tradition becomes reasoned truth. If the truth ascertained by inquiry conflict with the statements found in the scriptures, the latter must be explained in a way agreeable to truth. No scriptures can compel us to believe falsehoods. 'A thousand scriptures verily cannot convert a jar into a cloth.' We have much in the *Vedas* which is a product not of man's highest wisdom but of his wayward fancy. If we remember that revelation precedes its record, we will realize that the *Veda* may not be an accurate embodiment of the former. It has in it a good deal of inference and interpretation mixed up with intuition and experience. Insistence on Vedic authority is not an encouragement of credulity or an enslaving subjection to scriptural texts. It does not justify the conditions under which degrading religious despotisms grew up later.

The Vedic testimony, the logical truth, must become for us the present fact. We must recapture something of that energy of soul of which the *Vedas* are the creation by letting the thoughts and emotions of that still living past vibrate in our spirits. By *nididhyāsana* or contemplative meditation, ethical discipline, the truth is built into the substance of our life. What we accept on authority and test by logic is now proved by its power to sustain definite and unique type of life of supreme value. Thought completes itself in life and we thrill again with the creative experience of the first days of the founders of the religion.

God

If religion is experience, what is it that we experience? What is the nature of reality? In our knowledge of God, contact with the ultimate reality through religious experience plays the same part which contact with nature through sense perception plays in our knowledge of nature. In both we have a sense of the other, the trans-subjective, which controls our apprehension. It is so utterly given to us and not made by us. We build the concept of reality from the data of religious experience, even as we build the order of nature from the immediate data of sense.

In the long and diversified history of man's quest for reality represented by Hinduism, the object which haunts the human soul as a presence at once all-embracing and infinite is envisaged in many different ways. The Hindus are said to adopt polytheism, monotheism, and pantheism as well as belief in demons, heroes, and ancestors. It is easy to find texts in support of each of these views. The cults of Śiva and Śakti may have come down from the Indus people. Worship of trees, animals, rivers, and other cults associated with fertility ritual may have had the same origin, while the dark powers of the underworld, who are dreaded and propitiated, may be due to aboriginal sources. The Vedic Āryans contributed the higher gods comparable to the Olympians of the Greeks, like the Sky and the Earth, the Sun and the Fire. The Hindu religion deals with these different lines of thought and fuses them into a whole by means of its philosophical synthesis. A religion is judged by what it tends towards. Those who note the facts and miss the truth are unfair to the Hindu attempt.

The reality we experience cannot be fully expressed in terms of logic and language. It defies all description. The seer is as certain of the objective reality he apprehends as he is of the inadequacy of thought to express it. A God comprehended is no God, but an artificial construction of our minds. Individuality, weather human or divine, can only be accepted as given fact and not described. It is not wholly transparent to logic. It is inexhaustible by analysis.[12] It inexhaustibility is the proof of objectivity. However far we may carry our logical analysis, the given object in all its uniqueness is there constituting a limit to our analysis. Our thinking is controlled by something beyond itself which is perception in physical science and the intuition of God in the science of religion. The eternal being of God cannot be described by categories. An attitude of reticence is adopted regarding the question of the nature of the Supreme. Those who know it tell it not; those who tell it know it not. The *Kena Upanishad* says: 'The eye does not go thither, nor speech nor mind. We do not known, we do not understand how one can teach it. It is different from the known, it is also above the unknown.'[13] Śamkara quotes a Vedic passage where the teacher tells the pupil the secret of the self keeping silent about it. 'Verily, I tell you, but you understand not, the self is silence.'[14] The deeper experience is a 'wordless' doctrine. The sages declare that 'wonderful is the man that can speak of him, and wonderful is also the man that can understand him'.[15] Buddha maintained silence about the nature of ultimate reality. 'Silent are the Tathāgatas. O, Blessed one.'[16] The *Mādhyamikas,* declare that the truth in free from such descriptions as 'it is', 'it is not' 'bath', and 'neither'. Nāgārjuna says that Buddha did not give any definition of the ultimate reality. 'Nowhere and to nobody has ever anything been preached by the Buddha.'[17] A verse attributed to Śamkara reads: 'It is wonderful that there under the Banyan tree the pupil is old while the teacher is young. The explanation of the teacher is silence but the doubts of the pupil are dispersed.' This attitude is truer and nobler than that of the theologians, who construct elaborate mansions and show us round with the air of God's own estate agents.

When, however, attempts are made to give expression to the ineffable reality, negative descriptions are employed. The real is the wholly other, the utterly transcendent, the mysterious being which awakens in us a sense of awe and wonder, dread and desire. It not only fascinates us but produces a sense of abasement in us. Whatever is true of empirical being is denied of the Real. 'The Ātman can only be described by "no, no". It is incomprehensible for it cannot be comprehended,'[18] It is not in space or time; it is free from cause necessity. It is above all conceptions and conceptional differentiations. But on this account it is not to be confused with non-being.[19] It is being in a more satisfying sense than empirical being. The inadequacy of intellectual analysis is the outcome of the incomparable wealth of intrinsic reality in the supreme being. The eternal being is utterly beyond all personal limitation, is beyond all forms though the sustainer of all forms. All religious systems in which mankind has sought to confine the reality of God are inadequate. They make of God and 'idol'.

While the negative characteristics indicate the transcendent character of the real, there is a sense in which the real is also immanent. The very fact that we able to apprehend the real means that there is something in us capable of apprehending it. The deepest part of our nature responds to the call of the reality. In spiritual life the law holds that only like can know like. We can only know what is akin to ourselves. Above and beyond our rational being lies hidden the ultimate and highest part of our nature. What the mystics call the 'basis' or 'ground' of the soul is not satisfied by the transitory of the temporal, by the sensuous or the intellectual.[20] Naturally, the power by which we acquire the knowledge of God is not logical thought, but spirit, for spirit can only be spiritually discerned. While the real is utterly transcendent to the empirical individual, it is immanent in the ultimate part of our nature. God's revelation and man's contemplation are two aspects of one and the same experience. The Beyond is the Within. Brahman is Ātman. He is the *antaryāmin,* the inner controller. He is not only the incommunicable mystery standing for ever in his own perfect light, bliss, and peace but also is here in us, upholding, sustaining us; 'Whoever worships God as other than the self, thinking he is one and I am another, knows not,'[21] Religion arises out of the experience of the human spirit which feels its kinship and continuity with the Divine other. A purely immanent deity cannot be an object of worship and adoration; a purely transcendent one does not allow of any worship or adoration.

Hindu thinkers are not content with postulating a being unrelated to humanity, who is merely the Beyond, so far as the empirical world is concerned. From the beginnings of Hindu history, attempts are made to bring God closer to the needs of man. Though it is impossible to describe the ultimate reality, it is quite possible to indicate by means of symbols aspects of it, though the symbolic description is not a substitute for the experience of God. We are helpless in this matter and therefore are obliged to substitute symbols for substances, pictures for realities. We adopt a symbolic account when we regard the ultimate reality as the highest person, as the supreme personality, as the Father of us all, ready to respond to the needs of humanity. The *Rig-Veda* has it: 'All this is the person, that which is past and that which is future.'[22] It is the matrix of the entire being. The Vaishnava thinkers and the Saiva Siddhāntins make of the supreme, the fulfilment of our nature. He is knowledge that will enlighten the ignorant, strength for the weak, mercy for the guilty, patience for the sufferer, comfort for the comfortless. Strictly speaking, however, the supreme is not this or that personal from but is the being that is responsible for all that was, is and shall be. His temple is every world, every star that spins in the firmament. No element can contain him for he is all elements. Your life and mine are eveloped by him. Worship is the acknowledgement of the magnificence of this supreme reality.

We have account of the ultimate Reality as both Absolute and God, Brahman, and Iśvara. Only those who accept the view of the Supreme as personality admit that the unsearchableness of God cannot be measured by our feeble conceptions. The confess that there is an overplus of reality beyond the personal concept. To the worshipper, the personal god is the highest. No one can worship what is known as imperfect. Even the idol of the idolater stands for perfection, though he may toss it aside the movement he detects its imperfection.

It is wrong to assume that the Supreme is either the Absolute or God. It is both the Absolute and God. The impersonal and the personal conceptions are not to be regarded as rival claimants to the exclusive truth. They are different ways in which the single comprehensive pattern reveals itself to the spirit of man. One and the same Being is conceived now as the object of philosophical inquiry or *jnānā,* at another as an object of devotion or *upāsana.* The conception of ultimate reality and that of a personal God are reconciled in religious experience, though the reconciliation cannot be easily effected in the region of thought. We cannot help thinking of the Supreme under the analogy of self-consciousness and yet the Supreme is the absolutely simple, unchanging, free, spiritual reality in which the soul finds its home, its rest, and completion.

Hospitality of the Hindu Mind

A religion that is based on the central truth of a comprehensive universal spirit cannot support an inflexible dogmatism. It adopts an attitude of toleration not as a matter of policy or expediency but as principle of spiritual life. Toleration is a duty, not a mere concession. In pursuance of this duty Hinduism has accepted within its fold almost all varieties of belief and doctrine and treated them as authentic expressions of the spiritual endeavour, however antithetic they may appear to be. Hinduism warns us that each of us should be modest enough to realize that we may perhaps be mistaken in our views and what others hold with equal sincerity is not a matter for ridicule. If we believe that we have whole mind of God we are tempted to assume that any one who disagrees with us is wrong and ought to be silenced. The Hindu shared Aristotle's conviction that a view held strongly by many is not usually a pure delusion. If any view has ennobled and purified human life over a wide range of space, time, and circumstance, and is still doing the same for those who assimilate its concept, it must embody a real apprehension of the Supreme Being. For Hinduism, though God is formless, he yet informs and sustains countless forms. He is not small and partial, or remote and ineffable. He is not merely the God of Israel or Christendom but the crown and fulfilment of you and me, of all men and all women, of life and death, of joy and sorrow. No outward form can wholly contain the inward reality, though every form brings out an aspect of it. In all religions, from the lowest to the highest, man is in contact with an invisible environment and attempts to express his view of the Divine by means of images. The animist of the *Atharva-Veda,* who believes that nature is full of spirits, is religious to the extent that he is convinced of the Divine presence and interpenetration in the world and nature. The polytheist is true to the extent that the Divine is to be treated on the analogy of human consciousness rather than any other empirical thing. The gods of the *Vedas* resemble the Supreme no more than shadows resemble the sun, but even as the shadows indicate where the sun is, the Vedic deities point to the direction in which the Supreme reality is. All forms are directing their step towards the one God, though along different paths. The real is one, though it is expressed in different names, which are determined by climate, history, and temperament. If each one follows his own path with sincerity and devotion he will surely reach God. Even inadequate views help their adherents to adapt themselves more successfully to their environment, to order their experiences more satisfactorily, and act on their environment more creatively. In the great crises of life, our differences look petty and unworthy. All of us have the same urge towards something of permanent worth, the same sense of awe and fascination before the mystery that lies beyond and within the cosmos, the same passion for love and joy, peace and fortitude. If we judge the saving power of truth from its empirical effects we see that every form of worship and belief has a strange power which enables us to escape from our littleness and become radiant with a happiness that is not of this world, which transforms unhappy dens into beautiful homes and coverts men and women of easy virtue and little knowledge into suffering servants of God. All truth is God's truth and even a little of it can save us from great troubles.

Besides, the truth of religion is, as Troeltsch declared, 'polymorphic'. The light is scattered in many broken lights and there is not anywhere any full white ray of divine revelation. Truth is found in all religions, through in different measures. The different revelations do not contradict but on many points confirm one another. For the Hindu, religions differ not in their object but in their renderings of its nature.

The Hindu attitude to religious reform is based on an understanding of the place of religion in human life. A man's religion is something integral in his nature. It is like a limb, which grows from him, grows on him, and grows out of him. If we take it away from him we mutilate his humanity and force it into an unnatural shape. We are all prejudiced in favour of what is our own. In spite of all logic we are inclined to believe that the home into which we are born is the best on all possible homes, that our parents are not as others are, and we ourselves are perhaps the most reasonable excuse for the existence of the human race on earth. If strangers are sceptical, it is because they do not know. These prejudices serve a useful purpose within limits. Mankind would never have progressed to this high estate if it had not been for this partiality for our homes and parents, our art and culture, our religion and civilization. If each pushes this prejudice to the extreme point, competition and warfare will result, but the principle that each one should accept his own tradition as the best for him requires to be adopted with due care that it is not exaggerated into contempt and hatred for other traditions. Hinduism admits this principle of historical continuity, recognizes its importance for man's advancement, and at the same time insists on equal treatment for other's views. Trying to impose one's opinions on other is neither so exciting nor so fruitful as joining hands in a endeavour after a result much larger than we know.

Besides, truth will prevail and does not require our propaganda. The function of a religious teacher is only to assist the soul's natural movement towards life. The longing for an ideal life may be hidden deep, overlaid, distorted, misunderstood, ill epressed, but it is there and is never wholly lacking. It is man's birthright which he cannot barter away or squander. We have to reckon with it and build on its basis. It does not matter what conception of God we adopt so long as we keep up a perpetual search after truth. The great Hindu prayers are addressed to God as external truth to enlighten us, to enable us to grasp the secret of the universe better and better. There is no finality in this process of understanding. Toleration in Hinduism is not equivalent to indifference to truth. Hinduism does not say that truth does not matter. It affirms that all truth are shadows except the last, though all shadows are cast by the light of truth. It is one's duty to press forward until the highest truth is reached. The Hindu method of religious reform or conversion has this for its aim.

Conversion is not always by means of argument. By the witness of personal example, vital changes are produced in thought and life. Religious conviction is the result, not the cause of religious life. Hinduism deepens the life of spirit among the adherents who belong to it, without affecting its form. All the gods included in the Hindu pantheon stand for some aspect of the Supreme. Brahma, Vishnu, and Siva bring out the creative will, saving love and fearful judgement of the Supreme. Each of them to its worshippers becomes a name of the Supreme god. *Harivamśa,* for example, tells us that Vishnu is the Supreme God, taught in the whole range of the Scriptures, the *Vedas, the Rāmāyana,* the *Purānas,* and the Epics. The same description is given of Śiva, who has Rudra for his Vedic counterpart.[23] He becomes the highest God. Śakti, the Mother Goddess, in her different forms represents the dynamic side of Godhead. Whatever form of worship is taken up by the Hindu faith it is exalted into the highest. The multiplicity of divinities is traceable historically to the acceptance of Prexisting faiths in a great religious synthesis where the different forms are interpreted as modes, emanations, or aspects of the one Supreme. In the act of worship, however, every deity is given the same metaphysical and moral perfections. The labels on the bottles may vary, but the contents are exactly the same. That is why from the *Rig-Veda* Hindu thought has been characterized by a distinctive hospitality. As the *Bhagavadgītā* has it: 'Howsoever men approach me, so do I welcome them, for the path men take from every side is mine.' Hinduism did not shrink from the acceptance of every aspect of God conceived by the mind of man, and, as we shall see, of every form of devotion devised by his heart. For what counts is the attitude of sincerity and devotion and not the conception which is more or less intellectual. Kierkegaard says: 'If of two men one prays to the true God without sincerity of heart, and the other prays to an idol with all the passion of an infinite yearning, it is the first who really prays to an idol, while the second really prays to God.'[24] Dominated by such an ideal, Hinduism did not believe in either spiritual mass-production or a standardized religion for all.

The great wrong, that which we can the sin of idolatry, is to acquiesce in anything less than the highest open to us. Religion is not so much faith in the highest as faith in the highest one can reach. At whatever level our understanding may be, we must strive to transcend it. We must perpetually strive to lift up our eyes to the highest conception of God possible for us and our generation. The greatest gift of life is the dream of a higher life. To continue to grow is the mark of a religious soul. Hinduism is bound not by a creed but by a quest, not by a common belief but by a common search for truth. Every one is a Hindu who strives for truth by study and reflection, by purity of life and conduct, by devotion and consecration to high ideals, who believes that religion rests not on authority but on experience.

Perfection

Whatever view of god the Hindu may adopt, he believes that the Divine is in man. Every human being, irrespective of caste or colour, can attain to the knowledge of this truth and make his whole life an expression of it. The Divinity in us is to be realized in mind and spirit and made a power in life. The intellectual apprehension must become embodied in a regenerated being. The Divine must subdue us to its purpose, subject the rebellious flesh to a new rhythm, and use the body to give voice to its own speech. Life eternal or liberation or the kingdom of heaven is nothing more than making the ego with all its thought and desires get back to its source in spirit. The self still exists, but it is no more the individual self but a radian divine self, deeper than the individual being, a self which embraces all creation in a profound sympathy. The *Upanishad* says: 'the liberated soul enters into the All.'[25] The heart is released from its burden of care. The sorrows and errors of the past, the anxiety of unsatisfied desire, and the sullenness of resentment are no more. It is the destiny of man where there is a perfect flowering of the human being. To embody this eternal greatness in temporal fact is the aim of the world. The peace of perfection, the joy of heaven, is realizable on earth. Perfection is open to all. We are all members of the heavenly household, of the family of God. However low we may fall, we are not lost. There is no such thing as spiritual death. As long as there is a spark of spiritual life, we have hope. Even when we are on the brink of the abyss, the everlasting arms will sustain us, for the there is nothing, not even and atom of reality where God does not abide. Men of spiritual insight take upon themselves the cross of mankind. They crown themselves with thorns in order that others may be crowned with life immortal. They go about the world as vagrants despising the riches of the world to induce us to believe in the riches of their world. When they gaze into men's eyes, whatever their condition of life, they see something more than man. They see our faces not merely by the ordinary light of the world but by the transfiguring light of our divine possibilities. They therefore share our joys and sorrows.

Yoga

To gain this enlightenment, this living first-hand experience of spiritual illumination, the aspirants submit themselves to long years of distracted search, to periods of painful self-denial. To be made luminous within we have to pay a heavy price. We must reduce the vast complex of actions and reactions we call human nature to some order and harmony. The appetites which call for satisfaction, the zest for life and animal propensities, our unreasoned likes and dislikes, pull us in different directions. This raw material requires to be subdued into the pattern of self. We must attain an integrated vision, a whole life, health and strength of body, alertness of mind, and spiritual serenity. A complete synthesis of spirit, soul, flesh, and affections requires radical change over, so that we think and live differently. We have to endure a violent inward convulsion. As a first step we are called upon to withdraw from all outward things, to retreat into the ground of one's own soul and find in the inmost depth of the self the divine reality. The world of things in its multiplicity is revealed as a unity.

The vision of the true self is at the same time vision of unity *(ekatvam anupaśyati)*. He beholds all beings in himself and himself in all beings.[26] 'There one perceives no other, hears no other, recognizes no other, there is fulness.'[27] A life that is divided becomes a life that is unified. Yoga is the pathway to this rebirth or realization of the divine in us .

There are not only many mansions in God's house but many roads to the heavenly city. They are roughly distinguished into three-Jnāna, Bhakti, and Karma. God is wisdom, holiness, and love. He is the answer for the intellectual demands for unity and coherence, the source and sustainer of values, and the object of worship and prayer. Religion is morality, doctrine as well as a feeling of dependence. It includes the development of reason, conscience, and emotion. Knowledge, love and action, clear thinking, ardent feeling and conscientious life, all lead us to God and are necessary for spiritual growth. A relatively greater absorption in one or the other depends on the point we have reached in our inner development. When the goal is reached there is an advance in the whole being of man. Religion then ceases to be a rite or a refuge and becomes the attainment of reality.

Jñāna

When *jñāna* is said to lead to *moksha* or liberation, it is not intellectual knowledge that is meant but spiritual wisdom. It is that which enables us to know that the spirit is the knower and not the known. By philosophical analysis *(tattva-vichāra)* we realize that there is in us a principle of awareness by which we perceive all things, though it is itself not perceived as an object in the ordinary way. Not to know that by which we know is to cast away a treasure that is ours. Yoga in the sense of the stilling of outward activities and emotions and concentration on pure consciousness is adopted to help the process of development. When we attain this *jñāna* there is a feeling of exaltation and ecstasy and a burning rage to suffer for mankind.

Bhakti

While Hinduism is one of the most metaphysical of religions, it is also one that can be felt and lived by the poor and the ignorant.

By the pursuit of *bhakti* or devotion we reach the same goal that is attained by *jñāna*. The devotees require a concrete support to their worship and so believe in a personal God. *Bhakti* is not the love which expects to be reciprocated. Such a love is a human affection and no more. Prayer becomes meditation, the worshipful loyalty of will which identifies itself with the good of the world. If you are a true devotee of God you become a knowing and a virtuous soul as well. The *bhakta* knows how to identify himself completely with the object of devotion, by a process of self-surrender.

My self I've rendered up to thee;
I've cast it from me utterly.
Now here before thee, Lord, I stand,
Attentive to thy least command.
The self within me now is dead,
And thou enthroned in its stead
Yes, this, I, Tuka, testify,
No longer now is 'me' or 'my'.[28]

The distinction between God and worshipper is only relative. Love and knowledge have one and the same end. They can only be conceived as perfected when there is an identity between lover and beloved, knower and known.

Karma

Ethical obedience is also a pathway to salvation. Hinduism desires that one's life should be regulated by the conception of duties or debts which one has to discharge. The debts are fourfold: (i) To the Supreme Being. One's whole life is to be regarded as a sacrifice to God. (ii) To the seers. By their austerities and meditations the sages discovered truth. We become members of a cultured group only by absorbing the chief elements of the cultural tradition. (iii) To our ancestors. We repay these debts by having good progeny. The Hindu social code does not ask us to impose and unnatural order on the world. We discover the intentions of nature in the constitution of men and women and it is our duty to act agreeably to them. Marriage is not merely of bodies but of minds. It makes us richer, more human, more truly living, and becomes the cause of grater love, deeper tenderness, more perfect understanding. It is an achievement which requires discipline. If it is not the expression of spirit, it is mere lust. There are innumerable shades between love, the spiritual unity expressed in physical unity, and lust which is mere physical attraction without any spiritual basis, and which has created prostitution both within and without marriage. The great love stories of the world, even when they involve a breaking of human laws, are centred, lifted up, and glorified by their fidelity, by the fact that they do not pass. (iv) To humanity. We own a duty to humanity which we discharge by means of hospitality and goodwill. Those who adopt this view are not content with merely earning their bread or seeking their comfort, but believe that they are born not for themselves but for others. Hinduism does not believe that the use of force is immoral in all circumstances. The *Bhagavad-gītā,* for examples, lays stress on the duties of the warrior and the claims of the nation. There is a place for politics and heroism, but wisdom and love are more than politics and war. In order to remain within the bonds of a class or a nation we need not free ourselves from the bonds of humanity. Real democracy is that which gives to each man the fullness of personal life. Animals are also included under object to be treated with compassion. All life is sacred, whether of animals or of follow men. We shudder at cannibalism and condemn the savage who wishes to indulge in this habit of our ancestors, though the slaughtering of animals and birds for human consumption continues to be regarded as right. The Hindu custom allows meat-eating but prefers vegetarianism. On days dedicated to religious functions meat-eating is disallowed. Our right to take animal life is strictly limited by our right to self-preservation and defence. The true man is he in whom the mere pleasure of killing is killed. So long as it is there, man has no claim to call himself civilized. The time will soon come, I hope, when public opinion will not tolerate popular amusements which depend on the illtreatment of animals. While Hinduism has within its fold barbarians inheriting the habits of wild ancestors who slew each other with stone axes for a piece of raw flesh, it aims at converting them into men whose hearts are charged with an eager and unconquerable love for all that lives.

In the priestly codes there is a tendency to confuse virtue with ceremonial purity. To kill a man is bad, but to touch his corpse is worse. The great scriptures, however, disregard technical morality and insist on the spirit of self-control and love of humanity. The law of self-sacrifice is the law of development for man. To be able to fulfil the obligations expected of man he must exercise self-control. Not only what we accept but what we renounce contributes to our making. Threefold is the gate of hell that destroys the self: lust, anger, and greed. We must make war upon them with the weapons of spirit, opposing chastity to lust, love to anger, and generosity to greed. The *Veda* says: 'Cross the bridges hard to cross. Overcome anger by love, untruth by truth.' The *Mahābhārata* says: 'The rules of *dharma* or virtuous conduct taught by the great seers, each of whom relied on his own illumination, are manifold. The highest among them all is self-control.'[29] Unfortunately, in our times, the man of self-control is regarded as a weak man.[30] It is for developing self-control that austerities and asceticism are practised, but when self-control is attained these rigorous practices are unnecessary. Insistence on discipline or self-control avoids the two extremes of self-indulgence and asceticism. Discipline does not mean either the starving of the senses or the indulgence of them.[31]

There is enough scope for repentance also. 'If he repents after he commits the sin, the sin is destroyed. If he resolves that he will never commit the sin again, he will be purified.'

The *Sannyāsi* is not one who abstains from work. Meditation and action both express the same spirit. There is no conflict between wisdom and work. 'It is the children of this world and not the men of learning who think of wisdom and work as different. The peace that is won by the knower is likewise won by the worker. He sees in truth who sees that wisdom and work are one.'[32]

Karma and Rebirth

The world is not only spiritual but also moral. Life is an education. In the moral sphere no less than the physical, whatsoever a man soweth that shall he also reap. Every act produces its natural result in future character. The result of the act is not something external to it imposed from without on the actor by an external judge but is in very truth a part of the act itself. We cannot confuse belief in *karma* with an easy-going fatalism. It is the very opposite of fatalism. It deletes chance, for it says that even the smallest happening has its cause in the past and its result in the future. It does not accept the theory of predetermination or the idea of an over-ruling providence. If we find ourselves helpless and unhappy we are not condemned to it by a deity outside of ourselves. The *Garuda Purāna* says: 'No one gives joy or sorrow. That others give us these is an erroneous conception. Our own deeds bring to us their fruits. Body of mine, repay by suffering.' God does not bestow his favours capriciously. The law of morality is fundamental to the whole cosmic drama. Salvation is not a gift of capricious gods but is to be won by earnest seeking and self-discipline. The law of *karma* holds that man can control his future by creating in the present what will produce the desired effect. Man is the sole and absolute master of his fate. But so long as he is a victim of his desires and allows his activities to be governed by automatric attractions and repulsions he is not exercising his freedom. If chains fetter us, they are of our own forging and we ourselves may rend them as under. God works by persuasion rather than by force. Right and wrong are not the same thing and the choice we make is a real one.

About future life there are three alternatives possible: (i) The soul dies with the body since it is nothing more than a function of physical life. Hindu religion does not accept this mechanical view. (ii) The soul goes either to heaven or eternal bliss or to hell or eternal torment and remains there. For the Hindu, the doctrine that the soul has only one life, a few brief years, in the course of which it determines for itself an eternal heaven or an eternal hell, seems unreasonable and unethical. (iii) The soul may not be fit for eternal life and yet may not deserve eternal torment and so goes from life to life. This life is not the end of everything. We shall be provided with other chances. The soul does not begin with the body nor does it end with it. It pursues its long pilgrimage through dying bodies and decaying worlds. The great purpose of redemption is carried over without break from one life to another. All systems of Hindu thought accept the idea of the continuous existence of the individual human being as axiomatic. Our mental and emotional make-up is reborn with us in the next birth, forming what is called character. 'When a man dies, what does not forsake *(na jahāti)* him is his soul *(nāma)*.'[33] Our strivings and endeavours give us the start. We need not fear that the spiritual gains of a long and strenuous life go for nothing. This continuity will go on untill all souls attain their destiny of freedom, which is the goal of human evolution. If there is not a shred of empirical evidence for it the same is true of other theories of future life also.

Conclusion

From the beginnings of Hindu history the culture has been formed by new forces which it had to accept and overcome in the light of its own solid and enduring ideas. In every stage there is an attempt to reach a harmony. Only the harmony is a dynamic one. When this dynamic harmony or organic rhythm of life is missing it means that the religion stands in need of reform. We are now in a period of social upheaval and religious unsettlement the world over, in one of those great incalculable moments in which history takes its major turns. The traditional forms are unable to express the growing sense of the divine, the more sensitive insight into the right way of life.' It is wrong to confuse the technique of a religion with its central principles. We must reform the technique so as to make it embody the fertile seeds of truth. In my travels round the country and abroad I have learnt that there are thousands of men and women today who are hungry to hear the good news of the birth of a new order, eager to do and dare, ready to make sacrifices that a new society may be born, men and women who dimly understand that the principles of a true religion, of a just social order, of a great movement of generosity in human relations, domestic and industrial, economic and political, national and international, are to be found in the basic principles of the Hindu religion. Their presence in growing numbers is the pledge for the victory of the powers of light, life and love over those of darkness, death, and discord.

—*S. Radakrishnan*

REFERENCES

1. Sir John Marshall, *Mohenjo-Dāro* and the Indus Civilization (1931), Vol. i, p. 106.
2. Professor Child writes: 'India confronts Egypt and Babylonia by the third millennium with a thoroughly individual and independent civilization of her own, technically the peer of the rest. And plainly it is deeply rooted in the Indian soil.' Again 'it has endured; it is already specifically Indian, and forms the basis of modern Indian culture'. *New light on the Most Ancient East* (1934).
3. Sir John Marshall, *Mohenjo-daro and the Indus Civilization* (1931), Vol. i, p. viii.
4. *Bhāgavata Purāna, iv.* 2. In the *Padma Purāna,* pāshandins are said to be 'those who wear skulls, ashes, and bones, the symbols contrary to the Vedas, put on matted locks and the barks of trees, even without entering into the third order of life and engage in rites which are not sanctioned by the Vedas.' *Uttara-kbandu, ch. 235.*
5. *Census of India Report (1901),* Vol. i, pt. I, p. 508.
6. See Clement Webb, *Religion and Theism* (1934), p. 36.
7. See Rivers, *Instinct and the Unconscious.*
8. *Rig-Veda, x. 90. 9; Brihadāranyaka Upanishad,* ii. 4. 10.
9. Purushābhāvāt...nishthā, Mīmāmsā-nyāya-prakāśa, 6.
10. *Vivarana-prameya-samgraha,* p.1.
11. *Nirukta-parisishta,* XIII. ii.
12. Cf. Augustine's statement that if one knows the object of one's belief, it cannot be God one knows.
13. i. 2-4.
14. *Bhāsya on Brahma Sūtra, iii.* 2. 17.
15. See *Katba Up.* i. 2.7; also *Bhagavad-gītā,* ii. 29.
16. *Lankāvatāra-sūtra,* 16.
17. *Mādhyamika-kārikā,* xv. 24.
18. *Brbad-āranyaka Up.* iii. 9, 26.
19. See Śamkara's commentary on *Chāndōgya Upanishad,* viii.

20. 'In us too, all that we call person and personal, indeed all that we can know or name in ourselves at all is but one element in the whole. Beneath it lies even in us, that wholly other, whose profundity impenetrable to any concept can yet be grasped in the numinous self-feeling by one who has experience of the deeper life.' Rudolf Otto, *The Idea of the Holy,* E.T., P. 36.
21. *Brhad-āranyaka Upanishad,* i. 4, 10.
22. The Supreme is 'all that which ever is, on all the world' *(Sarvam idam yatkinca jagatyām jagat).*
23. *Atharva-śiras Up.* v. 3.
24. Quoted in *The Tragic Sense of Life* by Unamuno (3rd imp.), p. 178.
25. *Mumdaka Up.* iii. 2. 15.
26. *Īśa Up.* 6.
27. *Cbāndogya Up.* vii. 24.
28. Nicol Macnicol, *Psalms of Marātbā Saints,* p. 79.
29. *Śāntiparva,* clx. 6.
30. *Ibid.* 34.
31. See *Bhagavad-gītā,* vi. 16-18.
32. *Ibid* x. 3; v. 4-5.
33. *Bribad-āranyaka Upanishad,* iii. 2, 12.

5

DHARMA, THE FIRST END OF MAN

The older Brahmanism of the Samhitās and Brāhmanas, when faced with the popularity of the non-Brahmanic religions and the appeal among intellectuals of Upanishadic mysticism, began to consolidate, reorganize and revitalise the Bahmanic way of life and thought. In this process a synthesis waș achieved between the older Brahmanical ideal of action—of life viewed as a ritual—and the newer, quictistic ideal of withdrawal and renunciation developed in the Upanishadic period. This revivalist movement within Brahmanism touched all spheres of human life—religious, academic, domestic, and social. Indeed, it was then for the first time that conscious efforts were made to evolve a definite pattern of Brahmanical society. The movement found expression in the texts of the Sacred Law (*Smṛti* or *Dharma Śāstra*) as well as in the Epics, the *Mahābhārata* and *Rāmāyana*, and in literature generally, even that dedicated to such profane subjects as material gain or love.

For vast numbers of Hindus throughout the ages there has been no more inspiring symbol of dharma than the hero of the epic *Rāmāyana,* a text which gives expression to the two main tendencies of the new revivalist movement—social and devotional. Rāma, eldest son and rightful heir to Dasharatha, King of Ayodhyā, is deprived of the throne by his stepmother's sudden demand that Dasharatha, in fulfillment of a boon granted long before, crown her own son king and banish Rāma. So that his father may keep his pledge to his wife, Rāma voluntarily withdraws to live in the wilderness for fourteen years with his faithful wife Sītā. In the forest the sages who have been leading a life of penance and austerity seek help from the great warrior Rāma against demons who are harassing then. This brings Rāma into conflict with the demons, whose king abducts Sītā and keeps her captive in his stronghold, hoping to win her love. After many struggles Rāma and his allies, the monkeys, overcome Rāvana and rescue Sītā. Thereupon Rāma is restored to his throne in Ayodhyā and sets an example as king of the most righteous and benevolent rule.

Rāma's noble example of devotion to duty, to his father, and to his people, as well as Sītā's long-suffering fidelity to Rāma, have been looked to as religious and ethical ideals down through the ages. Rāma is seen as the embodiment of dharma, and his triumph over wicked Rāvana as the overcoming of vice (*adharma*) in order that virtue and the moral law might prevail in personal and public life. Rāma, the embodiment of dharma, is also adored as the incarnation of the Supreme Lord who has come into the world to restore the moral order. In this form he became the object of a great devotional movement which swept the country in the first centuries A.D. Generation after generation, poets have celebrated Rāma in poems and plays, in both Sanskrit and vernacular; temples have been built to him, where sculpture, song, and drama told of his glory and enthroned him in the hearts of the masses. Eventually the *Rāmāyana* spread to the whole world of Southeast Asia where one can still see Rāmāyana sculptures and Rāmāyana plays. Even today, the epic, in its original Sanskrit or its vernacular versions, is read and expounded to large gatherings of devout listeners and in the national struggle for freedom which Mahātmā Gandhi waged, he held forth the establishment of *Rāma-rājya,* a reign of truth and nonviolence, as the ideal.

The Sacred Law and the epics are viewed by the Hindus as only slightly less sacred than the Vedas and together form the body of semi-canonical scriptures called *Smriti* "(human) Tradition"—as opposed to the Vedas, which are *Shruti* "(divine) Revelation."

Smriti is supposed to be based on Shruti, as indeed it largely is, and its authority is therefore only derivative. It is best represented in the Lawbooks, namely, the earlier *Aphorisms on the Domestic Ritual (Grhya Sūtṛas)* and *Aphorisms on Dharma (Dharma Sūtras)* in prose, and the later expanded versified codes, called *Dharma Sūstras* or *Smrtis,* and related texts. The most famous of these latter codes are the *Lawbook of Manu* (*Manu Smrti,* Shunga period, second to first centuries B.C.) and that of Yājnavalkya (*Yājnavalkya Smrti,* early Gutpa period, c. fourth century A.D.).

In time the major period of Śmriti (the Lawbooks and epics) covers roughly a thousand years (c. 500 B.C. to A.D. c. 500). Smriti gave India an integrated philosophy of life and social organization which stood the test, on the one hand, of foreign invasions and rule over several centuries (second century B.C. to A.D. c. 300), and on the other, of the heterodox religions, furnishing a pattern for the integration and absorption of both. The same period of foreign invasions and rule saw the rapid spread of theistic devotional cults, which after early opposition came to accept the authority of the Sacred law and the Vedic scriptures, and in return gained the support of orthodox Brahmanism. The alliance soon grew into the single, dynamic movement—though divided into several schools and sects—known as Hinduism. In contrast to brahmanism, Hinduism was a mass movement, which brought together into a single culture and polity, presided over by the Sacred law of the brāhmans, various peoples, classes, and religious traditions. This fusion of diverse forces produced one of the world's great classical periods, that of Hindu culture in the Gupta Age (fourth and fifth centuries A.D.).

The central concept which was elaborated and emphasized by Smriti was that of dharma. The word has been used in most of the Brahmanic texts from the *Rig Veda* downwards, and in different contexts, as we have seen, it has denoted different ideas, such as, Vedic ritual, ethical conduct, caste rules, and civil and criminal law. The Sacred Law is the codification of dharma. Actually, the concept of dharma is all-comprehensive and may be, broadly speaking, said to comprise precepts which aim at securing the material and spiritual sustenance and growth of the individual and society. Another significant characteristic of dharma which deserves to be specially noted is that is was regarded as not being static. The content of dharma often changed is the changing contexts of time, place, and social environment.

In spite of the comprehensive character of dharma, in its most common connotation it was limited to two principal ideals, namely the organization of social life through well-defined and well-regulated classes (varnas) and the organization of an individual's life within those classes into definite stages (āhramas). Thus, in popular parlance, dharma almost came to mean just varna-āshrama-dharma, that is the dharma (ordained duties) of the four classes and the four stages of life.

The system of the four classes has come to be regarded as the most essential feature of Brahmanic society. Even later Hinduism, which differs from Brahmanism in many significant respects, has scrupulously preserved this peculiar social organization. Though the world *varṇa-vyavasthā* is generally translated as caste system, it should be remembered that, strictly speaking, varna does not denote caste as we understand it today. Caste system is *jāti-vyavasthā,* which, no doubt, represents a ramification of the original system of classes. From the early Brāhmanic texts we can derive but little historical information regarding the origin and development of classes and castes. The aim of those texts was avowedly to glorify and defend the social organization governed by the concepts of classes and castes. They either speak of the divine origin of those social phenomena or give some myethical accounts in respect to them. A complex social phenomenon such as the caste system must be the result of the interaction of a variety of factors. The world *varna* (colour, complexion) itself would indicate that one of these basic factors was racial distinction. In the *Rig Veda* we actually come across references to the *ārya varna* (the "Aryan colour," *i.e.,* the Vedic Aryans) and the *dāsa varna* ("the Dāsa colour," the name collectively given to all racial groups other than the Vedic Aryans). In territories where the Aryans were dominant, the colour-line dividing the three upper Aryan social orders from the fourth, that of the despised shūdras, was very strict. Draconian penalties were prescribed for the shūdra who struck or insulted an Aryan, or even presumed to sit on the same seat with him. This social cleavage was given religious sanction and was thus preserved to this day in the distinction between caste Hindus and shūdras. The shūdras were denied all access to the Veda, the Vedic sacrifices, and the Aryan sacraments, especially the investitute with the sacred thread symbolic of the Aryan child's admittance to membership in his class.

Another important factor was magico-ritualistic in character. The four main classes were distinguished from one another on account of the specific roles which they played in connection with the communal sacrifice. These were determined by certain definite concepts of taboo, pollution, and purification. Corresponding to their roles in the ritual these classes were assigned distinct colours, which fact also seems to have confirmed the use of the word *varṇa* with reference to them. This magico-ritualistic origin of the four classes is indirectly indicated by their mention in the Purusha Sūkta (*Rig Veda,* 10.90), as the limbs of the cosmic sacrificial Purusha. Then there was the impact on the social organization of the Vedic Aryans of the pattern of social life already evolved by the indigenous Indian communities, which must have also been responsible for the consolidation of this social phenomenon. In the initial stages, these classes were more or less fluid and elastic. But in course of time they hardened into a definite social system characterized by a large number of endogamous and commensal castes, sub-castes, and mixed castes. Elaborate discussions occur in texts of the Sacred Law regarding their respective duties, and social and legal privileges and disabilities.

Within these classes and castes, an individual's life was organized into four distinct stages, called āshramas, in such a manner that the individual should be enabled to realize, through a properly graded scheme, the four ends of life. These four stages of life are those of the student, the householder, the hermit or recluse, and the ascetic. It will be seen that the system of the four stages of life seeks to resolve the conflict between two ideals, namely, consolidation and progress of society on the one hand and the spiritual emancipation of the individual on the other. In connection with the scheme of the four stages the texts of the Sacred Law have stated clearly and at some length the Brahmanic ideals regarding such topics as education, position of woman, and family life. Attempts have also been made to render the broad scheme of the four stages more viable and effective by prescribing various sacraments (samskāras), which are, as it were, the lampposts on the road leading to the full-fledged growth of man's personality. These sacraments cover man's whole life, beginning from the prenatal and ending with the post-mortem condition.

It will thus be seen that the Brahmanists had developed a most comprehensive system of social thought. This system continues to constitute—though in a more or less modified form—the basis of Hindu society even to this day.

What is Dharma?

It is difficult to find any one single passage wherein the comprehensive character of dharma is adequately brought out. Some typical passages are, therefore, given below with the idea that they might cumulatively indicate some characteristic features of this highly significant concept in Brahmanism and Hinduism.

[From *Taittirīya Āranyaka,* 10.79]

Dharma is the foundation of the whole universe. In this world people go unto a person who is best versed in dharma for guidance. By means of dharma one drives away evil. Upon dharma everything is founded. Therefore, dharma is called the highest good.

[From *Mahābhārata,* 12,110,10-11]

For the sake of the promotion of strength and efficacy among beings the declaration of dharma is made. Whatever is attended with nonviolence (ahimsā),[1] that is dharma. Such is the fixed opinion.

Dharma [from a root *dhṛ,* "to sustain"] is so called on account of its capacity for the sustenance of the world. On account of dharma, people are sustained separately in their respective stations.[2]

[From *Vaiśeṣika Sūtra,* 1.1.2]

That from which result material gain and spiritual good is dharma.

[From *Manu Smrti,* 8.15]

Dharma, when violated, verily, destroys; dharma, when preserved, preserves: therefore, dharma should not be violated, lest the violated dharma destroy us.

The Sources and Extent of Dharma

A discussion about the more tangible nature and extent of dharma, as it is generally understood, is given in the following passages.

[From *Yājñavalkya Smṛti,* 1.1.1-3, 6-9]

Having paid homage to Yājnavalkya, the lord of yogins, the sages said: Please expound to us fully the dharmas of the four classes, the four stages of life, and others.

The lord of yogins, living in Mithilā [capital of Videha], having meditated for a moment, said to the sages: The laws of that country in which the black antelope roams freely,[3] do you understand carefully.

The four Vedas, together with the Purānas,[4] logic, the science of Vedic interpretation, the Sacred Law [Dharma Shāstra], and the [six] limbs of the Veda,[5] constitute the fourteen seats of sciences and of dharma...

In a certain country, at a certain time, through certain means, when a thing is given over to a deserving person with faith—then, in that case, all these items, among others, indicate the concept of dharma.[6]

The Vedic scriptures [Shruti], the Sacred Law [Smriti], the practices of the good, whatever is agreeable to one's own self, and the desire which has arisen out of wholesome resolve—all these are traditionally known to be the sources of dharma.

Over and above such acts as sacrifice, traditional practices, self-control, nonviolence, charity, and study of the Veda, this, verily, is the highest dharma, namely, the realization of the Self by means of yoga.

Four persons versed in the Vedas and dharma, or a group of those who are adept only in the three Vedas, constitute a court. Whatever that court declares would be dharma; or that, which even one person who is the best among the knowers of the lore of the Self declares, would be dharma.

This passage, which is of the nature of a table of contents, indicates the scope and extent of the Sacred Law, as it was traditionally understood.

[From *Manu Smrti,* 1.111-18]

The creation of the universe, the procedure in respect of the sacraments, the practices relating to the vow of studentship [the respectful behaviour toward teachers, etc.], the highest rule regarding the ceremonial bath [to be taken at the termination of studentship].

The taking of a bride, the definitions of various kinds of marriages, the regulations concerning the great sacrifices, the eternal rule of the obsequies.

The definition of the modes of gaining subsistence, the vows of a graduate in Vedic studies [*i.e.,* of a brāhman householder], the rules regarding what may be eaten and what may not be eaten, the purification of men and the purification of things.

The laws concerning women, the rules relating to a hermit's life, spiritual emancipation, renunciation of worldly life, the whole set of the duties of a king, the deciding of law-suits.

The rules regarding the examination of witnesses, the law governing the relation between husband and wife, the law of inheritance and partition of ancestral property, the law concerning gambling, the removal of men who prove to be thorns of society.

The behaviour of vaishyas and shūdras, the origin of mixed castes, the law for all four classes in times of distress, similarly the expiatory rites.

The threefold course of transmigration resulting from a person's karma, the spiritual good, the examination of merits and demerits of actions.

The laws of specific countries, the laws of specific castes, the eternal laws of individual families, the laws of heretics and [tribal] communities—all these topics Manu has expounded in this treatise.

Dharma is Not Static

The following passage brings out a very significant characteristic of dharma, namely, that the concept and content of dharma change in accordance with the changing circumstances. Ancient tradition speaks of four ages (yugas)—Krita, Tretā, Dvāpara, and Kali—their duration, respectively, 1,728,000; 1,296,000; 864,000; and 432,000 human years. It is believed that each of these four succeeding ages is characterized by an increasing physical and spiritual deterioration. No one uniform set of dharmas can, therefore, be made applicable to all the four ages. It is further believed that when one cycle of four ages is completed, there occurs the end of the universe, which is followed by a new creation and a new cycle.

[From *Manu Smṛit,* 1,81-86]

Four-footed and complete is dharma in the Krita age—it is, verily, identical with Truth. Through behaviour contrary to dharma, no gain of any kind accrues to men.

In the other three ages, by reason of some kind of gain [accruing to men even through behaviour contrary to dharma], dharma is deprived successively of one foot [*i.e.,* one-fourth]. On account of the prevalence of theft, falsehood, and deceitfulness, dharma disappears successively quarter by quarter.

In the Krita age men are free from disease, accomplish all their aims, and live four hundred years; but in the ages beginning with the Tretā, their span of life decreases successively by one quarter.

The span of life of mortals mentioned in the Veda, the desired results of sacrifical rites, and the special spiritual powers of the embodied souls (that is, of mortals)—these result as fruits of men's actions in this world in accordance with the character of a particular age.

One set of dharmas is prescribed for men in the Krita age, other sets of dharmas in the Tretā and the Dvāpara ages and still another set of dharmas in the Kali age, in accordance with the increasing deterioration characterizing each successive age.

Austerities [tapas] constitute the highest dharma in the Krita age; in the Tretā, sacred knowledge is declared to be the highest dharma; in the Dvāpara they speak of the performance of sacrifice as the highest dharma; giving alone is the highest dharma in the Kali age.[7]

Varna-Dharma or Organization of the Four Classes

As far as the Brahmanic-Hindu way of life was concerned, the essence of all dharma consisted in the proper functioning of the organization of the four classes or of its later complex development, namely, the caste system. Each class had its own set of duties and obligations (*sva-dharma*) definitely prescribed and, for the sake of the solidarity and progress of society as a whole, each class or social unit was expected to act up to the following teaching of the *Bhagavad Gitā* (3.35): "Far more conducive to the ultimate good is one's own code of conduct (*sva-dharma*), even though deficient in quality, than an alien code of conduct, far easier to be practiced though it may be."

The four classes of those born from the mouth and limbs of Purusha—the brāhman (priest), kshatriya (noble), vaishya (the bourgeois), the shūdra (serf)—formed a well-knit, almost self-sufficient society.[8]

Below the society, yet economically tied to it, were a number of "excluded" castes, whose contact, shadow, or even sight polluted. They performed impure work such as scavenging, disposing of the dead, leather-work, etc., and had to live outside Aryan communities. They were made to bear distinctive marks and to strike a piece of wood to warn people of their approach. The concept of excluded castes is continued today in the untouchable castes, some of which may go back to ancient times, others probably being added from time to time from primitive tribes coming to live near more settled communities.

Large parts of India were not conquered by the Aryans but were held by various indigenous peoples, some tribes or classes of whom were observed to have a status and occupations similar to those of the corresponding twice-born classes. These were called *Vrātyas* and were thought to be twice-born castes degraded by neglect of the Vedic rites. Though assimilated in principle to shūdras, they were eligible to admission into the caste system as brāhmans, kshatriyas, or vaishyas by having a special sacrifice performed by brāhman priests. This device may have been largely responsible for the integration among the twice-born both of the non-Aryan upper classes found in India by the Aryans and of later invaders such as the Huns. All other foreigners were despised "barbarians" (*Mlecchas*).

[From *Manu Smṛti,* 1,87-98, 102, 107, 108]

For the sake of the preservation of this entire creation, [Purusha], the exceedingly resplendent one, assigned separate duties to the classes which had sprung from his mouth, arms, things, and feet.[9]

Teaching, studying, performing sacrifical rites, so too making others perform sacrifical rites, and giving away and receiving gifts—these he assigned to the brāhmans.

Protection of the people, giving away of wealth, performance of sacrificial rites, study, and nonattachment to sensual pleasures—these are, in short, the duties of a kshatriya.

Tending of cattle, giving away of wealth, performance of sacrifical rites, study, trade and commerce, usury, and agriculture—these are the occupations of a vaishya.

The Lord has prescribed only one occupation [karma] for a shūdra, namely, service without malice of even these other three classes.

Man is stated to be purer above the navel than below it; hence his mouth has been declared to be the purest part by the Self-existent One.

On account of his origin from the best limb of the Cosmic Person, on account of his seniority, and on account of the preservation by him of the Veda [brahman]—the brāhman is in respect of dharma the lord of this entire creation.[10]

For the Self-Existent One, having performed penance, produced the brāhman first of all, from his own mouth, for the sake of the conveying of the offerings intended for the gods and those intended for the manes and for the sake of the preservation of this entire universe.

What created being can be superior to him through whose mouth the gods always consume the oblations intended for them and the manes those intended for them?

Of created beings, those which are animate are the best; of the animate, those who subsist by means of their intellect; of the intelligent, men are the best; and of men, the brāhmans are traditionally declared to be the best;

Of the brāhmans, the learned ones are the best; of the learned, those whose intellect is fixed upon ritual activity; of those whose intellect is fixed upon ritual activity, those who carry out ritual activity; of those who carry out ritual activity, those who realize the brahman.

The very birth of a brāhman is the eternal incarnation of dharma. For he is born for the sake of dharma and tends toward becoming one with the Brahman. . ..

For the sake of the discussion of the brāhman's duties and of those of the other classes according to their precedence, wise Manu, the son of the Self-existent One, produced this treatise. . . .

In this treatise there are expounded in entirety dharma, the merits and demerits of [human] actions, and the eternal code of conduct of the four classes.

The code of conduct—prescribed by scriptures and ordained by sacred tradition [the Sacred Law]—constitutes the highest dharma; hence a twice-born person, conscious of his own Self [seeking spiritual salvation], should be always scrupulous in respect of it.

The Origin of Mixed Castes

This is a conventional description of the origin and nature of the various castes and mixed castes. It can by no means be regarded as reflecting the complex system of more than three thousand real castes, subcastes, mixed castes, and exterior (untouchable) castes, which prevails in India at present. Only one factor is considered in relation to the complex variety of the caste system namely, mixed marriages; no reference is made to such other factors as occupations, specific religious functions, enforcement of deliberate economic and administrative policies, etc.

[From *Yājñavalkya Smṛti,* 1.90-96]

By husbands belonging to a particular class upon wives belonging to the same class—the husbands and wives having been united in unblemished marriages—are begotten sons who belong to the same caste as that of the father and the mother[11] and who are capable of continuing the line.

The son[12] begotten by a brāhamn upon a kshatriya woman is called *Mūrdhāvasikta;* upon a vaishya woman, *Ambaṣtha;* upon a shūdra woman, *Niṣāda* or even *Pāraśava.*[13]

The sons begotten upon vaishya and shūdra women by a kshatriya are known by tradition respectively as *Māhisya* and *Ugra.* The son begotten by a vaishya upon a shūdra woman is known as *Karana.* This rule is laid down only in respect of married persons.

The son[14] begotten upon a brāhman woman by a kshatriya is called *Sūta;* by a vaishya, *Vaidehaka;* by a shūdra, *Cāndāla,* who is excluded from all considerations of dharma.

A kshatriya woman procreates from a vaishya a son called *Māgadha;* and from a shūdra, *Kṣattr.* A vaishya woman procreates from a shūdra a son called *(Āyogava.*

By a Māhishya is begotten upon a Karana woman a son called *Rathakāra.*.[15] As bad and good are to be regarded respectively the sons born of hypogamous [pratiloma] and hypergamous [anuloma] marriages.

The progressive advance in the social status[16] [of the various mixed castes] should be known as resulting in the seventh or even in the fifth union.[17] In cases of inversion of duties one is reduced to the status equal [to that of the caste whose way of life he adopts also at the end of the same period]. The higher and lower [status of sons born of unions between real castes and mixed castes] is to be determined on the same principle as before [the principle of hypergamy].

Initiation to Studentship

A brāhman, kshatriya, or vaishya boy is formally taken to a preceptor to be initiated to the disciplined life of a student of sacred knowledge. This initiation (upanayana) constitutes his second or spiritual birth—his birth from his parents being only a physical birth. Persons belonging to the first three classes are therefore called *dvijas* or twice-born. With the initiation commences the first stage of life (āshrama), namely, Vedic studentship or brahmacharya. The different initiation ages for the various classes suggest that their courses of study were different. The brāhman boy's was without doubt intellectually the hardest and he was probably the only one expected to master a whole Veda. The kshatriya's education was also in the hands of a brāhman preceptor, but much emphasis must have been given to training in military arts and government. As we can see from the selection given below from a work dating several centuries before Christ, a long period of education was compulsory in principle for all Aryans, who thus learned a common language (Sanskrit) and acquired a common culture. The superior linguistic, cultural, and social cohesion of the Aryans vis-à-vis the various non-Aryan tribes and peoples insured Aryan domination—political, social, and cultural—over the greater part of India even more than their military victories.

[From *Āśvalāyana Gṛhya Sūtra,* 1.19.1-13; 20.1-7; 21.5-7; 22.1-5]

In the eighth year one should initiate a brāhman; or in the eighth year from the conception in the embryo; in the eleventh year, a kshatriya; in the twelfth, a vaishya. Until the sixteenth year the proper time for initiation has not passed for a brāhman; until the twenty-second year, for a kshatriya; until the twenty-fourth year, for a vaishya. After that they become banished from Sāvitrī.[18] One should not initiate them, nor teach them, nor officiate at their sacrifices; people should not have any dealings with them.

One should initiate a boy who has put on ornaments, the hair on whose head is properly taken care of, who is clothed in a new garment that has not yet been washed, or in an antelope skin if he is a brāhman, in the skin of a spotted deer if he is a kshatriya, in a goat's skin if he is a vaishya. If they put on garments, they should put on colored ones: a brāhman, a reddish-yellow one; a kshatriya, a light red one; a vaishya, a yellow one. As for their girdles: that of a brāhman should be made of *muñja* grass; that of a kshatriya, a bow-string; that of a vaishya, woollen. As for their staffs: that of a brāhman should be of *palāśa* wood; that of a kshatriya, of *uḍumbara* wood; that of a vaishya, of *bilva* wood; or all sorts of staffs are to be used by students belonging to all classes.

Having offered an oblation while the student touches him on the arm [implying participation in the offering], the teacher should station himself to the north of the sacred fire facing toward the east. To the east of the sacred fire facing toward the west should the student station himself. The teacher should then fill with water the two cavities of the hands of himself and of his student and with the formula *tat savitur vṛṇīmahe...* should make the water flow down upon the full cavity of the student's hands by menas of the full cavity of his own hands. Having thus poured out the water upon the student's hands, he should with his own hand take the student's hand together with the thumb with the words: "By the impulse of the god Savitar [the Impeller, *i.e.*, the sun god], with the arms of the two Ashvins [heavenly physicians], with Pūshan's hand [god of prosperity] I take thee by thy hand, O so-and-so!" The teacher should take the student's hand a second time with the words: "Savitar has taken your hand, O so-and-so." The teacher should take the student's hand a third time with the words: "Agni [Fire, the god of sacrifical rites] is thy teacher, O so-and-so!" The teacher should make the student look at the sun and should then say: "God Savitar, this is thy student of sacred knowledge [brahmachārī]; protect him; may he not die.". . .

Having seized the student's hands with the student's garment and his own hands, he teacher should recite the Sāvitrī verse firsty fourth by fourth, then verse-half by verse-half, and finally the whole of it. He should make the student recite the Sāvitrī after himself as far as he is able to do so. On the region of the student's heart the teacher should place his hand with he fingers stretched upwards and say: "Into my vow I put thy heart; after my mind may thy mind follow; with single-aimed vow do thou rejoice in my speech; may God Brihaspati [heavenly priest of the gods] join thee to me."

Having tied the girdle round the student and given him the staff, the teacher should instruct him in the disciplined life of a student of sacred knowledge (brahmacharya) with the words: "A student of sacred knowledge thou art; sip water [a purification rite]; do the ritual act (karma); do not sleep in the daytime; remaining under the direction of the teacher study the Veda." For twelve years lasts the studentship for the Veda; or until the student has properly learned it. The student should beg food in the evening and in the morning. He should put fuel on the sacred fires in the evening and in the morning.[19]

Marriage and Householder's Duties

The second stage of life, that of the householder, is often characterized as the basis and support of the other three. It is, indeed, the only stage which affords full scope for the realization of the first three ends of man, namely, pleasure (kāma), material gain (artha), and virtue (dharma).

[From *Āśvalāyana Gṛhya Sūtra,* 1.5.1-3; 6.1-8]

One should first examine the family [of the intended bride or bridegoom], those on the mother's side and on the father's side, as has been said above.[20] One should give his daughter in marriage to a young man endowed with intelligence. One should marry a girl who possess the characteristics of intelligence, beauty, and good character, and who is free from disease....

The father[21] may give away his daughter after decking her with ornaments and having first offered a libation of water: This is the *Brāhma* form of marriage. A son born to her after such a marriage purifies twelve descendants and twelve ancestors on both her husband's and her own sides. The father may give her away after decking her with ornaments to an officiating priest while a Vedic sacrifice is being performed: that is the *Daiva*[22] form of marriage. A son born of such a marriage purifies ten descendants and ten ancestors on both sides. "Practice dharma together,"—a marriage performed with this imposition on the bride and the bridegroom is the *Prajāpatya* form of marriage. A son born of such marriage purifies eight descendants and eight ancestors on both sides. A person may marry a girl after having first given a cow and a bull to her father: that is the *Ārṣa*[23] form of marriage. A son born of such marriage purifies seven descendants and seven ancestors on both sides. A person may marry a girl after having made a mutual agreement with her. That is the *Gāndharva*[24] form of marriage. A person may marry a girl after having satisfied her father with money: that is the *Āsura* ["demonic"] form of marriage.

A person may carry off a girl while her people are sleeping or are careless about her: that is the *Paiśāca* ["devilish"] form of marriage. Having killed her people and broken their heads, a person may carry off a girl, while she is weeping, from her relatives who are also weeping: that is the *Rākṣasa* ["fiendish"] form of marriage.

[From *Yājnavalkya Smṛti,* 1.97-105, 115-16]

A householder should perform every day a Smriti rite [*i.e.,* a domestic rite prescribed by the Sacred Law, Smriti] on the nuptial fire or on the fire brought in at the time of the partition of ancestral property. He should perform a Vedic rite on the sacred fires.

Having attended to the bodily calls, having performed the purificatory rites, and after having first washed the teeth, a twice-born [Aryan] man should offer the morning prayer.

Having offered oblations to the sacred fires, becoming spiritually composed, he should murmur the sacred verses addressed to the sun god. He should also learn the meaning of the Veda and various sciences.

He should then go to his lord for securing the means of maintenance and progress. Thereafter having bathed he should worship the gods and also offer libations of water to the manes.

He should study according to his capacity the three Vedas, the *Atharva Veda,* the Purānas, together with the Itihāsas [legendary histories], as also the lore relating to the knwoledge of the Self, with a view to accomplishing successfully the sacrifice of muttering prayers [*japa-yajna*].

Offering of the food oblation [bali], offering with the utterance *svadhā,* performance of Vedic sacrifices, study of the sacred texts, and honouring of guests—these constitute the five great daily sacrifices[25] dedicated respectively to the spirits, the manes, the gods, the Brahman, and men.

He should offer the food oblation to the spirits [by throwing it in the air] out of the remnant of the food offered to the gods.

He should also cast food on the ground for dogs, untouchables, and crows.

Food, as also water, should be offered by the householder to the manes and men day after day. He should continuously carry on his study. He should never cook for himself only.

Children, married daughters living in the father's house, old relatives, pregnant women, sick persons, and girls, as also guests and servants—only after having fed these should the householder and his wife eat the food that has remained...

Having risen before dawn the householder should ponder over what is good for the Self. He should not, as far as possible, neglect his duties in respect of the three ends of man, namely, virtue, material gain, and pleasure, at their proper times.

Learning, religious performances, age, family relations, and wealth—on account of these and in the order mentioned are men honoured in society. By means of these, if possessed in profusion, even a shūdra deserves respect in old age.

The Position of Women

Contradictory views have been expressed concerning the social status of a Hindu woman. On the one hand it is enjoined that he should be shown the utmost respect, while, on the other, she is said to deserve no freedom. This contradiction is more apparent than real, for the emphasis in the latter case is not so much on the denial of any freedom to a woman as on the duty of her near ones to protect her at all costs.

[From *Manu Smṛti,* 3.55-57; 9.3-7, 11, 26]

Women must be honoured and adorned by their fathers, brothers, husbands, and brothers-in-law who desire great good fortune.

Where women, verily, are honoured, there the gods rejoice; where, however, they are not honoured, there all sacred rites prove fruitless.

Where the female relations live in grief—that family soon perishes completely; where, however, they do not suffer from any grievance—that family always propers. . . .

Her father protects her in childhood, her husband protects her in youth, her sons protect her in old age—a woman does not deserve independence.

The father who does not give away his daughter in marriage at the proper time is censurable; censurable is the husband who does not approach his wife in due season; and after the husband is dead, the son, verily, is censurable, who does not protect his mother.

Even against the slightest provocations should women be particularly guarded; for unguarded they would bring grief to both the families.

Regarding this as the highest dharma of all four classes, husbands, though weak, must strive to protect their wives.

His own offspring, character, family, self, and dharma does one protect when he protects his wife scrupulously. . . .

His own offspring, character, family, self, and dharma does one protect when he protects his wife scrupulously. . . .

The husband should engage his wife in the collection and expenditure of his wealth, in cleanliness, in dharma,[26] in cooking food for the family, and in looking after the necessities of the household. . .

Women destined to bear children, enjoying great good fortune, deserving of worship, the resplendent lights of homes on the one hand and divinities of good luck who reside in the houses on the other—between these there is no difference whatsoever.

The Hermit and the Ascetic

In the third stage of life man is expected to retire from active family and social life and seek seclusion. But he should be available for advice and guidance to the family and society whenever they need them. In the last stage, namely, that of the life of an ascetic (sannyāsin), man completely renounces this worldy life and devotes himself exclusively to spiritual self-realization.

[From *Manu Smṛti,* 6.1-3, 8, 25, 33, 42, 87-89]

Having thus lived a householder's life according to the prescribed rules, a twice-born householder should, making a firm resolve and keeping his sense-organs in subjection, live in a forest as recommended in the Sacred Law.

When a householder sees his skin wrinkled and his hair gray and when he sees the son, then he should resort to the forest.

Having given up food produced in villages [by cultivation] and abandoning all his belongings, he should depart into the forest, either committing his wife to the care of his sons or departing together with her....

He should be constantly engaged in study and should be self-controlled, friendly toward all, spiritually composed, ever a liberal giver and never a receiver, and compassionate toward all begins....

Having consigned the sacred fires into himself[27] in accordance with the prescribed rules, he should live without a fire, without a house, a silent sage subsisting on roots and fruit. . .

Having thus passed the third part of his life in the forest, he should renounce all attachments to worldly objects and become an ascetic during the fourth part of his life....

He should always wander alone, without any companion, in order to achieve spiritual perfection—clearly seeing that such attainment is possible only in the case of the solitary man, who neither forsakes nor is forsaken...

The student, the householder, the hermit, and the ascetic—these constitute the four separate stages of life, originating from and depending upon the householder's life.

All these stages of life, adopted successively and in accordance with the Shāstras, lead the brāhman[28] following the prescribed rules to the highest state.

Of all these, verily, according to the precepts of the Veda and the Smriti the householder is said to be the most excellent, for he supports the other three.

The Sacraments

The sacraments (samskāras) help to render the scheme of the four stages of an individual's life more tangible and definite. They represent, as it were, the various landmarks in man's progress through the course of life, which aim at building up a full-fledged physical and spiritual personality. The following passage represents the earliest enumeration of the sacraments. Note the author's subordination of external ritual to moral qualities at the end of the passage.

[From *Gautama Dharma Sūtra*, 8.14-26]

(1) The ceremony relating to the conception of the embryo; (2) the ceremony relating to the desired birth of a male child; (3) the parting of the pregnant wife's hair by the husband [to ward off evil spirits]; (4) the ceremony relating to the birth of the child; (5) the naming of the child; (6) the first feeding; (7) the tonsure of the child's head; (8) the initiation; 9-12) the four vows taken in connection with the study of the Veda; (13) the ceremonial bath [graduation]; (14) the union with a mate who would practice dharma together with him [*i.e.*, marriage]; 15-19) the daily performance of the five sacrifices to gods, manes, men, spirits, and the Brahman; 20-26) and the performance of the following sacrifices, that is, of the seven cooked-food sacrifices. . . .; 27-33) the seven kinds of oblation sacrifices. . . .; 34-40) the seven kinds of soma sacrifices. . . .these are the forty sacraments.

Now follow the eight good qualities of the soul, namely, compassion to all begins, forbearance, absence of jealousy, purity, tranquillity, goodness, absence of meanness, and absence of covetousness. He who is sanctified by these forty sacraments but is not endowed with the eight good qualities of the soul does not become united with the Brahman, nor does he even reach the abode of the Brahman. On the other hand, he who is, verily, sanctified by a few only of the sacraments but is endowed with the eight good qualities of the soul becomes united with the Brahman, he dwells in the abode of the Brahman.

REFERENCES

1. In thought, word, and deed: violence of any kind disturbs the proper functioning of the individual and society, and, therefore, represents the negation of dharma.
2. Confusion regarding the respective duties and functions (and privileges and disabilities) of different classes unbalances society. One of the king's chief duties is to prevent such confusion.
3. That is, the open grazing lands of the north Indian plain. According to Manu (2.23), such a country alone is fit for sacrifice, that is, for Aryan habitation.
4. Semihistorical and religious legends.
5. They are science of correct pronunciation and accentuation, aphorisms concerning Vedic ritual, etc., grammar, Vedic etymology, Vedic metrics, and astronomy.
6. The various constituents of the activity of giving away, which is, indeed, the main basis of all dharma, at least in the final age of a cycle, form, according to the commentated the causative attributes of dharma.
7. Disparity (particularly in respect of material possessions), which is, indeed, the road cause of all evil and ill-will among men in the present Kali age, can be removed only by "giving away." It is interesting to view in this light such movements in modern India a *Bhū-dāna* (giving away of land), *Sampatti-dāna* (giving away of wealth), *ṣrama-dāna* (making physical labour available to society), etc.
8. The brāhman, kshatriyas, and vaishyas are called *dvija* or twice-born, because they are entitled as Aryans to the sacrament of initiation to the study of the Veda, which is regarded as their second or spiritual birth. The study or even overhearing of the Vedic scriptures by the non-Aryan shūdras was forbidden under the most drastic penalties.

9. Ci. *Rig. Veda,* 10,90. The divine origin of the four classes is indicated here. It is, therefore, almost sacrilegious for a lower order to assume the duties of a higher one.

10. Even from the point of view of civil law the brāhman enjoyed certain special privileges. In connection with the treasure-trove, for instance, the *Manu Smṛti* lays down (8.37) that a brāhman finds it he may keep the whole of it "for he is master of everything," while persons belonging to other classes cannot do so. The punishments prescribed for a brāhman dender are more lenient than those prescribed for the same offense by persons belonging to other classes. For perjury, persons of the three lower classes shall be fined and banished, but a brāhman shall only be banished. Similarly, a brāhman is not liable to corporal punishment (*Manu Smṛiti* 8.123-24).

11. There is a threefold division of Hindu marriage: (1) that in which the husband and the wife belong to the same class; (2) hypergamy, in which the husband belongs to a higher class than the wife; (3) hypogamy, in which the wife belongs to a higher class than the husband. The offspring of hypogamous unions was especially despised, in direct proportion to the disparity between the ranks of the parents: the Chāndāla, said to be the offspring of a shūdra by a brāhman woman, is the lowest untouchable.

12. This and the next stanza refer to the mixed castes resulting from hypergamous marriages. The sons of hypergamous unions between Aryan parents were also Aryan, though of mixed caste.

13. Two very low castes.

14. This and the next stanza refer to the mixed castes resulting from hypogamous unions.

15. The *Sūta* (charioteer, bard), *Ksattṛ* (doorkeeper), *Māhsya* (attendant on cattle), *Rathaara* (chariot-maker) must have originally had occupational significance. The Nishādas were an aboriginal tribe in origin and lived by fishing and hunting *Ambastha* (healer, doctor). *Vaidehaka,* and *Māgadha* (trader) are clearly regional names, implying that these castes came from Ambashtha, Videha, or Magadha. It may be seen how the castes named in this treatise had the most varied origins and were some how integrated into a hierarchical system based on the theory of hypergamy. We must admire, however, the Brāhman authorities ingenuity in choosing appropriate occupied caste for the offspring of different hybird unions.

16. This stanza is important in that it speaks of the possibility of a mixed caste being elevated to the status of the next higher real caste. It also

makes the significant point that a change in occupation (in normal circumstances) often implies a change in caste. In other words, birth is not the only factor which determines caste, for a Brāhman family which lives by the profession of a shūdra continuously through seven generations become shūdra. It is interesting that there is no mention of a person following the profession of a social order higher than his.

17. For instance a brāhman begets upon a shūdra wife of Nishāda daughter. Another brāhman marries this Nishāda daughter and be gets a daughter. Upon the daughter born in this way in the sixth generation a brāhman husband would be get a son who is himself a brāhman and not a member of any mixed caste.

18. From initiation and hence from class and Aryan society. Sāvitri being the Vedic verse used at initiations.

19. The student lived with the teacher at his residence and helped him in connection with among other things, his religious observances. He begged food daily for himself and his teacher. Society bore the responsibility for the maintenance of teachers and students.

20. That is, through ten generation, as has been prescribed in Āshvalāyana's *Aphorisms on the Vedic Ritual* (*Ā Śrauta Sitra* 9.3.20).

21. This passage describes the eight forms of marriage. The three main factors invovled in these different forms are money, love, and physical force. Traditionally, the first four forms of marriage are accepted as proper, while the remaining four are condemned. This becomes clear not only from the names given to the various forms but also from the conventional mention in respect of the first four forms of marriage of the purifying capacity of sons born of those marriages.

22. Lit, "pertaining to the [Vedic] gods."

23. Lit. "pertaining to the [Vedic] sages."

24. Lit. "pertaining to the heavenly musicians."

25. This is an expansion of the older and basic concept of Brahmanical thought, that of the three debt, to the ancestors or manes, to the gods, and to the rishis or sages. The debt to the manes was discharged by marrying and continuing the race and thus the ceremonies originally intended to feel the ancestors. The debt to the gods was discharged by sacrifice and worship and that to the sages through the study and preservation of the scriptures.

26. Ordained duty, especially here religious rites.

27. The three sacred fires are the symbol of a householder's life. During the latter part of his life as a forest hermit the Hindu gives up his sacred fires; these are not to be destroyed but are symbolically consigned into his own self.
28. And also persons belonging to the next two social orders.

6

BUDDHISM

An amazing number of popular or semi-popular books on Buddhism have been published during recent years. I am myself responsible for some of them. As a rule these books are built on the same pattern. They begin with an account of the religious and social life of eastern India before Śākyamuni, and then give a sketch of his life and work. Unfortunately the ideas, events, and men of this time can only be known by conjecture, and the reader is confronted, either by doubtful facts and questionable theories, or by a sceptical discussion about them. I shall dispense with some of those historical speculations and biographical accounts, which can be found in so many works, believing that it will be more useful to explain what we know about the internal constitution of Indian Buddhism, and about its changes during the eight or ten centuries of its early history.

The present work deals with the world's debt to India. In writing of Buddhism my first task will be to consider what that religion owes to the land in which Śākyamuni lived and taught.

Buddhism is not wholly original; it appears, during centuries, as a 'buddhification' of institution, ideas, or feelings, which were simply Indian: the asceticism and the clerical institutions took a special character in Buddhism; the Buddha doctrine of transmigration, of the action and the reward of actions, was a recast of the parallel Hindu doctrines; the cult or worship of Buddhism evolved according to the general transformation of cult and worship; the belief in a God Saviour, prominent in later Buddhism and less developed in early times, reflects also the gradual growth of devotion (*bhakti*). In short, Buddhism is only the 'buddhized' aspect of contemporaneous Hinduism.

It cannot be said that the most notable features of the Buddhist speculation—its 'rationalism' (I mean its antipathy to every kind of ritualism and superstition), its atheism (*i.e.* its negation of a God creator and providence), its high morality, its pessimism, its anti-caste tendency, its mildness and humanity, and so on—are specifically Buddhist.

But, on the other hand, I believe that Buddhism, owing to the 'solidity' of the Brotherhood, owing to the dialectical strength of its schools, gave to the ideas and feelings it adopted or patronized a great strength and *rayonnement*. The common Indian belief in the reward of good and bad actions was enforced by the Buddhist propaganda. The common Indian feeling of the misery of life, and the general Indian compassion and benevolence, had in the noble figures of the Buddhist saints very suggestive and attractive representations. The early brahmanic literature shows that many sages disapproved or clearly condemned social distinctions; but the Buddhist order was a living example of equality and mutual esteem. And so on.

Owing to Buddhism (as also owing to Brahmanism) many old things have conserved life and even vigour. The Buddhist monastic institution of Ceylon of today is probably very like the Buddhist monastic institution of pristine days: and this last was probably very like the institutions of the sects of Buddha's epoch.

Prefatory

(a) In early India, before the rise of the Brāhman speculation which is embodied in the treatises called *Upanishads*, Hindus knew only of gods to be worshipped, of paradises to be obtained through worship, rites, and good works. But there was later a great change. Many men admitted that paradises are perishable; that the gods themselves die; that beings transmigrate from the beginning: at one time they may be men, at another animals, they may suffer in hell, or rise to be gods. There is something better than paradise, there is a *summum bonum*, a highest good, a supreme happiness, known later as Nirvāna or Brahma-nirvāna, an abode beyond transmigration, change, consciousness, or personality; technically an abode 'supramundane' (*lokottara*) in contrast with the 'world' (*loka*), which includes paradises and hells.

This abode is not to be reached through the worship of any god, the doing of any good work, the acquisition of any merit, but by austerity or meditation or wisdom, in short by the discipline later known as *yoga*.

Henceforth, from the times of the *Upanishads* (sixth century B.C.) down to our days, every branch of the Indian faith, be it Brahmanism, Buddhism, Jainis, Vishuism, or Śivaism, has presented a twofold aspect. One is 'religious', or 'mundane' (*laukika*), and deals with paradises, happy rebirths, gods or God, worship, meritorious action. The other is 'transcendent' (supramundane, *lokottara*), or 'music', and makes man's chief object the attainment, through gnosis and ecstasy, of an abode of everlasting inconceivable happiness.[1]

The difference of the goal involves differences amongst the devotees. The men of mean aspirations, attached to sensual pleasures, wish for paradises. The 'few ones', the 'happy ones' wish for a 'better part' than paradises: they leave home and practise continence and religious life in order to achieve Nirvāna.

(b) The contrast between 'religion' and 'supramundane discipline' is a permanent feature of Buddhism. But both the 'religion' and the 'discipline' take a twofold aspect owing to the development of the Buddhology; that is, owing to the fundamental change that the doctrines concerning Buddha and Buddhahood underwent about the beginning of the Christian era.

Our knowledge of the feelings of the early Buddhist folk towards Śākyamuni, living or dead, is scanty.[2] But we feel sure that the general conviction of the monks was that Śākyamuni, no longer visible to gods or men, was lost in eternal quietude. A process of apotheosis began soon, both amongst the good folk and amongst some sections of the clergy. It resulted in a theory which constitutes the essential tenet of the later Buddhist faith (Mahāyāna): Buddhas, who are many in number, have been men, but their 'buddhification is an event of a primitive age; they are now, as they have been for centuries and will be for ever, divine beings enthroned in the highest heavens. The real Śākyamuni has been reigning for many cosmical periods on the celestial 'Peak of the Vultures'. The historical Śākyamuni, who was born at Lumbinī, left his home, obtained Buddhahood, preached and reached Nirvāna, is only an image, a fiction, a 'created body' of the real Śākyamuni.

It will be easy to understand the profound modification which Buddhist religion and Buddhist mysticism must undergo when such Buddhology is admitted.

I. Early Buddhist Religion

A number of good *recoupements*—Asoka's edicts, a few books of popular inspiration, monastic texts relative to laymen, archaeology—give an approximate idea of the true nature of early extra-monastic Buddhism.

1. *Upāsakas or Laymen.* Śākyamuni came rather late into a world where ascetic institutions had long been flourishing. This explains why the rules of the monastic Buddhist discipline were rapidly fixed (not without variants and recasts), and why the congregation of the laymen—the Upāsakas or 'devotees'-rapidly took the form of a *tiers ordre.*

The reader of Kipling is well aware that a holy man (*sādhū*) easily finds food and a roof. But the religious orders, with their little village-convents, could not live without regular and organized assistance: they had official friends, 'bourgeois' and villagers, who gave alms, clothing, houses, and fields.

The 'official' position of the laymen is more important than is often admitted. First, they are really 'Buddhists', not only generous alms-givers, but members of the Church: a man becomes a Upāsaka by taking liturgically the 'triple refuge' (I take refuge in the Buddha, in his Doctrine, in his Brotherhood); by binding himself to the observation of the fivefold morality (I shall not kill, steal, &c.). Secondly , while laymen are under the guidance of the clergy, they exercise on the clergy a right of control (legend or history of the Council of Vaiśālī), and the clergy have to submit to 'public opinion'. Buddha often says to his monks: 'Will such behaviour please the people?'

2. One character of the lay-Buddhism is that Nirvāna is of little importance. It opens the way to paradises or to a happy rebirth as a man. It is sometimes styled *devayāna,* the vehicle of the gods.

By a sinless life, by perseverance in the practice of family and social duties, by benevolence and kindness, by alms to the monks, by the worship of the Buddha and his relics, by the fortnightly fast, a man earns merit (*punya*) and enjoys the reward of this merit in a future life, either as a god or as a happy man.

It must be remembered that paradises (*svarga*) are only places of pleasure and sensual enjoyment. They present no Buddhist features, and are simply the Hindu paradises adopted by Buddhism, but not adapted. The idea that a man might be reborn in the palace of a Buddha, and enjoy his presence, is absolutely foreign to Asoka (third century B.C.).

3. *Buddhist elements in this early religion.* There is much in this religion which is properly Buddhist; its very pure morality, free from ritualism or superstition; the 'buddhification' of the path of paradise, which consists in the strict observance of morality, not in sacrifices; the gods have been ethically improved, they have been 'converted' by the Buddha, and learnt to favour the good and hate sinners; the cult of the dead has been metamorphized by Buddhism—they are helped by good deeds accomplished for their welfare by their relatives;

there is created a new and very white 'white magic': the best defence against evil spirits and serpents is to 'direct towards them the strength of benevolence'—'I am your friend, oh serpents' (as in Kipling's *Kim*).

The dogmatic basis of the system is the belief that man transmigrates, that good and evil deeds are rewarded and punished in a future life. We do not know exactly what stage of development the notions of reincarnation, transmigration, act, retribution, had reached in the Kośala-Magadha of the sixth century B.C. But we know that the Buddhist doctrines of transmigration and good works differ from the Brahmanic. Brāhmans have never conceived transmigration as the universal rule: they have always thought that the great gods at least are gods by nature.

Buddhists say that the person who is actually Brahmā has obtained this 'place' by his good works; that, after centuries, when the merit of his good works will be exhausted by the very enjoyment of the reward, the actual Brahmā will die and be reborn as a man or as a citizen of hell. Brāhmans teach that the good man obtains a happy rebirth, and reversely; but they do not object to the doctrine of 'fate' and they attach great importance to sacrificial or ritual 'good work'. According to Buddhists, 'fate' is only the former actions of every one, and the only good work is the moral act, the act accomplished with the purpose of benefiting oneself in a future life, and one's neighbour in the present one. Brāhmans admit the retribution of works, but they believe that the great god Brahmā is the 'retributor' and places beings in a high or a low rebirth according to their merit Buddhists strongly object to a God, to a Providence: they teach that actions, good or bad, bear their fruit, owing to their own (semi-magical) strength. As concerns deities, fairies, and spirits, Buddhism admits not only their existence, but also their power; they are very useful and must be properly worshipped: they care for a number of things too mean to attract the attention of the Buddhist Persons. But they nevertheless hold a very humble position in Buddhism.

It is very probable that these moral and rationalist views have exercised a notable influence on the old India.

Śākyamuni has often been described as a social reformer: 'He attacked the system of caste and conquered for the poor and the outcasts a place in his spiritual kingdom.' Oldenberg has said in so many words that this description is a misrepresentation. He observed that he man who has abandoned the worldly life in order to be a monk has no longer any interest in worldly or social affairs.

Let us observe that the Buddhist Brotherhood is open to men of low extraction. True, the Buddhists followed the example of other sects. But the fact remains that orthodox Brahmanism scarcely approved this contempt of the caste principle: it condemns the men 'who bear by imposture the dress of ascetics and are professional thieves'. The liberalism of the Brotherhood was clearly anti-caste.

Again, the Buddhist monks became the spiritual advisers of their lay supporters. The moral systems they taught contradicts the Brahmanic tradition and the system of caste. Bloody sacrifices are murders; funeral ceremonies are of no use since the defunct is already reborn either in hell or in paradise. Brāhmans are conceived and born like other men, they do not differ from them in colour or physique. The best 'fields of merit' (the alms receivers who give efficacy to charities) are the Buddhist monks, not the Brāhmans.

4. *Buddhism owes much to its non-clerical elements.* According to tradition the worship of the relics was at first the business of the laymen. Ascetics or monks who have in Nirvāna their goal and in the preparation for Nirvāna the rule of their religious life, consider Śākyamuni as the sage who has discovered the Way, no more. The worship of the relics and of the stūpas, all-important in historical Buddhism, has in itself no specially Buddhist character.

Scholars believe that the legend of Śākyamuni-his descent from the Tushita heaven into the womb of Māyā, his miraculous birth, the poetiç and mythological features of his 'conquest of Buddhahood' under the Sacred Tree, and so on—is the work of popular speculation. When we are told that Śākyamuni in his former birth has been the good elephant, the patient bear, the generous King Sibi, &c., we feel sure that the history of the former

Śākyamuni has been embellished with Hindu stories wherein the popular faith had embodied its conception of the good man; we are even justified when we admit that the chief characteristic of Śākyamuni, his universal benevolence, his pity for all creatures, has its origin in the kindly and generous feelings of the folk of Magadha, rather than in the speculation of the clerical part of the Church. For monks Śākyamjuni is the 'great Ascetic' (*mahāśramana*). India has venerated and loved Śākyamuni as the 'Great Compassionate One' (*mahākārunika*). Of course the true personality and the psychological figure of Śākyamuni remain a riddle. His 'goodness' was probably fascinating; but India was prepared to worship an incarnation of goodness. The monkish ideal was quite different, and ideal of stoic tranquillity, and the clerical tradition is that Śākyamuni first decided to keep to himself the truths which he had discovered, in order to avoid the trouble of preaching.

5. *Buddhist lay-religion and brahmano-hinduism.* Buddhism was a *pūjā*, worship, also a *dharma*, code of ethics. But it had no rites for marriage, birth, death, or ceremonies for the welfare of the dead, Not that it did not enforce precepts for conjugal morality, for the preparation for death, for benefiting the dead by gifts to the monks and by pious works; but the Brāhmans continued to officiate at marriage, birth and death; they continued to be the guests at the funeral banquets.

As Buddhism did not impose or even propose any *substituta* for the traditional rites of the family life, it did not destroy these rites or jeopardize the position they assured to Brāhmans. To destroy them, it was not enough to preach that, 'although they might be useful for the present life, they are without utility for the next one' (Aśoka).

Brahmanism catered for happiness here below and hereafter. Buddhism professed to be and indeed was much more concerned with the future life; but as an established religion it was deficient in supernatural devices for the welfare of everyday life. Kings, merchants villagers did not find in Buddhism the manifold contrivances of Brahmanism for victory, profit, or bringing rain. Of course Buddhist women implore Hāritī for children, villagers implore Serpents for rain: Hāritī and Serpents have been admitted into the Buddhist pantheon; but they are no more Buddhist for that. The consequence is that a lay Buddhist is not a Buddhist as concerns familiar life; as concerns all the needs of the daily life, he remains a Hindu.

II. The Religion of Mahāyāna

1. This Buddhist religion which until the present time is the religion of the Buddhists of the Far East (Churches of 'Pure Land') is generally styled Mahāyāna, 'Great Vehicle; (but this term means exactly the form of mysticism described in IV); it is in short a hagiolatry with saints who possess all the power and all the benevolence of really godly persons.

From about the beginning of the Christian era Buddhism had gods of its own (celestial Buddhas, celestial Future Buddhas or bodhisattvas)[3] and therefore paradises of its own. The devotee hopes and tries to be reborn in one of the paradises, which are no longer places of sensual pleasures, but abodes worthy of their kings: eternal abodes of music, light, worship and contemplation.

Morality and worship continue to be the chief requirements from the candidate to a rebirth in paradise. But devotion (just as in Vishnuism) becomes more and more important. According to the 'low' section of Mahāyāna, a man, even a sinner, is saved and goes to paradise if he only has one unique thought for the Buddha (just as in the Pāncharātra section of the Vishnuist Church).

Chinese translations give dates; religions of the Mahāyāna cannot be later than the first Christian century, and are probably earlier. The original places cannot be ascertained. But the definition of the Buddhas as true living gods is the natural development of the primitive belief in the supernatural character of Śākyamuni: therefore the theist Mahāyānist system probably took growth and importance at the same moment in all the provinces of Buddhist India. The literary testimonies do not indicate the real evolution of the religious ideas, but only the gradual admission by the clergy of ideas probably born outside its pale. It is probable that the Mahāsamghika sect was the first to give an official theology to the adorers of the Buddhas namely the distinction between the true heavenly Buddha and his human substitute or avatar (see above, p. 165). But we remain in the dark concerning the place, the date, the diffusion, and the way by which religious ideas obtained literary and iconographic expression. Art is an important feature.

The problem is the more complex because there are several religions of the Mahāyāna. All have the same doctrine, but the Buddha-God is sometimes Maitreya, sometimes Śākyamuni, sometimes Amitābha, sometimes Avalokiteśvara. Our knowledge of the origin of these Persons (Śākyamuni excepted) is less than scanty. There is some probability that many figures of the Buddhist hagiolatry have been adapted from non-Buddhist beliefs: many scholars observe that Amitābha, the most popular of the Buddhas of the Far East, bears the mark of Iranism and of the solar religion.

Maitreya, Ajita Maitreya, Invictus Maitreya, is not a Buddha, but the Buddha who is to come. He reigns in the Tushita heaven, in the heaven which according to an early tradition Śākyamuni inhabited before incarnating himself in the womb of Māyā. Devotees either desire to be reborn in Tushita or make the 'resolve' to be reborn on earth when Maitreya will 'descend' and become a Buddha. Early Buddhism ignores this 'Messiah': he only appears in the latest part of the old Canon; but he is certainly an interesting figure.[4]

In early sources there are two disciples of Śākyamuni, of no particular importance, one named Ajita, the second Maitreya. Later Ajita, *invictus*, is the name or 'surname' of Maitreya. The idea that many Buddhas came before Śākyamkuni is an old one; the idea that a new Buddha is to come is not early, although it is natural. When it developed the beneficiary was a person the name of whom is like the name of the Vedic Mitra ('Sun' and 'Friend') and the name of the Iranian Sun God.

III. Buddhism as a 'supramundane' discipline; early form: the Vehicle to Nirvāna

1. In early days the disciples of Śākyamuni who were 'men of ascetic or spiritual dispositions' aimed at Nirvāna, or 'end of misery', 'deliverance from rebirth', the state or the abode of eternal peace which after death will be the lot of the saint, the Arhat.

This form of Buddhism ought to be styled *nirvānayāna*, Vehicle leading to Nirvāna. It is generally named *Hīnayāna*, 'inferior or low vehicle', from the designation used by the adherents of the form of Buddhism described under IV; because these new philosophers thought that Nirvāna (an unconscious beatitude) is not worthy to be sought for, or that the Arhat, an egoist saint, is not really a saint.

This form of Buddhism still survives in Ceylon, Burma, &c.; it has practically disappeared in the Far East.

We believe that it is early: the Buddhist Nirvāna is nothing else than a certain aspect of the 'deliverance' or of the 'supramundane abode' aimed at by a great number of ascetics or ecstatics; Śākyamuni is one of the doctors or saints who fixed the practical means of reaching Nirvāna.

In short, Nirvāna, is to be reached by the suppression of passion, by ecstatic or hypnotic devices. Therefore a candidate for Nirvāna, according to Buddhist principles (which are marked by a high morality), must lead a continent and frugal life, he must be a monk or, more exactly, a 'beggar, son of Śākya'. The Brotherhood is one, since it has only one master and one goal; but owing to minutiae in monastic discipline (or to unknown circumstances) it was early divided into a number of sects. Their number is said to have been eighteen.

Śākyamuni's path to Nirvāna is known to use by the canonical texts, which are comparatively late. Scholars are confronted with the same difficulty as regards the disciplinary (or monastic) rules: there is little doubt that the early; Brotherhood had fixed rules and was distinguished from the contemporaneous sects; but the disciplinary books we possess are the result of long growth and regularisation.

We feel sure that the early Buddhist candidate for Nirvāna must be a monk, a gook monk, must practise frugality, continence, meditation on the corpse, meditation on the transitiveness of pleasure, must concentrate his thought and wishes on the eternal peace of Nirvāna. But we also feel sure that the clerical (or scholastical) speculations on Nirvāna and the way thereof do not correspond exactly to the early state of Buddhist philosophy and mysticism. To give an example. A few early narrations certainly prove the habit of religious suicide. Many saints of the primitive Brotherhood 'took the knife' in order to reach Nirvāna. The orthodox theory and rule is that 'a saint does not wish for life or death', and patiently waits for his natural time. This detail shows that scholars who describe early Buddhism as a 'rationalisms' misrepresent Buddhism, and have an inexact (or incomplete) idea of the intellectual and moral 'climate' of old ascetic India.

2. It is probable that, even at an early date, there was a contrast between the monks who attached great importance to ecstasy (and to mystic experiences) and the monks who relied on 'wisdom'. There is a Buddhism centred on the 'true meditation', the meditation which destroys the opposition of 'subject' and 'object', knower and known; this meditation is the fruit of a transcendent agnosticism. There is a Buddhism which teaches that liberation from desire and existence is the fruit of the 'knowledge of the nature of things', Both have a long history. We owe to the second a number of theories.

A. *Nihilism.* According to the teaching of many canonical texts there is not in man any permanent principle—what we style a soul—capable of going through successive existences and of reaching Nirvāna. Man, like a chariot, has not real unity: he is made of pieces (*skandha*): material atoms, spiritual or mental atoms (sensations, perceptions, actions, &c.).

Several theories have been concocted in order to explain how such a 'complex' can commit acts, eat the fruit of its acts, pass into a new existence where it enjoys the fruit of its acts. These theories cannot be early, nor indeed is philosophy of the negation of a living and permanent and free soul. In early days Buddhists probably believed simply in transmigration and release. Now this philosophy, according to the Canon, is the truth which must be meditated upon in order to eradicate desire. It is the 'corner-stone' of wisdom and holiness. But an irresistible progress it turned not a system of universal nihilism: the material or mental atoms have no more reality than the material or mental compounds. This is 'acosmism'.

It is well known that the great monist philosopher of Brahmanism, Samkara, who taught the existence of the Brāhman only and the non-existence of the world, of souls, of God, has been criticized by theist Brāhmans as a 'Buddhist in disguise'. And scholars agree that Samkara's philosophy is the result of the synthesis so the old Brahmanic faith in an Absolute (Brāhman) and the Buddhist nihilism. Thus Śamkara appears as one of the heirs of Buddhism.

We shall see (p. 180) that Buddhist philosophers also adopted the notion of an Absolute.

B. *Nirvāna*. During the nineteenth century and the first decade of the twentieth European scholars believed that the early Buddhist Nirvāna was annihilation.

They now feel sure that early Nirvāna was not eternal death, but 'immortality', an imperishable abode of undefinable peace, above thought and consciousness. The Canon contains testimonies to this early view, for it describes Nirvāna as 'the unborn which is the refuge of what is born', also as the 'Immortal element' which is 'touched' during trances by the living saint.

But owing to the nihilistic theory (above, A), the Buddhist schools went very far in the way of negation, and sometimes proclaimed an annihilation-Nirvāna.

Some schools preserved the doctrine of the 'immortal element', the eternal entity, which is 'touched' by the living saint. But they believed that a saint is only a compound of transient atoms and therefore completely perishes at death. The Nirvāna of a saint is only the annihilation of this saint.

Some scholars wholly rejected the notion of the 'immortal element' and said in so many words that Nirvāna is only 'nonexistence following existence'.

A third view is that Nirvāna is eternal happiness; the dead saint possesses beatitude (*sukha*) for he no longer suffers: but he has no feeling of beatitude (*sukhasamvedana*). This Nirvāna is, according to a school of Mahāyāna, the Nirvāna of the ordinary saints.

Lastly, according to the Mahāyāna, the Buddhas have a Nirvāna of their own: perfectly calm and free, they are in Nirvāna: but they are nevertheless compassionate and active. They do not abandon existence, and will continue for ever.

3. It has been said above that a monk is 'by definition' a candidate for Nirvāna. But, in fact, Nirvāna, when we consider the majority of the monks, is only the ideal of a distant future.

All the immediate disciples of the Master reached sainthood and Nirvāna. But already, at the time of the compilation of the Scriptures, the great object was not to reach Nirvāna, but to enter into the path leading to Nirvāna: a man who has entered into this path must be reborn eight times before attaining the goal. In fact the only candidate for Nirvāna is the ascetic who practises mortification and penances, and the faculty of *dhyāna* or ecstatic trance, more than are enjoined by the rules of his order, thus acquiring supernatural powers. To pretend falsely to have realized such spiritual progress is one of the four sins (together with murder, &c.) which are punished by expulsion from the Brotherhood: this shows that any pretence to holiness was looked upon with suspicion. We are told that in the early days saints were many and disciplinary rules few: later the position was reversed, and it was commonly admitted that sainthood had disappeared.

The conclusion is that we cannot give an absolute value to the opposition of the monk and the layman, in regard to the spiritual dignity or the goal which they try to reach. As a rule, a monk only wishes to 'earn merit' by the practice of his professional duties (abstinence, continence, preaching—the most excellent work of charity, receiving alms, or worship), just as a layman earns merit by the practice of his professional duties (abstention from murder, 'home-chastity'—that is, conjugal fidelity—giving alms, worship): in both cases the fruit of merit is rebirth as a god, or as a human being who is capable of entering into the Path that leads to Nirvāna.

IV. Buddhism as a 'supramundane discipline'. Later Form: The Vehicle of Buddhahood

1. From the beginning of the Christian era and probably earlier a number of Buddhist monks came to despise Nirvāna, and entered into the path which had been followed by the man who was to become Śākyamuni, the path leading to Buddhahood. The second form of 'supramundane Buddhism' is a *Bodhisattvayāna* or a *Buddhayāna*, the Vehicle of the future Buddhas, the Vehicle of the Buddhas, the path that leads to the possession of Buddhahood.

This Buddhism differs from the Buddhism of III. The devotee no longer aims at Nirvāna but at Buddhahood; therefore his discipline is no longer the egoistical virtue and impassibility of the Arhat[5], but the charitable practices of the future Buddha. The Arhat reaches Nirvāna by his own unique exertion: Buddhahood is obtained by personal exertion coupled with the help of the Buddhas and heavenly Bodhisattvas who are living gods.

This Buddhism may be considered as the 'learned', mystical branch of the Buddhism of II. It differs: the candidate for Buddhahood loves and worships the Buddhas and does not despise a rebirth in the paradise of a Buddha (as in II): but such a rebirth is regarded by him as a temporary stage in his progress towards

Buddhahood. The devotee of II is only a *bhakta, a dévot*; he is not a future Buddha.

The vehicle of the Bodhisattvas is nothing new in Buddhism. Buddhist antiquity was well aware of the fact that Śākyamuni has obtained Buddhahood in his last existence because during many (552) previous existences he had followed the path of the future Buddhas, that is, because he had heaped up heroic deeds of virtue and self-sacrifice (narrated in the *Fātaka*).

But the general opinion was that Śākyamuni is 'exceptional', that Buddhas are very rare.

There was (before the compilation of the *Saddharmapundarīka*, Lotus of the true Law, perhaps about the beginning of the Christian era) a new departure: the discovery of a new truth, namely that all men can or must imitate Śākyamuni, can pronounce (as did Śākyamuni) the vow of becoming Buddha, in other words can become 'future Buddhas'.

2. At the time of Asanga (fourth century A.D.) a monk was always a member of one of the eighteen early sects. But a number of monks, not satisfied with the mystical goal (Nirvāna) and the moral ideal (impassibility of the *Arhat*) of these sects, added to the obligations of the traditionary clerical life (old disciplinary rules) the obligation of a future Buddha, heroic charity and self-sacrifice; they took the vow of Buddhahood. There was a ceremony, a private one, in the presence of a man (monk or layman) already equipped with this vow.

Later on, as the new spirit developed, as the candidates to Buddhahood became more numerous and influential, the adhesion to an early sect was no longer necessary. A special discipline for the Bodhisattva-monks had been delineated, and they had monasteries of their own.

The chief innovation, as concerns discipline, was probably the prohibition of meat. The worship of the Buddhas, which from of old was admitted by some at least of the early sects, became more pompous and general. There was also a new or renewed spirit of charity and propaganda: a spiritual life more noble, intense, and profound. One cannot read without respect and admiration the formulas of the eigthtfold supreme worship (confession of sins, &c.) and the homilies on patience, love of one's neighbour, considering a neighbour as one's own self and one's own egoist self as an enemy to be humiliated and destroyed.[6]

There is sometimes much wisdom and moderation in Mahāyāna teaching. We are beginners in the path of self-sacrifice. To save others we must not jeopardize our own welfare: therefore we must first avoid sin and exert ourselves in the humble virtues of everyday life; such is the right way to prepare oneself for the heroic deeds of future rebirths.[7]

But this wisdom is not general. A future Buddha must imitate the habit of self-sacrifice which characterized the future Śākyamuni when he gave to beggars or to tigresses his eyes or his flesh. Hence an epidemic of religious suicides.[8] As the Church officially deprecates suicide, an orthodox method of self-sacrifice was created. The initiation into the Mahāyānist community (*i.e.* the solemn vow of Buddhahood) was accompanied by the 'burning of the skull' (China): a number of incense-sticks are fixed on the skull of the candidate and lighted; the candidate is looked upon as a man who has burned his body for the welfare of mankind.[9]

During all his former existences Śākyamuni was not a monk, but a layman. A future Buddha may be a layman. A consequence of this doctrine is that the clerical life lost its prestige and that Buddhism, hitherto essentially a clerical brotherhood, became more and more a popular religion. This religion was more and more open to Hindu (*Sivaist*) influences: this is one of the causes of the disintegration and disappearance of Indian Buddhism.

3. The popular and sincere belief in the divine power and providence of the Buddhas was not to satisfy the intellectual needs of the learned monks. The Mahāyāna has elaborated systems of metaphysics and Buddhology.

A. *Tathatā*. The first Buddhist speculation resulted in a nihilistic or quasi-nihilistic attitude (III); but, while admitting the conclusions of the Ancients—namely absence of a soul, unsubstantiality of all phenomena (or 'caused contingent things')—some of the eighteen early sects and the schools of the Mahāyānist Church recognized an 'absolute' which is probably derived from the absolute of the Brāhmans (*brāhman*). There is an immutable element (dhātu*) below the changing flow of phenomena; more precisely a 'nature of things'* (dharmatā) or 'true reality' (*tathatā),* which is a spiritual or meta-mental reality, a transcendent thought free from the opposition of 'subject' and 'object'.

All beings are metaphysically the *tathatā*. But only a few beings (the Buddhas) have attained knowledge of the *tathatā* by personal experience: they have attained the perfect 'equation' of their individual thought to the very nature of thought. This sort of identification is the cause of Buddhahood, is Buddhahood itself.

We are the *tathatā;* therefore we are Buddhas *en puissance;* we shall become actually Buddhas when we attain the consciousness of our identity with the *tathatā*. It is a long business: a long endeavour in self-sacrifice and contemplation, the career of a future Buddha: to conceive the vow of Buddhahood, to progress during many rebirths before entering upon the first of the ten stages of a future Buddha.[10]

B. *The four bodies*. Early Mahāyāna taught that Buddhas have two bodies: there is a quasi-eternal and divine Śākyamuni; there is a human Śākyamuni who is only a 'creation body', a magical contrivance managed in order to guide men towards happiness.

Later a Buddha is said to possess four bodies: (1) a transcendent one, the *tathatā,* the same, of course, for all the Buddhas; (2) the 'body of personal enjoyment', that is, the real thought and form which constitutes a certain Buddha, Amitābha, Śākyamuni, and so on: this body, which is the Buddha himself, will last for eternity; (3) the 'body of altruistic enjoyment': the form under which a Buddha manifests himself to saints in the heavens: this body of course is manifold, since saints differ in holiness and needs; (4) the 'creation-body', the form under which a Buddha manifests himself to very imperfect beings, men, devils, and so forth. The best creation-body is the human Buddha.

C. The Buddhology just described is a compromise between two notions: (1) the early dogma that Buddha and is obtained through long exertion by beings who have been transmigrating 'since a time which has not begun'; (2) the metaphysical view of the universal and immutable *tathatā,* which is the transcendent body realized by each Buddha.

Mahāyāna sometimes abandoned the early dogma. According to many schools, some of which are certainly old (possibly fourth century A.D.) there is a primeval eternal Buddha—Vajrasattva, the 'diamond or the thunderbolt', Adibuddha, the 'Buddha of the beginning'—from which the Buddhas issue by a process of meditative emanation; the Bodhisattvas are no longer 'future Buddhas' but 'spiritual sons' of the Buddhas. Tantric and Tibetan Buddhism illustrate this new aspect of the religion of Śākyamuni.

Some Remarks on the Disappearance of Indian Buddhism

Scholars have given many explanations of the gradual decay and final disappearance of Indian Buddhism. Of course, epigraphical literary sources are not wanting, and it is not impossible to follow, province by province, the process of decay: this preliminary and necessary work has not been carefully done, and the problem remains terribly obscure. Nevertheless a few general observations may be useful.

(a) For centuries and almost everywhere Buddhism had numbered its monks by thousands, enjoyed the most vigorous life in devotional and philosophical directions, obtained the patronage of kings and sometimes the advantages of being the state religion. But, as we have seen, it had never and nowhere taken the place of Brahmanism.

(b) The bonds which for a time strongly attached laymen to Buddhism were the worship of the Buddhist saints and the veneration of the monks—who were not 'priests' but moral advisers and excellent 'fields of merit'.

Śākyamuni has been for centuries a most popular figures: the history of his previous births, of his miracles and deeds, enjoyed the favour of the people at large. Later on Sākyamuni was superseded in learned and lay Buddhist circles by other Buddhas or saints: Maitreya, Amitābha, Mañjurśrī, Avalokita, Tārā or Tārās. These figures lacked the personal character of Śākyamuni, never possessed his prestige, or, again, had features which established between them and Hindu gods an undeniable likeness.

The presence of fairies and minor useful deities in the Buddhist pantheon was not in itself a great danger, but, with centuries, the Hindu infiltration took a new character. We know that the monks of the conservative party accused their brethren of philośivaism (eight century A.D.); in Bengal, after the Mohammedan destruction of the Buddhist monasteries, the Buddhists exchanged their worship of Buddhist figures for the worship of Vishnuist ones; the Buddhism of present-day Nepal is a mixture of Buddhism and Brāhmano-śivaism.

Buddhism admitted into its pantheon and worshipped under the title of Buddhas or Bodhisattvas or Vajradevatās figures deeply stamped with the Hindu (Vishnu-śivaite) mark. Its theology too had been penetrated by Hindu conceptions. One of the favourite deities of later Buddhism is Tārā, 'the Star' or 'the Saviouress', who owes all her 'Budhism' to her kindness, to her title of 'future Buddha', or of wife of a Buddha.

(c) The strength of Buddhism is in its clergy, in the Brotherhood. For centuries the brotherhood flourished in the East, in the Deccan; in the West, in the Konkan and the Telugu country. Buddhist pilgrims and archaeology slow the gradual decay of the Buddhist communities almost everywhere.

One lesson of the Mahāyāna (see II and IV) is that a layman has the same right to holiness and salvation as a monk: the

Mahāyāna to some extent deprecates clerical life. Can we say that asceticism—at least this form of comfortable asceticism which characterized the Buddhist clergy—was losing its prestige and its hold on religious India?

Buddhist casuists have always admitted that a monk commits no sin when he officially declares that he is not capable of keeping his vows: he then becomes a Buddhist layman and can marry. With the Mahāyāna this casuistry turned into a historical feature: we have evidence of the growing habit of young men to take the monastic vows (a meritorious act), only to proclaim immediately after the ceremony that they renounce the vows of a monk in order to take the vows of a lay Bodhisattva. Kashmir and Nepal have had or have a married clergy.

Another cause of weakness in the Brotherhood was the declined of intellectual activity (already visible during the sixth and the seventh centuries), and the development of the Tantric (or magic) form of Buddhism: pure Śivaism in disguise. The master or teacher (*guru*) who gives the initiation and shows the way to a rapid acquisition of Buddhahood or of worldly advantages is no longer a monk, but a *siddha,* a magician, a *vajrāchārya* (often of very low moral habits).

(*d*) The fate of Indian Buddhism must be explained by its own internal faults. At least this aspect of the problem deserves attention. But external circumstances also had no little effect.

The advantage of official or kingly patronage is great. Inversely, when kings were strongly 'Śivaizing' (like Śaśānka or the Cholas), or 'jainizing' (as in Malwa), or 'lingaīzing' (as in the Telugu country), or simply 'anticlerical' (as the Hun kings, some potentates of Kashmir, the Mohammedans), Buddhism suffered.

Greater importance than that of the occasional bias of the civil power in favour of non-Buddhist creeds and clergy must probably be attached to the change that Brahmanism underwent during the Middle Ages under the guidance of many religious reformers.

Formerly Brāhmans were domestic priests or held liturgical duties in the ceremonies of the temples; but they had no 'cure of souls', they were not preachers nor propagandists, as the Buddhists and Jains were of old. But with Śamkara, Rāmānuja, many other saints and their disciples, Śivaism and Vishnuism acquired an active clergy. While the vital energies of Buddhism were declining, the Brahmano-Hinduist religion enjoyed a sort of revival.

—*De La Vallée Poussin.*

REFERENCES

1. The first aspect corresponds to what is called 'Lower Hinduism', the second to what is called 'Higher Hinduism'.
2. I am inclined to believe that laymen and ordinary devotees never thought that the death of the Holy Man had deprived the world of a superhuman protector. But, to tell the truth, we have no information. It is difficult to understand the ideas which found their expression in the worship of relics and stūpas—we know that Asoka never speaks of a 'paradise of Śākyamuni' but only of *svargas*, paradises according to the ideas of Hindu mythology.
3. The Buddhas are not creators, but they are providences: Mahāyāna is a particular sort of theism. The Bodhisattvas often take the aspects of Saviors: at the beginning of their career they have practised self-sacrifice for the welfare of all beings; later they are occupied in benefiting creatures by every kind of boon. The descent of Avalokita into hell is a well-known topic.
4. Emil Abegg, *Der Messiasglauhe in Indian und Iran,* 1928; J. Przyluski, 'La croyance au Messie', *Revue de l'Ilistoire des Religions,* juillet, 1929.
5. Altruistic virtues have a place in the preparation for Nirvāna, for peace of soul presupposes the suppression of anger, the culture (*bhāvanā*) of feelings of universal benevolence; but this place is a small and a prefatory one, since the candidate for Nirvāna must destroy hate and love.
6. L.D. Barnett, *The Path of Light* (Wisdom of the East Series) (John Murray, 1909).
7. *Sāntideva's Śiksbāsamuccaya,* tr. by W.H.D. Rouse (Indian Texts Series) (John Murray, 1922).
8. I-tsing, *Records of the Buddhist Religion* (Claredon Press, Oxford, 1896).

9. De Groot, *Code du Mahāyāna en Chine* (Amsterdam, 1893).

10. Such is the early and orthodox view; but the thesis that all living beings have the nature of a Buddha could not but result in the hope of quickly actualizing this nature. Hence a number of magical or ecstatic devices in order to acquire the body, the voice, and the thought of a Buddha. See La Vallée Poussin, *Le dogme et la philosophie du Bouddhisme* (Paris, Beauchesne, 1930).

7

RELIGIOUS TENSION UNDER THE MUGHALS

The religious unity of Islam in India suffered its greatest stresses during the century from A.D. C.150 to 1650, the period of the establishment of Mughal rule and of its apogee. Many forces, some political and more religious, were conspiring to weaken the holdover Indian Muslims of Sunni orthodoxy and of "moderate" mysticism.

The Mughals were by ancestry, taste, and conviction seekers and eclectics in religion, characteristics which their political necessities and ambitions tended to confirm. The family of Chingis Khān are reported to have joined in Nestorian, Christian, Muslim, and Buddhist religious observances. Tīmūr showed greater respect to Sufi shaikhs than to the Sunniulamā. Bābur and his son Humāyūn had been constrained to accept Shī'ism outwardly while negotiating for the support of the Persian. Shiite Safavids. Moreover, during the sixteenth and seventeenth centuries, Shī'ism in India enjoyed political patronage. In the Deccan, Yūsuf 'ādil Shāh of Bijapur (1489-1510) pronounced himself a Shīa as did Burhān ud-dīn of Ahmadnagar and Qūlī Qutb Shāh of Golkonda. In North India, Bairam Khān, the guardian and minister of the young Akbar, was a Shī'a with a large Persian Shī'a following who settled down in India.

Furthermore, significant religious developments within the penumbra dividing Muslim from Hindu had softened religious accrbities in India. If from within Islam the mystic had appeared to reach out toward Hinduism, from within Hinduism, Kabīr (b. 1398), Nānak (b. 1469), and Chaitanya (b. 1485), with their condemnation of caste, Hindu rituals, and idolatry appeared to be reaching out toward Islam.

Important changes also occurred in the character of Muslim mysticism in India. New orders were introduced from Persia—the Shattārī, whose shaikh Muhammad Ghawth was Humāyūn's spiritual preceptor; the Qādirī, whose shaikh Mir Muhammad was tutor to the Mughal prince Dārā Shikōh; and the Naqshbandī order, whose greatest luminary was Shaikh Ahmad of Sirhind. Members of the first two orders in particular were deeply influenced by the frankly pantheistic doctrines of the Spanish Muslim mystic Ibn 'Arabī (1164-1240); they observed few of the restraints in expression characteristic of the earlier Chishtī and Suhrawardī orders. What is more, their adherents were often intimately acquainted with Hindu mysticism.

None of these challenges to Sunni orthodoxy was exactly new; what was new was the political climate in India in which they had to be met. Under the Mughals, until Aurangziīb's time, the Sunni ulamā could not be confident of the exclusive support and patronage of the ruling power. Akbar came to an understanding with the Hindu Rajputs, who served to underpin his empire, and with policy reinforcing his own personal religious inclinations, set his face against Muslim militancy. The orthodox were scandalized not so much by the presence of un-Islamic ideas and practices in the Indian Muslim community as by the absence of political support in resisting them.

But resist they did, and, in the end successfully, though not without the help of a Sunni Mughal emperor, Aurangzīb (1658-1707). Readings have already been given from the works of a great traditionist of the Mughal period, 'Abd ul-Haqq al-Dihlawī. However, the greatest figure in the reaction against Akbar's and the mystics' religious syncretism was Shaikh Ahmad of Sirhind (1564-1624) who, arguing from within mystic experience itself against the pantheism of Ibn 'Arabī, recalled Muslims to a fresh realization of the religious value of traditional observance.

Akbar's Religious Outlook

Akbar, apparently by deliberate, mature choice, could neither read nor write; it is possible, therefore, only dimly to perceive his religious attitudes through the testimony of witnesses violently prejudiced either in his favour, as was Abū'l Fazl, his friend and confidant; or against him, as was the historian 'Abd ul-Qādir Badā'ūnī, his secret orthodox Sunni opponent, or partly through the testimony of the Jesuit fathers and of a Parsi student of religion, Muhsin-i-Fānī, who wrote half a century after Akbar's death.

As a boy in Kabul, Akbar had been open to Shīa teachings and to the mysticism of the Persian poets. Although at the outset of his reign, however, his religious officials—the *sadr* ("minister for religious endowments") and the *qādīs* (religious judges)—were Sunni, Akbar himself visited Sufi retreats at Ajmir and Sikri. He seems to have been offended by the persecution of the Shī'a by his Sunni *sadr* and chief muftī (canon jurist) which grew violent about 1570. Meanwhile, in 1562, he had married a Hindu Rajput princess, Bihārī Mal of Amber, and had admitted Rajput princes, *e.g.,* Rājā Mān Singh and Todar Mal, to high political and administrative office. After 1574 he was influenced by Abū'l Fazl and his brother Faizī, sons of Shaikh Mubārak Nāgōrī, and all students of Hinduism, indeed of "comparative religion." From this time, they led the discussions in the Hall of Worship which Akbar had built at Fathpur Sikri. These discussions, over which Akbar presided, were attended by Sunni ulamā, Sufi shaikhs, Hindu pundits, Parsees, Zoroastrians, Jains, and Catholic priests from Portuguese Goa. The mere fact of such discussions—in which apparently the Sunni ulamā did not shine—is the measure of the bias against orthodoxy at court. Akbar's personal religious searchings were followed by the Declaration (*Mahzar*) of 1579 that Akbar was accepted by the ulamā as the arbiter in religious disputes, by the enunciation of the "Divine Faith" (*Din-i-Ilāhi*), Akbar's own eclectic faith of 1582, and by a series of conciliatory gestures toward the Hindus. The Divine Faith, however, was accepted by only a small number of courtiers and was not enforced throughout the empire by political and administrative pressure.

Akbar ordered the translation of the *Atharva Veda,* the *Rāmāyana,* and the *Mahābhārata*. According to Badā'ūnī he prohibited the killing of cows, refrained from eating meat on certain days and celebrated non-Islamic festivals. However, Akbar emphatically did not wish to destroy Islam in India, as Badā'ūnī implies. His quest for religious truth was that of an eclectic, not of a fanatic. Looking back, the consensus of the community appears to have pronounced against his activities, but this does not mean that they necessarily flouted the consensus at the time.

The following readings will illustrate Akbar's religious quest and the Divine Faith. The Declaration will be given in the next chapter on Muslim political thought.

The Discussion in the Hall of Worship

Readers must recall that the author of these passages is hostile to Akbar.

[Badā'ūnī, *Muntakha but-Tawārīkh,* II, 200-201, 255-61 *passim,* 324]

In the year nine hundred and eighty-three the buildings of the 'Ibādatkhāna were completed. The cause was this. For many years previously the emperor had gained in succession remarkable and decisive victories. The empire had grown in extent from day to day; everything turned out well, and no opponent was left in the whole world. His Majesty had thus leisure to come into nearer contact with ascetics and the disciples of his reverence [the late] Mu'īn, and passed much of his time in discussing the World of God and the word of the Prophet. Questions of Sufism, scientific discussions, inquiries into philosophy and law, were the order of the day. [II, 200-201].

* * *

And later that day the emperor came to Fathpūr. There he used to spend much time in the Hall of Worship in the company of learned men and Shaikhs and especially on Friday nights, when he would sit up there the whole night continually occupied in discussing questions of religion, whether fundamental or collateral. The learned men used to draw the sword of the tongue on the battle-field of mutual contradiction and opposition, and the antagonism of the sects reached such a pitch that they would call one another fools and heretics. The controversies used to pass beyond the differences of Sunni, and Shī'a, of Hanafī and Shāfi'ī, of lawyer and divine, and they would attack the very bases of belief. And Makhdūm-ul-Mulk wrote a treatise to the effect that Shaikh 'Abd-al-Nabī had unjustly killed Khizr Khān Sarwānī, who had been suspected of blaspheming the Prophet [peace be upon him!], and Mīr Habsh, who had been suspected of being a Shī'a, and saying that it was no right to repeat the prayers after him, because he was undutiful toward his father, and was himself afflicted with hemorrhoids. Shaikh 'Abd-al-Nabī replied to him that he was a fool and a heretic. Tehn the mullās [Muslim theologians] became divided into two parties, and one party took one side and one the other, and became very Jews and Egyptians for hatred of each other. And persons of novel and whimsical opinions, in accordance with their pernicious ideas and vain doubts, coming out of ambush, decked the false in the garb of the true, and wrong in the dress of right, and cast the emperor, who was possessed of an excellent disposition, and was an earnest searcher after truth, but very ignorant and a mere tyro, and used to the company of infidels and base persons, into perplexity, till doubt was heaped upon doubt, and he lost all definite aim, and the straight wall of the clear law and of firm religion was broken down, so that after five or six years not a trace of Islam was left in him: and everything was turned topsy-turvy....

And Samanas [Hindu or Buddhist ascetics] and Brahmans (who as far as the matter of private interviews is concerned gained the advantage over every one in attaining the honour of interviews with His Majesty, and in associating with him, and were in every way superior in reputation to all learned and trained men for their treatises on morals, and on physical and religious sciences, and in religious ecstasies, and stages of spiritual progress and human perfections) brought forward proofs, based on reason and traditional testimony, for the truth of their own, and the fallacy of our religion, and inculcated their doctrine with such firmness and assurance, that they affirmed mere imaginations as though they were self-evident facts, the truth of which the doubts of the sceptic could no more shake "Than the mountains crumble, and the heavens be cleft!" And the Resurrection, and Judgment, and other details and traditions, of which the Prophet was the repository, he laid all aside. And he made his courtiers continually listen to those revilings and attacks against our pure and easy, bright and holy faith… .

Sometime before this a Brahman, named Puruk'hotam, who had written a commentary on the Book, *Increase of Wisdom* (*Khirad-afzā*), had private interviews with him, and he had asked him to invent particular Sanskrit names for all things is existence. And at one time a Brahman, named Debi., who was one of the interpreters of the *Mahābhārata,* was pulled up the wall of the castle sitting on a bedstead till he arrived near a balcony, which the emperor had made his bed-chamber. Whilst thus suspended he instructed His Majesty in the secrets and legends of Hinduism, in the manner of worshipping idols, the fire, the sun and stars, and of revering the chief gods of these unbelievers, such as Brahma, Mahadev [Shiva], Bishn [Vishnu], Kishn [Krishna], Ram, and Mahama (whose existence as sons of the human race is a supposition, but whose nonexistence is a certainly, though in their idle belief they look on some of them as gods, and some as angels). His Majesty, on hearing further how much the people of the country prized their institutions, began to look upon them with afflection….

Sometimes again it was Shaikh Tāj ud-dīn whom he sent for. This shaikh was son of Shaikh Zakarīya of Ajodhan…. He had been a pupil of Rashīd Shaikh Zamān of Panipat, author of a commentary on the *Paths* (*Lawā'ih*), and of other excellent works, was most excellent in Sufism, and in the knowledge of theology second only to Shaikh Ibn 'Arabī and had written a comprehensive commentary on the *Joy of the Souls* (*Nuzhat ul-Arwāh*). Like the preceding he was drawn up the wall of the castle in a blanket, and His Majesty listened the whole night to his Sufic obscenities and follies. The shaikh, since he did not in any great degree feel himself bound by the injunctions of the law, introduced arguments concerning the unity of existence, such as idle Sufix discuss, and which eventually lead to license and open heresy….

Learned monks also from Europe, who are called *Padre,* and have an infallible head, called *Papa,* who is able to change religious ordinances as he may deem advisable for the moment, and to whose authority kings must submit, brought the Gospel, and advanced proofs for the Trinity. His Majesty firmly believed in the truth of the Christian religion, and wishing to spread the doctrines of Jesus, ordered Prince Murād to take a few lessons in Christianity under good auspices, and charged Abū'l Fazl to translate the Gospel....

Fire worshipers also came from Nousarī in Gujarat, proclaimed the religion of Zardusht [Zarathustra] as the true one, and declared reverence to fire to be superior to every other kind of worship. They also attracted the emperor's regard, and taught him the peculiar terms, the ordinances, the rites and ceremonies of the Kaianians [a pre-Muslim Persian dynasty]. At last he ordered that the sacred fire should be made over to the charge of Abū'l Fazl, and that after the manner of the kings of Persia, in whose temples blazed perpetual fires, he should take care it was never extinguished night or day, for that it is one of the signs of God, and one light from His lights….

His Majesty also called some of the yogis, and gave them at night private interviews, inquiring into abstract truths; their articles of faith; their occupation; the influence of pensiveness; their several practices and usages; the power of being absent from the body; or into alchemy, physiognomy, and the power of omnipresence of the soul. [II, 255-261 *passim.* 324].

Note in the next readings the condemnation of prophethood by a philosopher at Akbar's court, which is said to have gone uncensured.

[From Muhsin-i-Fānī, *Dabistān-i-Mazāhib,* III, 78-81]

But the greatest injury comprehended in a prophetic mission is the obligation to submit to one like ourselves of the human species, who is subject to the incidental distempers and imperfections of mankind; and who nevertheless controls others with severity, in eating, drinking, and in all their other possessions, and drives them about like brutes, in every direction which he pleases; who declares every follower's wife he desires legal for himself and forbidden to the husband; who takes to himself nine wives, whilst he allows no more than four to his followers, and even of these wives he takes whichever he pleases for himself; and who grants impunity for shedding blood to whomsoever he chooses. On account of what excellency, on account of what science, is it necessary to follow that man's command; and what proof is thereby his simple word? His word, because it is only a word, has no claim of superiority over the words of others. Nor is it possible to know which of the sayings be correctly his own, on account of the multiplicity of contradictions in the professions of faith. If he be a prophet on the strength of miracles, then the deference to it is very dependent; because a miracle is not firmly established, and rests only upon tradition or a demon's romances. . . .

But if it be said that every intellect has not the power of comprehending the sublime precepts, but that the bounty of the Almighty God created degrees of reason and a particular order of spirits, so that he blessed a few of the number with superior sagacity; and that the merciful light of lights, by diffusion and guidance, exalted the prophets even above these intellects—If it be so, then a prophet is of the little service to men; for he gives instruction which they do not understand, or which their reason does not approve. Then the prophet will propagate his doctrine by the sword; he says to the inferiors: "My words are above your understanding, and your study will not comprehend them." To the intelligent he says: "My faith is above the mode of reason". Thus, his religion suits neither the ignorant nor the wise.

The Divine Faith

The Divine Faith was Sufi in conception, with ceremonial expressions borrowed from Zoraoastrianism. It was strictly monotheistic and incorporated Shī'ite ideas of the role of the mujtahid or interpreter of the faith. In brief, it appears to owe more to Islam than to Hinduism. Unfortunately the beliefs and practices of the divine Faith are nowhere comprehensively stated. They have to be pieced together from Abū'l Fazl's *Institutes of Akbar* (*āin-i-Akbarī*), Badā-ūnī's *Selected Histories* (*Muntakhab ut-Tawārīkh*) and Muhsin-i-Fānī's *School of Religions* (*Dabistān-i-Mazāhib*).

The Divine Faith's Monotheism

[From Muhsin-i-Fānī, *Dabistān-i-Mazāhib,* III, 74-75]

Know for certain that the perfect prophet and learned apostle, the possessor of fame, Akbar, that is, the lord of wisdom, directs us to acknowledge that the self-existent being is the wisest teacher, and ordains the creatures with absolute power, so that the intelligent among them may be able to understand his precepts; and as reason renders it evident that the world has a Creator, all-mighty and all-wise, who has diffused upon the field of events among the servants, subject to vicissitudes, numerous and various benefits which are worthy of praise and thanks giving; therefore, according to the lights of our reason, let us investigate the mysteries of his creation, and, according to our knowledge, pour out the praises of his benefit.

The Divine Faith's Sufi Piety

[From Muhsin-i-Fānī, *Dabistān-i-Mazāhib,* III, 82-84]

In the sequel it became evident to wise men that emancipation is to be obtained only by the knowledge of truth conformably with the precepts of the perfect prophet, the perfect lord of fame, Akbar, "the Wise"; the practices enjoined by him are: renouncing and abandoning the world; refraining from lust, sensuality, entertainment, slaughter of what possesses life; and from appropriating to one's self the riche of other men; abstaining from women, deceit, false accusation, oppression, intimidation, foolishness, and giving [to others] opprobrious titles. The endeavors for the recompense of the other world, and the forms of the true religion may be comprised in ten virtues, namely, (1) liberality and beneficence; (2) forbearance from bad actions and repulsion of anger with mildness; (3) abstinence from worldy desires; (4) care of freedom from the bonds of the worldly existence and violence, as well as accumulating previous stores for the future real and perpetual world; (5) piety, wisdom, and devotion, with frequent meditations on the consequences of actions; (6) strength of dexterous prudence in the desire of sublime actions; (7) soft voice, gentle words, and pleasing speeches for everybody; (8) good society with brothers, so that their will may have the precedence to our own; (9) a perfect alienation from the creatures, and a perfect attachment to the supreme Being; (10) purification of the soul by the yearning after God the all-just, and the union with the merciful Lord, in such a manner that, as long as the soul dwells in the body, it may think itself one with him and long to join him, until the hour of separation from the body arrives.

The Influence of Zoroastrianism

[From Badā'ūnī, *Muntakhab ut-Tawārīkh,* II, 322]

A second order was given that the sun should be worshipped four times a day, in he morning and evening, and at noon and midnight. His Majesty had also one thousand and one Sanskrit names for the sun collected, and read them daily at noon, devoutly turning toward the sun; he then used to get hold of both ears, and turning himself quickly round about, used to strike the lower ends of his ears with his fists. He also adopted several other practices connected with sun-worship.

Dārā Shikōh and Pantheism

Akbar's mantle as a religious seeker fell not on his son Jahāngīr or his grandson Shāh Jahān, but on his great-grandson Dārā Shikōh (1615-1659). Dārā Shikoh addressed himself, with perhaps more enthusiasm than insight, to the study of Hindu philosophy and mystical practices. This was the more congenial because he himself was a follower of the Qādirī order of Sufis in the persons of Miān Mīrzā (d. 1635) and Mullā Shāh Badakhshānī (d. 1661).

Dārā Shikōh is important from the present standpoint because he symbolizes the major danger threatening the religious integrity of Islam in India, a mingling of the two seas of Muslim mystical pantheism and Hindu pantheism to batter down the defences of orthodoxy. He symbolized but did not intend that threat; he himself would have rejected a charge of heresy or unbelief. The widespread Sufi acceptance of Ibn 'Arabī's mystical philosophy and their interest in Hindu mysticism should be condemned as infidelity if Dārā Shikō is to be condemned for infidelity. However, the subsequent consensus of the Muslim community was that Dārā Shikōh's activities were dangerous to it and there is a strong presumption that Aurangzib's political instincts were finely tuned to strong waves of Muslim sentiment when, after the war of succession, for his own ambitious purposes he had ḌārāShikōh condemned as a hectic and executed.

The readings which follow are intended to illustrate first the pantheistic tendency in Dārā Shikōh's thought—tendency, not fulfilment, for he appears to stop short of asserting the complete absorption of the mystic in God's essence—and second his efforts to find common ground between Hindu and Muslim.

The Mystic Path

[From Dārā Shikōh, *Risāla-yi-Haqq-Numā,* pp. 24, 26]

Here is the secret of unity (tawhīd), O friend, understand it;
Nowhere exists anything but God.
All that you see or know other than Him,
Verily is separate in name, but in essence one with God.

* * * *

Like an ocean is the essence of the supreme self,
Like forms in water are all souls and objects;
The ocean heaving and stirring within,
Transforms itself into drops, waves and bubbles, [p. 24]

So long as it does not realize its separation from the ocean,
The drop remains a drop;
So long he does not know himself to be the Creator,
The created remains a created.

* * * *

O you, in quest of God, you seek Him everywhere,
You verily are the God, not apart from Him!
Already in the midst of the boundless ocean,
Your quest resembles the search of a drop for the ocean! [p. 26]

[From Dārā Shikōh, *Hasanat ul-'ārifin,* p. 16]

Dost thou wish to enter the circle of men of illumination?
Then cease talking and be in the "state";
By professing the unity of God, thou can not become a monotheist,
As the tongue cannot taste sugar by only uttering its name.

[From JRASB, Vol. V, No. 1, p. 168]

Paradise is there where no mullā exists—
Where the noise of his discussions and debate is not heard.

May the world become free from the noise of mullā,
And none should pay any heed to his decrees!

In the city where a mullā resides,
No wise man ever stays.

The Upanishads: God's Most Perfect Revelation

The following is taken from Dārā Shikōh's translation of fifty-two Upanishads, completed in 1657. He uses the third person in referring to himself.

[From Hasrat, *Dārā Shikōh*, pp. 260-68)]

Praised be the Being, that one among whose eternal secrets is the dot in the [letter] of the bismallāh in all the heavenly books, and glorified be the mother of books. In the holy Qur'ān is the token of His glorious name; and the angels and the heavenly books and the prophets and the saints are all comprehended in this name. And be the blessings of the Almighty upon the best of His creatures, Muhammad, and upon all his children and upon his companions universally!

To proceed; whereas this unsolicitous faqir [a religious mendicant], Muhammad Dārā Shikōh in the year 1050 after Hijra [A.D. 1640] went to Kashmir, the resemblance of paradise, and by the grace of God and the favour of the Infinite, he there obtained the auspicious opportunity of meeting the most perfect of the perfects, the flower of the gnostics, the tutor of the tutors, the sage of the sages, the guide of the guides, the unitarian accomplished in the Truth, Mullā Shaāh, on whom be the peace of God.

And whereas, he was impressed with a longing to behold the gnostics of every sect, and to hear the lofty expressions of monotheism, and had cast his eyes upon many books of mysticism and had written a number of treatises thereon, and as the thirst of investigation for unity, which is a boundless ocean, became every moment increased, subtle doubts came into his mind for which he had no possibility of solution, except by the world of the Lord and the direction of the Infinite. And whereas the holy Qur'ān is mostly allegorical, and at the present day, persons thoroughly conversant with the subtleties thereof are very rare, he became desirous of bringing in view all the heavenly books, for the very words of God themselves are their own commentary; and what might be in one book compendious, in another might be found diffusive, and from the detail of one, the conciseness of the other might become comprehensible. He had, therefore, cast his eyes on the Book of Moses, the Gospel, the Psalms, and other scriptures, but the explanation of monotheism in them also was compendious and enigmatical, and from the slovenly translations which selfish persons had made, their purport was not intelligible.

Thereafter he considered, as to why the discussion about monotheism is so conspicuous in India, and why the Indian theologians and mystics of the ancient school do not disavow the Unity of God nor do they find any fault with the unitarians, but their belief is perfect in this respect; on the other hand, the ignoramuses of the present age—the highwaymen in the path of

God—who have established themselves for erudites and who, falling into the traces of polemics and molestation, and apostatizing through disavowal of the true proficients in God and monotheism, display resistance against all the words of unitarianism, which are most evident from the glorious Qur'ān and the authentic traditions of indubitable prophecy.

And after verifications of these circumstances, it appeared that among this ancient people, of all their heavenly books, which are the *Rig Veda,* the *Yajur Veda,* the *Sama Veda,* and the *Atharva Veda,* together with a number of ordinances, descended upon the prophets of those times, the most ancient of whom was Brahman or Adam, or whom be the peace of God, this purport is manifest from these books. And it can also be ascertained from the holy Qur'ān, that there is no nation without a prophet and without a revealed scripture, for it hath been said: "Nor do We chastise until We raise an apostle" (Qur'ān 17-15). And in another verse: "And there is not a people but a warner has gone among them" (Qur'ān 35.24). And at another place: "Certainly we sent Our apostles with clear arguments, and sent down with them the Book and the measure" (Qur'ān 57.25).

And the *summum bonum* of these four books, which contain all the secrets of the Path and the contemplative exercises of pure monotheism, are called the *Upanekhats* [*Upanishads*], and the people of that time have written commentaries with complete and diffusive interpretations thereon; and being still understood as the best part of their religious worship, they are always studied. And whereas this unsolicitous seeker after the Truth had in view the principle of the fundamental unity of the personality and not Arabic, Syriac, Hebrew, and Sanskrit languages, he wanted to make without any worldly motive, in a clear style, an exact and literal translation of the *Upanekhat* into Persian. For it is a treasure of monotheism and there are few thoroughly conversant with it even among the Indians. Thereby he also wanted to solve the mystery which underlies their effort to conceal it from the Muslims.

And as at this period the city of Banares, which is the centre of the sciences of this community, was in certain relations with this seeker of the Truth, he assembled together the pandits [Hindu scholars] and the sannyasis [Hindu ascetics or monks], who were the most learned of their time and proficient in the *Upanekhat*... in the year 1067 after Hijra; and thus every difficulty and every sublime topic which he had desired or thought and had looked for and not found, he obtained from these essences of the most ancient books, and without doubt or suspicion, these books are first of all heavenly books in point of time, and the source and the fountainhead of the ocean of unity, in conformity with the holy Qur'ān.

Happy is he, who having abandoned the prejudices of vile selfishness, sincerely and with the grace of God, renouncing all partiality, shall study and comprehend this translation entitled *The Great Secret (Sirr-i-Akbar)*, knowing it to be a translation of the words of God. He shall become imperishable, fearless, unsolicitous, and eternally liberated.

The Reaction against Pantheistic Mysticism

The leader of the religious opposition to pantheistic mysticism and to neglect of the Sharī'a was Shaikh Ahmad Sirhindī al-Mujaddid-i-Alf-i-Thānī (the Renewer of Islam at the Beginning of the Second Muslim Millennium). Born at Sirhind in the East Punjab in 1564, he frequented the society of Abū'l Fazl and his brother Faizī at Agra. In 1599 he was initiated into the Naqshbandī order of mystics. He incurred the displeasure of Jahāngīr for this unbending opposition to the Shī'a who were powerful at court, but was restored to favour before his death in 1624.

Shaikh Ahmad Sirhind's great achievement was paradoxically to win Indian Islam away from Sufi extremism by means of mysticism itself. Perhaps his success was due to deep personal understanding of the meaning and value of what he rejected. To explain briefly; the mystical school of Ibn 'Arabī holds that Being is one; is Alllāh, and that everything is His manifestation or emanation. God is neither transcendent nor immanent. He is all. Creation is only God's yearning to know Himself by expressing

Himself. At the end of the mystic path (fanā) the mystic knows himself to be Himself. God's essence and His attributes (*e.g.*, individual Sufi seekers) are One.

Shaikh Ahmad of Sirhind replied that Ibn 'Arabī and his school were merely talking of the mystic stage of annihilation (fanā) and that this is not the final stage of reality. At the stage of annihilation the mystic is *ipso facto* absorbed in the being of God and utterly oblivious to anything other than God. Ibn 'Arabī is confusing the subjective with the objective. In fact, says Shaikh Ahmad, Ibn 'Arabī must still be aware of the world in order to identify is with God, otherwise he would have talked only of God. Shaikh Ahmad argues that beyond annihilation is a state which, he says, Ibn 'Arabī did not reach, in which the mytic experiences the truth that God is beyond comprehension through intuition. Hence man must revert to revelation and to the religious sciences based on revelation, in other words to the Sharī'a of the ulamā. Shaikh Ahmad insists that the only relation between God and the world is that of Creator and created and all talk of union or identity is hereby born of subjective mystic misconceptions.

These views Shaikh Ahmad propagated in his *Letters* (*Maktūbāt*), written to his disciples and others. About five hundred and thirty in all, they form a great classic of Indo-Muslim religious literature.

Mystic Union With God Is Only Subjective

[From Shaikh Ahmad Sirhindi, *Maktubat,* folios 52-53b]

The divine unity which Sufis encounter on their way is of two kinds, "unity of experience" (*tauhid-i-shuhūdī*) and "unity of existence" (*tauhid-i-wujūdī*). "Unity of experience" is seeing only one thing, that is to say, the traveler on the mystic path witnesses only oneness. "Unity of existence" is considering that only one thing exists and conceiving all else as non-existent, believing that nonexistence is a mere reverse and antithesis [logically] of that one existence. "Unity of existence" is of the order of positive knowledge and "unity of experience" is of the order of absolutely certain knowledge. "Unity of experience" is among the necessary stages of the mystic path because annihilation of the self is not established without this oneness and without that real insight is not possible.

The overwhelming power of the vision of the unity of God is such that it is impossible to see what is beyond the state of annihilation of the self (fanā). Contrary to that is the "unity of existence"; . . . . There is nothing in the heart which shall cause the denial of knowledge of what is beyond at the time of attaining knowledge of the unity of God. For example, when someone obtains a certain knowledge of the existence of the sun, the attainment of that knowledge does not cause him to think that the stars do not also exist at the same time. But at the time when he saw the sun he will certainly not see the stars, what he has witnessed will only be the sun. At the time when he does not see the stars, he knows that he stars are not nonexistent; indeed he knows they exist, but are hidden and overcome by the brilliance of the sun. This person is in a position to contradict those who deny the existence of the stars for the knows it was only that the knowledge of their existence had not yet been attained by him. Then the doctrine of unity of existence, which is the denial of everything except the Self of the Divine, is at war with both reason and the Sharī'a in contradistinction to unity of experience in which in its visualizing of unity no opposition to them occurs. For example, at the time of sunrise to deny the existence of the stars is to deny fact. At the same time when the stars are not seen, there is no opposition; rather their invisibility is due to the superiority of the light of the sun; if one's vision becomes so powerful as not to be affected by the light of the sun, the stars will be seen separately from the sun. This power of vision is possible in the "station" of absolute truth.

Thus the statements of some shaikhs who are apparently opposed to the True Way, and lead some men toward the doctrine of unity of existence as, for example, Abū Mansūr al-Hallāj in his statement, "I am God," and Abū Yazīd Bistāmī, "Praise be to Me!" and such like. It is proper that people must be led toward "unity of experience" and that opposition to that doctrine be repelled. Whenever what is other than God Most High was hidden to them, they uttered those phrases in the grip of ecstasy and they did not affirm anything but God. The meaning of "I am the Truth" is that He is the Truth, not "I" [al-Hallāj]; since he does not see himself be [al-Hallāj] does not establish that it is he who sees himself and he calls what he sees God. This is unbelief,. Here no one may speak because not to affirm a thing is not [necessarily] to deny its existence and this is exactly what "unity of existence" does. For I say that to affirm nothing is not to deny anything. Indeed at this stage on the mystic path there is utter amazement [at the Glory of God] and all commands become ineffective.

And in "Praise be to Me!" the holiness of God is meant, not the holiness of the mystic, because God has become completely raised beyond the mystic's sight. . . . Some mystics do not give vent to such expressions in the state of real certainty, which is a state of amazement. When they pass beyond this stage and arrive at absolute certainty, they avoid such expressions altogether and do not transgress proper bounds.

In these times, many of those who claim to live as Sufis have propagated "unity of existence" and do not know anything beyond that; they have remained behind in real knowledge and have reduced the statements of the shaikhs to meanings of their own imagining and have held them up as guides for their own generation making current their own wicked secrets by means of these conceptions. If there are expressions in the statements of some of these shaikhs which lead to unity of existence, they must be attacked. . . .

The Sharī'a Is the True Religious Way

[From Shaikh Ahmad Sirhindī, *Maktūbāt,* folios 46a-b]

The Prophet says that there are three parts to the Sharī'a, knowledge, action, and sincere belief. Until these three parts are verified the Sharī'a is not verified. When the Sharī'a is verified God's satisfaction is obtained and this is superior to all else, "May

God Most High be satisfied with all of them!" Therefore the Sharī'a is a guarantee of all these blessings and there is no purpose in seeking anything beyond the Sharī'a. The Way and the Truth, which for the Sufis have become distinct, both are servants of the Sharī'a. On the perfection of the third part of the Sharī'a which is sincere belief—the aim in acquiring the first two parts of the Sharī'a is the perfection of the Sharī'a and not anything else. The states and stations and gnosis which happen to the Sufi along his way are not among the purposes of the Sharī'a. The imaginings, the ideas, and the dark thoughts of the novice of the Way, having passed beyond all these must reach the stage of acquiescence in God, the end of the stages of the pilgrims of the mystic path and the object of the greatest desire. Unfortunately, the aim of passing beyond the stages of the Way to the reality beyond is not just to obtain that sincere belief which is the real cause of acquiescence in God. ... Short-sighted people count the attainment of the various states and stages of the mystic path among their aims and consider the appearance of God and His manifestations among the things to be most desired. In the end, they remain imprisoned in their thoughts and in their imagining and deprive themselves of the perfections of the Sharī'a.

Revelation and Inspiration Reconciled

[From Shaikh Ahmad Sirhindī, *Maktūbāt,* folios 50-51b]

The Prophet of God is the beloved of God; everything which is good and desired is for the sake of the beloved of God. As God has said in the holy Qur'ān, "No doubt your conduct and character is the best," and "You are without doubt among the prophets and on the right path," and . "This is the only right path that you follow, and you do not follow the wrong path." His people have called him the straight road and what is outside his way of life is forbidden. As the Prophet has said, "Thanks should be given that the Prophet has shown a right path for the people." He also said that inner belief perfects outward observance and that there is not a hair-breadth of contradiction between the two. For example, not to tell lies is Sharī'a and to condemn lying thoughts in the heart is the Way (tarīqa) and inner reality (*haqīqat*). If this condemnation is possible but with hesitation and great effort, it is the Way and if it comes about without great hesitation it is inner reality. Then in truth, interior belief, which is both the Way and the Truth, is shown forth; this is the Sharī'a. When the travellers who follow the way of reproach encounter anything which is openly at war with the Sharī'a and adopt it, they fall victim to intoxication and are overcome by the mystic state (*hāl*). If they pass beyond that stage and return to sobriety, opposition to the Sharī'a is completely removed and destroyed.

For example, a group of the intoxicated limit their imagination to themselves and consider the Person of God to be encompassed by the world. This view is opposed to the opinion of the orthodox ulamā. They assert the way of (traditional) knowledge. Whenever, despite the fact that the Person of God is unlimited by any categorical mandates, and despite the fact that to inject something into the Person of God is to oppose the clear statement that He is ineffable and inscrutable, the Sufis assert that His Person is limitrophe with the world, then indeed they dwell in confusion, folly, and mere ignorance. What has God to do with the injection of human ideas and limitations into His Person? The Sufis must give the excuse that their intention is to understand the first manifestation of God and that when they see that manifestation they do not know it for what it is, and they interpret it as God Himself....

The Person of God Most High is most nearly understood by the orthodox ulamā when they say that He is ineffable and incomparable and that whatever is beyond Him is something additional to that manifestation. If that manifestation of Him is proved it will be known that it is beyond the bounds of His essence and it will not be said that the limit of that manifestation are the limits of God's essence. Thus the viewpoint of the ulamā is more lofty than the viewpoint of the Sufis. The Person of God according to the Sufis is in fact implied in the essence of God according to the orthodox ulamā. Nearness and association with the Person of God and the agreement of interior knowledge with the sciences of the Shafī'a is perfect and complete....

The station of truth is higher than the station of saintship; higher than that still is the station of prophethood and the knowledge which came by inspiration and by revelation to the holy Prophet. Between knowledge by revelation and knowledge by inspiration there is only a difference of process.... Revelation is clear cut and inspiration, opinion. For revelation is through the medium of angels and angels are innocent; there is no imputation of error to them.

Although inspiration has a high religious status and is of the heart, and the heart is of the Divine Order, nevertheless, it is connected with the reason and the lower self and however much one is on guard against the lower self, it never rises beyond its own qualities. The ability to err finds a home in it. But one must know that the survival of the qualities of the lower self and its contentment is a benefit and an advantage. It the lower self is completely forbidden from manifesting its qualities, the way of moral and spiritual development is obstructed. The soul would attain the rank of an angel and it would be imprisoned. Its progress is by means of opposition between it and the lower self. If no opposition remains how shall development occur?

Against Rulers Misled by Wicked Ulamā

[From Shaikh Ahmad Sirhindī, *Maktūbāt,* folios 58b-59b]

The Sultan in relation to the world is like the soul in relation to the body. If the soul is healthy, the body is healthy, and if the soul is sick, the body is sick. The integrity of the ruler means the integrity of the world; his corruption, the corruption of the world. It is known what has befallen the people of Islam. Notwithstanding the presence of Islam in a foreign land, the infirmity of the Muslim community in previous generations did not go beyond the point where the Muslims followed their religion and the unbelievers followed theirs. As the Qur'ān says, "For you, your way, for me, my way."...

In the previous generation, in the very sight of men, unbelievers turned to the way of domination, the rites of unbelief prevailed in the abode of Islam, and Muslims were too weak to show forth the mandates of the faith. If they did, they were killed. Crying aloud their troubles to Muhammad, the beloved of God, those who believed in him lived in ignominy and disgrace; those who denied him enjoyed the prestige and respect due to Muslims, and with their feather brains condoled with Islam. The disobedient and those who denied Muhammad used to rub the salt of derision and scorn into the wounds of the faithful. The sun of guidance was hidden behind the veil of error and the light of truth was shut out and obscured behind the curtain of absurdity.

Today, when the good tidings of the downfall of what was prohibiting islam [*i.e.*, the death of Akbar] and the accession of the king of Islam [*i.e.*, Jahāngīr] is reaching every corner, the community of the faithful have made it their duty to be the helpers and assistants of the ruler and to take as their guide the spreading of the Holy Law and the strengthening of the community. This assistance and support is becoming effective both by word and deed. In the very early days of Islam the most successful pens were those which clarified problems of Holy Law and which propagated theological opinions in accordance with the Qur'ān, the Sunna, and the consensus of the community, so that such errors and innovations as did appear did not lead people astray and end in their corruption. This role is peculiar to the orthodox ulamā who should always look to the invisible world.

Worldly ulamā whose worldly aspirations are their religion—indeed their conversation is a fatal poison and their corruption is contagious.... In the generation before this, every calamity which appeared arose from the evil desires of these people. They misled rulers. The seventy-two sects who went on the road of error were lost because the ruler enforced his errors on others and the majority of the so-called ignorant Sufis of this time upheld the decisions of the wicked ulamā—their corruption was also contagious. Obviously, if someone, notwithstanding assistance of every kind, commits an error, and a schism occurs in Islam, that error should be reprehended. But these hateful people of little capital always wish to enroll themselves among the helpers of Islam and to beg importunately.... These disobedient people worm their way into the confidence of the generous and consider themselves to be like heroes.... It is hoped that in these times, if God wills, the worthy will be honoured with royal company.

Shah Walī-Ullāh

The instinct of Indian Islam for tolerance and flexibility as a condition of its survival is symbolized in the life and thought of Shah Walī-Ullāh of Delhi (1703-1762), who wrote during the decline of the Mughal empire and before Indian Islam felt the impact of Western thought. He translated the Qur'ān into Persian, wrote Qur'anic commentaries, was a student of tradition, scholastic theology, and jurisdprudence, and practiced Sufism. His significance as a religious thinker is still being estimated but his writings indicate that Indian Islam had survived the intellectual and religious trials of the sixteenth and seventeenth centuries without loss of vitality and catholicity. Shah Walī-Ullāh helped to insure that at least among Muslims there was no bitter religious strife to complement the political strife in India after Aurangzīb's death. Shah Walī-Ullah, in the readings which follow, is to be observed teaching the old lessons of devotion to the Sunna of the Prophet and the need for breadth and tolerance in interpreting the mandates of the Sharī'a.

The Imitation of Muhammad

[From *The Muslim World,* Vol. XLV, No. 4 (tr. by Rahbar), pp. 326-27]

Know that the key of happiness is following the Sunna and imitating God's apostle in all his goings out and comings in, in his movements and times of quiescence, even in the manner of his eating, his deportment, his sleep, and his speech. I do not say that concerning his manners in matters of religious observances alone, because there is no reason to neglect the traditions which have come down concerning them; nay. that has to do with all the matters of use and wont, for in that way unrestricted following arises. God said, "Say, If you love God, follow me and God will love you" (Qur'ān 3-29). And He said, "What the apostle has brought you receive, and what he has forbidden you refrain from" (Qur'ān 59.7). So you must sit while putting on trousers and stand while putting on a turban; you must begin with the right foot when putting on your sandals, and eat with your right hand; when cutting your nails you must begin with the forefinger of the right hand and finish with its thumb; in the foot you must begin with the little toe of the right foot and finish with the little toe of the left. It is the same in all your movements and times of quiescence. Muhammad b. Aslām used not to eat a melon because the manner in which God's apostle ate it had not been transmitted to him. A certain man was unmindful and began to put on the left shoe first, so he made atonement for that with *a kurr* [a measure] of wheat. Now it is not fitting to be lax in such matters and say that this is one of the things which pertain to use and wont, so that there is no point in following the Prophet regarding it, because that will lock against you an important gate of happiness.

Legal Interpretation

Ijtihād or legal interpretation is the process whereby the student of the Sharī'a arrives at determinations of the Holy Law in circumstances not already covered by previous decisions. Legal interpretation is the sole means of adapting the Sharī'a to changing social circumstances while yet preserving the ideal of orthodoxy, *i.e.,* of following in the footsteps of the Prophet in obedience to a God-revealed law. The problems of legal interpretation has come to the fore in every period of crisis for the Indo-Muslim community, whether in the newly founded state of Pakistan or in Shah Walī-Ullāh's eighteenth century, when Muslim power was rapidly disintegrating. Shah Walī-Ullāh advises interpreters of the law to avoid arbitrariness and destructive controversy, and rather to apply the Golden Mean.

[From *The Muslim World,* Vol. XLV, No. 4, pp. 347-54 *passim;* 357-58]

The true nature of legal interpretation (*ijtihād*), as understood from the discourse of scholars, is exhaustive endeavour in understanding the derivative principles of the Holy Canon Law by means of detailed arguments, their genera being based on four departments· I) The Holy Book [the Qur'ān]; (2) The example and precept of the Prophet [the Sunna]; (3) The consensus of opinion of the Muslim community; (4) The application of analogy.

Let it be understood from this that legal interpretation is wider than [*i.e.* not confined to] the exhaustive endeavour to perceive the principle worked out by earlier scholars, no matter whether such an endeavour leads to disagreement or agreement with these earlier scholars. It is not limited by the consideration whether this endeavour is made with or without aid received from some of the earlier scholars in their notification of the aspects of questions involved in a given issue and their notification over the sources of the principles through detailed arguments. . . .

[Al-Baghawī said] "An interpreter of the Law is one who combines in himself five types of knowledge: (1) the knowledge of the Book of God the Glorious; (2) the knowledge of the example and precept of the Prophet (peace be on him and his descendants); (3) the knowledge of the speeches of the scholars of yore recording their consensus of opinion and their difference of opinion; (4) the knowledge of the Arabic language; and (5) the knowledge of analogy, which is the method of eliciting the principle from the Qur'ān or the Hadīth when the principle is not found unequivocally in the statures of the Qur'ān, the Hadith, and the consensus of opinion.

"It is incumbent that of the knowledge of the Holy Book he should possess the knowledge of the abrogating and the abrogated passages, the summary expressions and the full expressions, the general ordinances and the particular ones, the sound verses and the ambiguous verses, the disapprovals, prohibitions, permissions and approvals, and obligations.

"And of the Hadth he must recognize the perfectly sound Hadth, the weak ones, the ones supported by complete chains of narrators going back to the Prophet, the ones in which the chains of narrators omit the names of the Companions who transmitted the Hadīth. And he must know the application of the Hadith upon the Qur'ān and of the Qur'ān upon the Hadīth, so that if he finds a Hadith, the outward meanings of which do not conform to the meanings of the Book, he should get guided rightly to bring out its bearing, for the Hadīth is an exposition of the Book, and does not contradict it. Of the Hadīth it is obligatory upon him to know only those which relate to the principles of the Holy Law, and not the rest which contain stories, accounts of events, and admonitions.

"And likewise, it is incumbent that he should possess the lexical knowledge necessary to understand the passages in the Qur'ān and the Hadīth. But it is not required that he should encompass the entire vocabulary of Arabic. He should so polish up his linguistic knowledge that he may be in a position to understand the real import of Arabic phrases to an extent which may guide him to the intended meanings in different contexts and circumstances. This requirement is there because the Holy Canon Law is addressed in Arabic. He who does not know Arabic will not recognize the meaning intended by the Law-giver [*i.e.,* the Prophet], nor will be understand what the companions and the successors of the companions said of principles, nor will he understand the most important judgments given by the jurisconsults of the community. He should know Arabic well so that his judgment does not stand opposed to theirs, in which case his judgment will involve violation of the consensus. And when he knows the major portion of each of these departments of knowledge, he is an interpreter of the Law, and the exhaustive knowledge of all these is not a condition. And if he is ignorant of one of these five departments then his path is to follow [*i.e.,* not to indulge in legal interpretation], even if he is profoundly learned in the school of one of the bygone Imāms [the founders of one of the four schools of Muslim law]. It is not allowable for such a man to be invested with the status of a judge, or to be a candidate for a position in which he might give judgments. And if these sciences are combined in him, and he shuns evil passions and innovations, clothes himself with robes of piety, and abstains from major sins, not persisting in minor sins, then it is allowable that he may take up the responsibility of the office of a judge and may exercise his personal discretion in the Holy law using legal interpretation and may pronounce his judgment. And he who does not combine in himself these conditions must, in matters that might concern him, follow him who does combine them." [The quotation from al-Baghawī ends here.]...

Scholars have differed in the matter of ratification of interpreters of the law, pronouncing differently on the derivative issues where no conclusive judgement is to be found. Is each of these interpreters of the law correct or is only one of them correct?... [The author reviews the opinions of various authorities, and finally quotes al-Baidāwī.]

Al-Baidāwī said in *The Stages* (*Al-Minhāj*): "The most preferable view is that which comes soundly from al-Shāfi'i: 'In every occurrence there is a fixed verdict upon which there is an indication.' Whichever interpreter of the law finds out that indication, hits the target, and whichever fails to find it out, misses the target, although he is not sinful on that account, for legal interpretation, which is the sum total of the search of arguments, is preceded by arguments; and the indication upon the error made comes after the verdict. If two different legal interpretations were to be regarded true, this would be a concurrence of two contradictions. And the interpreter of the law, missing the target of truth is not sinful either because the Prophet (peace be on him!) said: 'Who so hits the target, shall have two rewards, and who so misses it, shall have only one reward'.

"It is said that if the verdict is fixed, then he whose position is contrary to it does not judge according to what Allāh had revealed, and so is a transgressor, for Allāh the Exalted says; 'Who so judges not in accordance with what Allāh has revealed, they are the transgressors.' We say answering this objection that he [*i.e.*, the error-maker] pronounced judgments in accordance with what he thought was right, even though his judgment mistook the meaning of what God has revealed."...

And in reality the opinion attributed to the four Imams [the opinion that only one legal interpreter out of many, pronouncing on the same issue, is correct] is drawn out from some of their statements and there is no final unequivocal ruling (*nass*) given by them on this matter.

And in fact that community of Islam has not differed from the position that you can ratify legal interpreters pronouncing judgement in a matter wherein the community is given choice by an unequivocal holy text or by consensus (ijmā‘), *e.g.*, the Seven Variant Readings of the Qur'ān, the formulae of invocations, and the number of prostrations in Witr Prayers, which may be seven, nine, or eleven. And likewise the ulamā [i.e., scholars] should not differ [from the position that both the legal interpreters could be ratified] in matters wherein choice is given by some indication [if not by an unequivocal text or by consensus].

And the truth is that there are four types of difference: (1) That in which the truth is decisively determined, and it is necessary in such a case that its opposite be contradicted for it is false; (2) That in which the truth is determined by the dominant opinion. The opposite of it is false by dominant opinion; (3) That is which definite choice has been given to adopt any of the two alternative sides of difference; and (4) That is which the above choice is given by the dominant opinion.

And the detailed explanation of the above is that if the issue at hand is such that the verdict of the verdict giver is violated by both the alternative ways of settling it, *i.e.*, if there is found an unequivocal, sound, and well-known Hadīth of the Prophet, and both legal interpretations stand opposed to it, then both will be false. But yes. The legal interpreter in such a matter will sometimes be excused upon grounds of his ignorance of the unequivocal Hadīth of the Prophet (peace be upon him) until that Hadīth reaches him, and the argument gets established. And if the legal interpretation is exercised in the ascertainment of an event which happened but the state whereof becomes dubious, like in the question whether Mr. A is dead or alive, unquestionably the truth in such a case will be one of the two alternatives. But the interpreter making a mistake in such a case will sometimes be excused in his legal interpretation.... The important cases of difference are of many types:

1. One interpreter of the law receives a Hadith and the other one does not. Now in this case the right interpreter is already known.
2. Every interpreter engaged in the same issue has some conflicting Hadīth and the exercises legal interpretation in bringing about congruence between some of them and preference of some over others, and his legal interpretation leads to a certain judgment of his own and so difference of this nature appears.
3. They may differ in the explanation of the words used and their logical definitions, or regarding the supply of what might be considered omitted in speech [and left to be understood], or in eliciting the *manat* [*i.e.,* the common factor which justifies the application of a primary principle from the Qur'ān or the Hadīth to a derivative situation, or in application of general to particulars, etc.].
4. They may differ in primary principles leading to difference in derivative principles.

In all these cases each of any two interpreters of the law will be right provided the sources from which they get support are easily acceptable to intellects....

Now whoever recognizes the true nature of this problem will realize: (1) that in the majority of cases of legal interpretation the truth lies somewhere between the two extremes of difference; (2) that in the matter of religion there is breadth and not narrowness; (3) that being unreasonably stubborn and determined to deny what the opponent says is ridiculous; (4) that the construing of definitions if it aims at bringing concepts closer to the understanding of every literate person, assists knowledge. But if these definitions are far-fetched and try to discriminate between involved matters by means of innovated premises, it will soon lead to an unworthy and innovated system of Sharī'a; (5) the true opinion is that pronounced by Izz al-Din 'Abd al-Salām who says: "He attains the goal who stands firm on what is agreed upon by scholars and abstains from what they have unanimously disallowed, and regards allowable that which is unanimously thus regarded by scholars, and does that which is unanimously approved by scholars, and keeps away from that which they have unanimously regarded as hateful."

Shah Walī-Ullāh and Mysticism

In his attitude toward mysticism, Shah Wali-Ullāh was conciliatory. For him, Ibn 'Arabi's doctrine of the unity of existence and Shaikh Ahmad of Sirhind's doctrine of the unity of experience, *i.e.*, the apparent but illusory unity of existence are both true statements about the same thing. In a letter to one Afandī Ismīl he writes:

[Adapted from *Visva-Bharati Annals*, IV 35-36 (tr. by Asiri), 1951]

Unity of existence and unity of experience are two relative terms used at two different places in an argument about God. Unity of existence here implies scrutiny of the encompassing truth which has filled the universe by unfolding itself with various commands on which is based knowledge about good and evil. Both revelation and reason support it. One should know that created things are one in one respect and different in another. This can only be perceived by the saints who are really perfect. The stage of unity of experience is higher than unity of existence.... Now some Sufis saw the contingent and created as connected with the eternal; also they perceived the modes of God's existence combined with His essence.

This can be explained by the example of wax forms of man, horse and ass, which have wax in common, but different shapes. This is the belief of the real panthesis. But the others maintain that the Universe is a reflection of the names and attributes of the necessary being [God] reflected in their opposite, nonexistence. These attributes and names are reflected in the mirror of nonexistence which is powerless.

In the same manner one can imagine the appearance of each name and attribute of God in the mirror of non-being. The former is unity of existence, and the latter unity of experience. To me both are based on true revelations. Unity of experience of Shaikh Ahmad does not contradict but confirms Ibn 'Arabī's unity of existence. In short, if real facts are taken into account and studied without their garb of simile and metaphor, both doctrines will appear almost the same.

8

SIKHISM

In dealing with Sikhism we are in face of what many be called a double movement. Fundamentally religious in its beginnings, it was forced by the pressure of circumstances into a militant organization. Most people in thinking of the Sikh think of a gallant warrior, of a splendid fighter. But we shall err very seriously if we look on him, we who are students of religion, as only, or even fundamentally, a fighter. That came by the pressure of circumstances, by the pressure of his environment; but the movement itself, in its lasting character, is fundamentally a religious movement. It a movement which grew up in the midst of Hinduism, having in the mind of its great Founder, Guru Nānak, the idea of joining together the Hindus and the Musalmans in one league of love to God and service to man. The thought of Guru Nānak—as we find it expressed not only in his words, but far more in his life—was to join together these warring elements of the Indian people on a platform that both could accept.

That platform is fundamentally love to God, Bhakti, devotion-Bhakti to God and also to the Guru, the Teacher, for the very name Sikh comes from the world sishya, disciple, and this idea of love to God and to the Teacher is the very basis and the very root of Sikhism. It is movement, then primarily of devotion. In its philosophy it is Hindu, but as a movement it is reformatory in its nature, striving against the formalism of the time, against the ceremonialism of the time, in order to find the life which lay below the form, the essence of the truth that had inspired the ceremonies. In the time of guru Nānak, as too often in the history of the world, a great religion had grow more and more formal and men were starving on the husk of the grain rather than eating the grain itself. Guru Nanak sought to find the grain, and in so doing threw aside, to a large extent the husk; he strove to lead men to see the reality of religion, the life of religion, the essence of religion, and to see that life and essence in love of God and the Guru, in love to men as children of the one God. You may almost sum up in that phrase the very essence of Sikhism. We shall find presently in his life how he tried to draw together the warring elements around him. We shall see presently in his life how it was one song of praise and love to God, how he was ever seeking the Supreme and, having found Him, strove to teach his fellows how they too, by devotion, might reach the same knowledge. That is the thought that I would have in your minds in the study of Sikhism, and I shall show you presently how that is carried out by the teachings in Sikh scriptures.

But before I do that, and before I speak of the life of the great saint, I must hastily sketch for you, as it were, the historic setting of Sikhism, so that you may understand how it came to pass that from a movement essentially of Bhakti, it became identified with the most gallant military spirit. And in doing this, I cannot, of course, give all the details that you may read for yourselves. But there is ever the difficulty in the minds of most that they lay too much stress on details in their study and lose sight of the broad outlines that alone render the whole intelligible. Professor Huxley used to complain of students of science that they lost sight of the forest in studying the trees, and that is continually true. Men lose themselves in a maze of details and they fail to grasp the unifying principles in history, and to see the main trend and current and meaning of events. Now all that I want to do, as regards the history of the Sikhs, is to give you a broad outline which will make you understand how it came to be what it was.

There were ten Gurus, one after the other, in unbroken succession, Guru Nānak being the first, the purest, the saintliest and the noblest of all, the life, the heart and soul of his followers.

We will take his life presently (A.D. 1469-1539); for the movement I but name him. He was followed by the second, Guru Angad (1539-52) of whom there is little to be said, save that he gathered together many of the songs and the teachings of his predecessor and so began the compilation of the Sikh Scriptures, the Ādi Grantha Sāhab. Then comes the third, Guru Amār Dās (1552-74), of whom one point is specially noticeable—that he met in conference the Musalman Emperor, Akbar, on matters of religion; showing how the spirit of Guru Nānak was ruling, and the attempt was being carried on to bring about peace between the great rival faiths of Hinduism and Islam. Then there the next Guru, the fourth, Guru Rām Dās (1574-81), still on terms of friendship with the liberal- minded and magnanimous Akbar, who gives him a piece of land at Amritsar, where he digs out the famous tank. Then the fifth, Guru Arjunmal (1581-1606), the builder of the famous Golden Temple, marks a point in the history of the Sikhs; for this building gives them a centre, a home, a rallying-place. The temple is first dedicated to Hari, Hari Mandir it was called, for Guru Nānak ever taught that in the name of Hari lay salvation. Later it became the Darbār Sāhab. Now the Sikhs have got, as it were, their own place. they begin to gather round the temple; They begin to form a definite community. Arjunmal, the religious teacher, becomes the head of the definitely organized religious community gathered at a special spot—the beginning of the Sikh State. His great work, again, is to gather together the teachings of his predecessors, and it is he who definitely compiles and who gives out the Ādi Grantha Sāhab; composed partly of the songs and the teachings of the preceding Gurus, partly also from the songs of the Saints in the Sikh movement, and so on.

Now comes the first touch which tells of the future struggle. Jehangir is on the throne of Akbar, less liberal, less magnanimous than his predecessor. His son rebels against him. Guru Arjunmal, apparently without any reason, or for a reason which really was no reason at all, was accused of sympathizing with the rebel son. I say "no reason," because the root of the accusation appears to have lain in the anger and the jealousy of the powerful minister to whom he had refused his child in marriage; and this minister, stirring up the suspicions of Jehangir against him, induces the Emperor to seize the Guru and imprison him. He dies from the hardships of the imprisonment.

There is the point where the community, which was purely religious and peaceful, begins to be led by this aggression on its Teacher and its Ruler, into the path that will make it a great military body. Jehangir is followed by Aurangzib, and things grow worse and worse under that fanatical ruler. The succeeding Guru, the sixth, Guru Har Govind (1606-45). begins definitely in self-defence to organize the Sikh; he binds them into a body apart alike from Hindu and Musalman, no longer a body to join the two, but a body apart and separate from both. The State of the Sikh is beginning to grow up, and now commence warfare and struggle, scattered skirmishing, scattered fighting, a sharing in the fights around them, ever welding the Sikhs more and more together as a fighting body. The seventh Guru, Guru Har Rai (1645-61), of whom little is said, is quiet and peaceful, but around are more struggles, still increasing war, increasing strife, increasing military spirit, until the religious side, as it were, almost goes into the background, save for the inspiration and the binding force it gives. Then comes a Guru, Guru Har Kisan (1661-64), who is but a child, a child of six years, dying when he is nine years old, to be followed by the ninth Guru, Guru Tegh Bahādur (1664-75). His life is very troubled, and he is cruelly murdered by Aurangzib, and is succeeded by his son, the last, the tenth Guru, Guru Govind (1675-1708), who gives to the Sikhs their great military organization, and makes them into the body that raised, under Ranjit Singh, the Sikh Empire in the Punjab.

On this tenth Guru we must pause for a while. A mere boy, he flies for his life after his father's murder, and for some twenty years he remains in retirement, thinking out his mission. Naturally, he broods over his father's murder, naturally he is bitter against his father's enemies; the hatred of the Musalman seems to become almost a duty for the son, for the Guru, and therefore for the Sikh. The old friendship has vanished; the blood of a father lies between the Guru and the Musalman Emperor. For some twenty years, as I say, he remains in retirement, thinking over the work that lies before him, thinking over his work as a religious teacher, but still more as a military organizer. And at last, he comes out from his retirement ready to do a mighty work, prepared for his life's mission. He is determined definitely to separate off the Sikhs from all possibility of confusion with men of any other faith. Five devoted disciples he calls around him, and with these five men and himself in the midst, he institutes the ceremony of Pahul, initiation, simple, warrior-like. He takes water; his wife happens to be passing with five kinds of sweetmeats, and he takes of the five sweet-meats, a little of each, and throws them into water. He stirs the water with a two-edged knife; he sprinkles it on the five men around him, and gives to each of them to drink, and they in turn sprinkle him and give him to drink, and he proclaims them as the Khālsā, the pure, and bids them add to their names the epithet of Singh, the Lion. These are the first initiated disciples, marked out from all others by special signs that every Sikh must carry on his person. The long hair, dividing him from the shaven Hindu; the comb; the two-edged dagger or knife; the steel bangle; the short breeches, coming to the knee. These are the five marks—the five K's as they are called, because each because begins with a 'K' in the vernacular—whereby he separates every Sikh from all surrounding him, and which true Sikhs bear today. That is the ceremony which he lays down as the ceremony of initiation, and wherever five Sikhs are gathered together, there he said, would be his spirit, and there the power of initiation. He is to be the last of the Gurus; after him no other teacher is to come; the power is to go into the hands of the Khālsā to be exercised by the council of its chiefs, the Guru Mātā; the authority for the Sikhs lies in the sacred book which, later, Guru Govind completes.

Now he is the warrior chief and the Sikhs flock around his standard. He fights, he struggles, he builds up a great army, his men are known by their marvellous courage, by the way they face great odds in battle; the same passion that we saw animating the Musalman in his conquering career after his great Prophet, is seen also in the warrior Sikh, and they died as joyfully as other men lived. No wonder that at first they carried all before them; yet, after much struggling, being put a few, after all, amid myriads, we find them beaten back in the struggle that they undertook with such heroism against overwhelming numbers, for these few had set themselves against the mighty Musalman Empire in the North.

They are but a few against myriads, but they are never discouraged, never terrified, never disheartened; their Guru is with them wherever they go, and where he is they are confident—he is beaten back, back, back until at last, by a splendid effort, he turns and drives off the troops of the enemy; they pursue him no further. The Well of Salvation the place is called, where that saving battle was fought.

It is after this, to encourage his followers, that he gives out the last of the Sikh Scriptures, the *Book of the Tenth King, or Guru, Daswin Pādshāhi,* the completion of the Ādi Grantha Sāhab.

Then comes the end. He is attacked by a Pathan, who quarrels with him over a matter of trade, a mere trifle, but the man threatens his life, and the warrior Guru strikes him down. He is dead. The sons of this man come, and he addresses them with kindness and favour; remembering the murder of his own father, he pities the sons whom he has made fatherless; he takes them into service and confidence, and when he knows that his time is come, there is a stranger scene. He speaks to one of these sons about the duty of revenge, about the slaying of the slayer of the kinsman, until at last he provokes him to strike him his own deathblow; he saves the young man from the anger of his followers, saying that he has but avenged his father's blood, and he must go free. He bids them follow the Scripture, bids them be faithful to the Khālsā, and dies.

Then, after he is gone, there is no more the Teacher; but, as I said, the real authority is the Ādi Grantha Sāhab, with the council of chiefs, and the Khālsā, the whole community of the Sikhs, wherein there was to be no difference of caste, no difference between man and man, all were to be brothers and were to be equal.

Then a brilliant story of military struggle and military success, crowned at last by the splendid victories of Ranjit Singh, the Lion of the Panjab (1797), who makes the Panjab practically the Sikh Empire. He dies in 1839. And then, ah! the saddest history of treachery, of betrayal, of brave warrior-souled and gallant men deceived and sold, struggling on desperately against all. The saddest of all stories, but the story of India over and over again, where brother has sold brother, where friend has sold friend, where Indian has betrayed Indian—that was all repeated in this story of the fall of the Sikh Empire. Never a story more heroic, never a story more pathetic, brave men struggling against overwhelming odds, so that even their own heroism could not save them, until the Empire broke entirely and the Panjab passed into the hands of the British troops in 1849. That is the outside setting.

Let us pass from that; let us see what was the faith, what the life, that gave to Sikhism its binding power, its marvellous heroism, its splendid strength. It is the life and the teaching of Guru Nānak, the sweetest of characters, and the saintliest of men.

From childhood a boy marked out, as all God's Prophets are marked out, as different from his fellow-men. The story of his childhood is not eventful, but it is very pathetic and very quaint. Quaint in this way, that he was born into a family of good people, of the commonest quality, like an eagle in the nest of a sparrow and the sparrows did not understand the eagle, and they could not make out what manner of creature this was. Quiet, reserved, silent, wandering away to meditate when other boys would be at play; what strange child is this, who will not learn as other boys learn, who will not play as other boys play, who when he goes to his teacher wants to know the mystic meaning of the letters, and angers the Pandit by asking questions that the Pandit—good man—cannot answer? Always coming athwart his surroundings because he must know what is within, he cannot be satisfied with what is without. And there is nothing more troublesome to the commonplace man or woman than to be pressed. With questions as to realities, when he finds himself quite comfortable on the safe cushions of formulae; and so Nānak, in his childhood, is a great trial to his father. Surely he must be mad; he is sitting for hours meditating and taking no food; he must be having fever. They bring a doctor to see him. Nānak asks the doctor whether he could cure the diseases of his soul. What kind of patient is this who greets his physician in that manner? Or take him when the ceremony of the sacred thread is to be performed. The story is so characteristic that I will give it to you, and I ought to say here that for all the quotations I am making, I am depending upon my Sikh friends, who have been good enough to translate them for me from their own books, so that I may have ground to go on which is sure.

"When everything was ready and the Purohit (the family priest) was about to invest him with it, Nānak turned round and enquired: 'Tell me, Panditji, of what use is this thread? What are the duties of the man who is invested with it? Why is it necessary to put it on?'

"'Nobody can perform any sacrificial ceremonies without putting it on,' said the Purohit, who was merely a village Pandit, and did not know the secret signification of the sacred thread; 'this thread purifies the wearer and entitle him to attend and perform all ceremonies.'"

"'If a man who has put on this sacred thread,' said Nānak,'does not change his ways, and leads an impure life, does this thread purify him and help him in any way in the end? Does not he reap the fruit of his actions?'"

"'I do not know,' replied the Purohit, 'but it is ordained in the Shāstras, and we must follow our for-fathers.'"

"From the cotton of compassion spin out the thread of love; make the knots of abstinence and truth: led your mind put on this thread; it is not broken, nor soiled, nor burned, nor lost. Praised be they who have put this on,' said Nānak.

"'You have spoken well,' said the Purohit, 'but look at all the expense and trouble your father has been put to, see all these friends and relations; they will be all disappointed if you won't put this on.'"

"'I am truly sorry that I cannot oblige you,' said Nānak;'I cannot put it on, and I will advise you also to think more about the essence of things than the form. Only by true conviction one gains respect, and by praising God and by living truthfully man reaches perfection.'"

"At last his mother entreated him for her sake not to disappoint her. Then Nānak simply said: 'Mother, I obey,' took the thread and put it on."[1]

There you have a very characteristic story of this Youth with the marks of a Prophet upon him, ever seeking the inner truth through the outer shows.

He grows into youth, and is a most unsatisfactory son to the good dull father, for he will not take up agriculture, he won't have a shop, and he won't travel in commerce. His trade consists in giving money or rather food to Sannyāsis, which his father thinks is not a good bargain, and finds little satisfactory, although Nānak thinks that it is the best bargain that can be made. What is to be done with such a young man. He sends him to his sister and her husband who love him. He takes services under a Nawāb, and serves faithfully and well; but he is ever giving away in charity, and at last wearies of the world, and determines to give up service, to give up the household life into which he has entered, to wander seeking for God, and for the realization of His love, There comes another characteristic scene with the Nawāb after he had left his service. The Nawāb sends for the young man, and after a time he comes. The Nawāb is angry because he has not come at once.

"'I am not now your servant. Nawāb Sāhab,' was Nānak's reply. 'Now I am a servant of God,'"

"'Do you believe in one God or many Gods?' Enquired the Nawāb."

"'Only in one, indivisible, self-existent, incompressible and all-pervading adorable God do I believe.'" Replied Nānak.

"'Then since you believe in one God, and I too believe in one God, Your God must be the same as mine; so then if you are a firm believer, come with me to the mosque and offer prayers with us.'

"'I am ready.' Said Nānak.

"His father-in-law was struck dumb with amazement, and he at once left the Court believing that Nānak had embraced Islām."

"It was Friday, and as the time for prayer was at hand the nawāb got up and, accompanied by Nānak, proceeded to the mosque. When the Kāzi began to repeat the prayer the Nawāb and his party began to go through the usual bowing ceremony, but Nānak stood silently still. When the prayer was over the Nawāb turned towards Nānak, and indignantly asked: 'Why did you not go trough the usual ceremonies? You are a liar and your pretensions are false. You did not come here to stand like a log.'

"'You put your face to earth,' observed Nānak, 'while your mind was running wild in the skies; you were thinking of getting horses from Candahār, not offering prayers; and your priest, sir, while going automatically through the bowing process, was thinking of the safety of the mare which foaled only the other day. How can I offer prayers with those who go through customary bows and repeat words like a parrot?'

"The Nawāb acknowledged that he was really thinking of getting horses and all the time he was praying the thought harassed him, but the Kāzi was greatly displeased and turning towards Nānak showered a volley of questions."[1]

There is the spirit of the seeker for reality coming out again. He begins his wanderings. He goes wandering about, singing with a musician and a friend who follow him. Mardāna and Bālā, and he comes to a village where he needs food. There is a poor man. Lālu, a carpenter. A man of pure life, who welcomes the wandering Sannyasi, gives him his own bed, brings him warm food, and Nānak eats. Next day a rich banker in the town gives a great feast to Brahmanas, and invites Nānak to come and eat with them. Nānak goes, but he will not take the food. Says the host:

"'Why don't you take my food?'

"'Because,' said Nānak,' 'Your food is not pure, for you have cooked this food for self-glorification; it is a tāmasic gift and therefore impure.'

"'You call my food impure while that of the low caste Lālu is pure? How is that?' asked Rai Bhag contemptuously.

"'You treat your guests irreverently and contemptuously,' said Nānak, 'that shows your tāmasic aims. I eat food cooked by Lālu, for it was cooked with love and brought with reverence, with no desire for repayment. You must learn a lesson from humble Lālu. Your food is full of blood.'

"'What proof have you that my food is impure,' demanded Rai Bhag angrily.

Nānak took Rai Bhag's food in one hand while in the other he took the food cooked by Lālu, and, as he pressed each, from Rai Bhag's food oozed out drops of blood while from that of Lālu oozed out milk.'[1]

Such was the way in which Guru Nānak taught the teaching ever bearing on reality and exposing show. Was he a Hindu? Was he a Musalman? Men quarrel as to which he was, for he was above the distinctions of outer creed and he loved all men and called himself nothing. When he came to die, after seventy years of noble life and priceless teaching, his disciples disputed as to what faith he really belonged; should he be burned as a Hindu, or should he buried as a Musalman? And as they disputed, one lifted the sheet over the corpse, and the body had disappeared, and he was neither burned nor buried.

Such was the spirit of the great teacher, as shown in his life and conduct, and in the teachings that he left behind him; they show the spirit that moved him—that profound devotion to the Supreme, that love for god that worldly men call madness, that passion and devotion that the Saints in every age and in every religion have felt. Philosophically he was a Hindu; his speciality is this profound Bhakti and his hatred of sham. Let us take his teaching and the teaching of his successors, for here we can make no difference, and see how they taught, and see the spirit of the teaching. I have, here, a large number of extracts from the Ādi Grantha Sāhab, classified under certain headings on which I had asked for specific Sikh teaching, so as to be able to give you an authoritative outline of that teaching, and I take passages from these Sikh translations, to show you exactly the nature of the teachings.[1]

First as to the Supreme. "Thou art I, I am Thou. Of what kind is the difference?" "In all the Once dwells, the One is contained." "He Himself is One. and He Himself is many. He does not die not perish. He neither comes nor goes. Nānak says that He is always contained in all."

You can catch the echo of the Upanishads thrown into more popular language, the deep thought of Hindu philosophy, put into a form for popular use.

One Omkāra, true Name, Maker, Sprit, fearless, unmalevolent, timeless Form. Form no womb, Self-existent, great-bliss (or through Guru's favour) (to be realized). True from before; true from before the ages (Yugas); true is and true to be, O Nānak.

[Japa I.]

Signless, that none may cross, unreachable (or unknowable); No object (for the sense); Untouched by time or action; Of unborn essence; From no womb; Self-existent; Unconditioned; Unwavering; May I unto this True Verity be sacrifice. He hath no form, nor colour, nor outline; by the true Word. He is to be pointed out. He hath no mother, father, son, nor kindred, nor lust, nor wife, nor clan; Untinged (by Māyā); Untranscended; Higher than highest; Thou Light of all; Brahm in all vessels hid; His Light complete in every vehicle (heart). By Guru's teaching the adamant Portals throw ajar, with fearless gaze fixed firm. Having created beings, he placed over them time, (death), and kept all regulation under (His) control. By Guru's service the true wealth (they) find; by acting on (His) world freedom (they) gain. In a pure vessel (heart) only Truth may live; rare are they conduct pure. Essence in the highest Essence merged; Nānak in Three doth refuge find.

[Sorath I.]

I bow down (or glorify) the primal One, Omkāra;

Who hath spread out (this) water, land and sky;

The first Spirit, unmanifest, imperishable;

Whose light illuminates the fourteen lokas;

Abiding in the elephant and the ant alike;

Who knoweth as equal the ruler and pauper;

From form duality; the signless Spirit

Directly knowing; the inner controller of every vessel (heart).

[Guru.]

He himself, the Formless (and) the form; That One without qualities and with qualities; One alone is spoken of, O Nānak. That one alone is many.

[Guru v. Bavanakhhri.]

The Parabrahman, Supreme Lord, cometh not into wombs.

With Thy word createst Thou creation, and after making Thou pervadest it.

Thy form could not be seen, how shall I meditate on Thee?

Thou functionest in all; Thy power showeth (this)

Thy love fills treasures which are inexhaustible;

These jewels (of peace, etc.), are priceless.

[Guru v. Var-Maru.]

Countless (lit. Crores) Avatāras of Vishnu didst Thou make.

Countless Brahmāṇḍas are the abodes of Thy Law;

Countless Maheshvaras are created and absorbed;

Countless Brahmās Thou didst set to fashion the worlds:

So rich is my Lord,
Whose great qualities I cannot speak of in details;
Whom countless Māyās attend.
(The hearts of) countless beings are His resting place;
Countless are (the devotees) who embrace (lit. or draw close to) Thy limbs (personified for worship).
Countless the devotees who dwell with Hari.
Countless the Kings (lit. Lords of Umbrellas) who pay Thee homage.
Countless Indras standing at Thy portals;
Countless Heavens in Thy glance;
Countless (Thy) priceless Names;
Whose countless resonance sounded forth;
Countless journeys of wondrous action;
Countless Shakṭis and Shivās obedient to His will;
Countless the beings whom Thou nourishest;
In whose feet are countless Tirthas (sacred places);
Countless pure ones repeat Thy dear name;
Countless worshippers render Thee worship;
Infinite Thy Expanse; there is no second;
Whose pure and spotless glories are countless;
Whose praise is sung by countless Brahmā-Rṣhis;
In the winking of an eye whose creations and absorption are countless;
Countless Thy qualities that may not be numbered;
Countless wise men declare Thy knowledge;
Countless meditators meditate on Thee;
Countless ascetics perform austerities;
Countless Munīs sit in silence;
Unmanifest Lord, imperceptible Master,

Filling all hearts and controlling from within,

Wherever I look Thou dwellest there;

The Guru (or great one) illumined Nānak (with this knowledge).

[Guru v. Bharon.]

Who hath no discus, mark, nor class, nor caste, not sub-caste,

Of whome none can say: "He hath form, colour, outline or vesture,"

Changeless form shining through Anubhava (direct perception of innermost spiritual consciousness),

Whom we might call the Indra (Lord) of countless Indras, and King of kings.

Three worlds, lords of earth. Gods, men, demons and forest grass are saying, neti neti (not this, not this).

Who can utter all Thy names? The wise declare Thy functional names (alone).

[Guru x, Japa.]

In every way I said, there was no other, O friend,

He dwells in all the continents and islands (dvipas),

He fills all lokas,

[Guru v. Devagandhāri]

His greatness the Veda doth not know;

Brahmā knoweth not His Mystery;

Avatāras know not His limit;

The supreme Lord, Parabrahm, is boundless.

[Guru v. Rāmkali.]

All are made liable to errors, the Maker alone does not err.

[Guru i. Śri Rāga.]

And then for worship; every Hindu knows the Ārati and the way in which light, and one thing after another, are offered to the image of the worshipped God. Guru Nānak deprecates the use of images in worship, and in his own Ārati offers the whole universe in the worship of Brahman, the Supreme,

Space itself (Thy) salver; the sun and moon (Thy) lamps;
The starry host thy pearls, O father,

The fragrant breeze of the Malaya mountains (Thy) incense;
The wind waving (its) chawri (over Thee);

All forest vegetation (lit. vegetable kingdom) as flowers, O Light!

What a rejoicing (Ārati or hymn of praise) O Destroyer of fear (or samsāra); the Anāhat Shabda (the soundless or unstruck sound) sounds as (Thy) kettle-drum.

Thousands are Thy eyes; Nay! Nay! Thou hast none;
Thousands are Thy forms; Nay! Nay! Thou hast none;

Thousands are Thy holy feet; Nay! Nay! Thou hast none;

Thou art without nostril (lit. sense of smell) yet Thou hast a thousand nostrils;

This wondrous working of Thine bewilders (us),

In everything, O Glory! is Thy Light.

In every one the Light of That (Light) shines.

In Guru's presence (or by Guru's teaching) shineth forth that Light;

That is rejoicing Ārati) which to Him is pleasing.

Such is his teaching. It breathes the purest spirit of devotion, that reaches beyond all forms, to the One Formless; and now and then a heart is found that feels greater passion of devotion for the ideal of the One than in dwelling on any of the forms in which the One manifests Himself. In Guru Nānak there is no denial of all the forms in which the Supreme is shown, but he takes the view of the Upanishads, that there is one Brahman, supreme over all, of whom all the Gods are but the partial manifestations, of whom the highest forms are but reflections of the Beauty.

When we are asked what it is he teaches us to creation, we find that the pure Vedāntic teaching, that the creation is but Māyā and by the power of Ishvara and Māyā all things come forth.

By will (lit. order) the forms come forth.

[Guru i. Japa.]

One Mother (Māyā united with (God) gave birth (to) three acceptable children (lit. disciples);

One of them sends forth samsāra, the other provides and the third habitually dissolves.

As it pleaseth Him so (He) directeth (them), according to (His) will.

He looketh on but is not seen; great is the marvel, Hail to Him, Hail!

The primal, the unstained, without beginning, the indestructible, in every age (assuming) the same vesture.

[Guru i. Japa]

When the Maker causes emanation (or expansion),

Then the creation takes up infinite bodies;

Whenever Thou drawest in,

Then all the embodied merge in Thee.

[Guru x. Chaupai.]

There are hundreds of thousands of Ākāṣhas and Pātālas.

[Guru i. Japa.]

The limits of His creation cannot be known.

[Guru i. Japa.]

This world is the house of the True (one), the True (one) dwells therein.

[Guru ii. Asavar.]

This world is the temple of Hari, but awful darkness without the Guru.

Those who are led by the mind (lit. mind facing), these blind rustics worship Him as being distinct (lit. another).

[Guru iii. Prabhati]

Here is Siddhā question:

How is the world produced O man, (and) how can pain be destroyed?

Answer of Guru Nānak:

In Egoism the world has its birth, by forgetting the name (we) suffer.

[Guru i. Sidhgosht.]

As to the Jiva he teaches that the Jīva is the same in essence with the Supreme, and that by reincarnation and by karma, the Jīva can realize himself and know that there is no difference. Endless births he speaks of, and he repeats that phrase that we find with the Jaina as with the Hindu, that human birth is difficult to gain and that in human birth is liberation to be found.

This Jiva is not subject to death.

[Guru v. Gauri.]

In the body is mind, in the mind is the True [one]

That True one merging in [uniting with] the True one is absorbed.

[Guru i. Rāg Dhanāsri.]

The same thing is in the body which is in the Brahmānda;
Whosoever seeks finds.

[Pippa Bhakta Dhanasri.]

Neither caste nor birth is asked; enquire at the House of the True.
According to one's actions are caste and birth.

[Guru i. Prabhati.]

The man who performs good actions,

He is called a Deva [in this] world:

He who does evil deeds in this world,

Men call him an Asura [demon].

[Guru x. Vichiṭra Nātak.]

On karma, the teaching is very clear:

Soweth himself, eateth himself.

[Guru i. Japaji.]

In the field of karma he reapeth whatever he soweth.

[Guru v. Baramah Majh.]

Let us not blame anyone,

Whatever we act that we enjoy (and suffer);

Karmas (actions) are ours, bondage is ours too,

Coming and going is the activity (business) of Māyā.

[Guru v.]

In many births [we] became insects and moths;

In many births [we] became elephants, fish, and deer;

In many births [we] became birds and serpents;

In many births [we] were yoked as steeds and bullocks;

Seek the Lord! It is the surer [opportunity] of seeking;

after long ages this [human] body has been attained.

Many lives [have we] wandered over mountains.

Many lives [have we] been miscarried from the womb.

Many live [have we] been created as herbage.

We have been made to wander through eight-four lakhs of wombs.

The association of the good hath let us attain [this] birth.

Serve thou devotedly, says Hari. This is the Guru's teaching.

If he cast off vanity, falsehood and pride

And die living, then is he accepted in [that] court *[i.e.,* presence].

[Guru v. Gauri Rāg].

As iron placed on an anvil is beaten into shape,

So is deluded [or ignorant] soul thrown into wombs and made to wander, [so that] it may bend (or turn to the Right Path).

[Guru i. Suhi Rāg Kafi 4.]

Here is a beautiful description of the Jivan-Mukta:

Who in his mind knows the Lord's will to be for the best,

He is verily called Jivan-Mukta.

To him jou is the same as sorrow.

He is ever blissful; to him there is no separation.

Gold to him is the same as clay.

To him nectar is the same as bitter poison.

Honour and dishonour are the same to him.

The pauper and the king are equal for him.

Whatever is made to happen (by the Lord), that same.

[he considers] fit and proper.

O Nānak, such a man is called a Jivan-Mukta.

[Guru v. Sukhmani.]

And here is a fine poem on the Brahmajnāni:

Brahmajnāni is ever unstained, like the lotus which is not wetted by water.

Brahmjnāni is ever free from fault (or evil), as the sun dries up all things;

Brahmajnāni looks upon every one equally, as wind touches the king and pauper alike.

Brahmajnāni suffers, endures all equally, as the earth dug by some and smeared with sandal by others.

Such is the quality of Brahmajnāni as the (burning) power of fire is innate.

Brahmajnāni is purer than the pure, as impurity touches not water.

In the mind of Brahmajnāni shines light, as the sky (shines) above earth.

To the Brahmajnāni friend and foe are equal, Brahmajnāni hath no pride.

Brahmajnāni is higher than the high, but he thinks himself lower than every one.

Those men become Brahmajnāni, O Nānak, whom the Lord Himself makes (such).

Brahmajnāni is the dust (of the feet) of every one;

Brahmajnāni has gathered (or known) the essence of ātmā.

Brahmajnāni is compassionate to all; no evil cometh from the Brahmajnāni.

Brahmajnāni always looks upon all equally, on whatever he looks he showers nectar.

Brahmajnāni is free from bondage, Brahmajnāni's yoga is pure.

Brahmajnāni's food is wisdom; O Nānak, the meditation of Brahmajnāni is Brahmā.

Brahmajnāni [fixes his] hope on the One, Brahmajnāni doth never perish.

Brahmajnāni is pervaded by humility, Brahmajnāni delights in doing good to others.

Brahmajnāni is free from activity [of the three Gunas].

Brahmajnāni makes [his own mind] prisoner.

Whatever befalls a Brahmajnāni (he considers) it good,

Divine qualities fructify in a Brahmajnāni.

Everything is uplifted along with a Brahnajnāni, O Nānak; the whole world repeats [the name of] the Brahmajnāni.

Brahmajnāni has one colour [state of the mind, *i.e.* Love]. The Lord dwells with the Brahmajnāni.

Brahmajnāni is supported by the name, to the Brahmajnāni the Name is his all in all.

Brahmajnāni is ever awake in the Real, Brahmajnāni relinquishes egoism.

In the heart of Brahmajnāni there is the highest bliss; in the Brahmajnāni's house there is ever peace.

Brahmajnāni dwells in happiness; O Nānak, there is no destruction for the Brahmajnāni.

Brahmajnāni is the knower of Brahmā; Brahmajnāni is ever in love with the One.

Brahmajnāni is free from anxiety, Brahmajnāni's belief is pure.

He is Brahmajnāni whom the Lord Himself makes [such]; the glory of the Brahmajnāni is great.

A very fortunate person may see [meet] a Brahmajnāni.

We should offer ourselves as a sacrifice for (lit. go round) a Brahmajnāni.

Maheshvara (Shiva the great Lord) seeks a Brahmajnāni, O Nānak.

The Brahmajnāni is the Supreme Lord Himself.

The Brahmajnāni is a priceless treasure.

Everything is in the heart of Brahmajnāni, he who knows the secret of the Brahmajnāni.

Let us ever salute the Brahmajnāni; we could not pronounce half a letter of the Brahmajnāni.

Brahmajnāni is the Lord of all; who can measure in speech the Brahmajnāni!

A Brahmajnāni alone knows the Goal of the Brahmajnāni.

Of the Brahmajnāni there is neither limit nor the other shore.
O Nānak, we ever salute the Brahmajnāni.

Brahmajnāni is the maker of all creation. Brahmajnāni is the giver of mukti, yoga and life.

Brahmajnāni is the whole Spirit (Purusha) and ordainer.

Brahmajnāni is the protector of the unprotected,

Brahmajnāni guards every one.

All this is the form of Brahmajnāni. Brahmajnāni is the Formless [Supreme Self] Himself.

The splendour (or grace) of the Brahmajnāni befits a Brahmajnāni alone. Bramajnāni is the treasure of all.

[Guru v. Sukhmani.]

He who causes no fear to others, and fears no one.

Say Nānak! hear O mind, call him Jnāni [wise].

[Guru ix.]

Here are some are some slokas on devotion to the Gurudeva:

O Nānak! know that to be the true Guru who unites (thee) with all, my dear.

[Guru i. Sri Rāg.]

Every day a hundred times would [1] sacrifice [myself] unto [my] own Guru;

Who transformed me into God, and it did not take him long to do so.

[Guru i. Vara Asā]

If a hundred moons and a thousand suns were to rise,

And there were so much light. Without Guru there would be (still) awful darkness.

[Guru ii. āsavara.]

Blessed by my true Guru, knower of Hari, Who showed us friend and foe equal in our sight.

[Guru iv. Vara Vadhans.]

Gurudeva is mother, Gurudeva is father, Gurudeva is the Supreme Lord;

Gurudeva is friend, destroyer of ignorance, Gurudeva is relative and real brother;

Gurudeva is the giver and teacher of Hari's name;

Gurudeva has realized the mantra;

Gurudeva is the embodiment of peace, truth and enlightenment; Gurudeva's touch is higher than that of the philosopher's stone.

Gurudeva is the Tirtha (place of pilgrimage), the tank of nectar (immortality), there is nothing beyond immersion in Guru's knowledge.

Gurudeva the maker is the destroyer of all evil.

Gurudeva is the purifier of all fallen ones.

Gurudeva is primal, before ages, in every age; by repeating his Hari-Mantra [we] are saved (lit. uplifted from the ocean of Samsāra)

O Lord, favour us with Gurudev's company, so that linked (attached) to him we deluded sinners may swim (across).

Gurudeva, the true Guru, is Parabrahman, Supreme Lord; Nānak bows to Gurudeva Hari.

[Guru v. Bavanakhhri.]

O mother! I rejoice, for I have found the true Guru.

[Guru iii, Rāmkali.]

Let him fix the Guru's word in his heart.

And cease to associate with the five persons (desire, wrath, etc,)

Keep the ten organs under control.

Then in his self the light shall shine forth.

[Guru v. Gauri.]

To conclude these perhaps too numerous quotations,

I will give some miscellaneous ones, full of beauty:

Think thou on the great qualities of the true Name at the ambrosial time (morning).

[Guru i. Japa.]

Even if we rub and scrub our body with water, still O Brother! It is impure;

Let us bathe in the mighty waters of knowledge, O Brother! so that the mind and body be purified.

[Guru i. Sorath.]

O heart! Love Hari as the lotus loves the waters;

It is buffeted by waves, but (the petals of) its love unfold.

[Guru i. Sri Rāga.]

I forgot all distinctions (lit. anotherness, or I forgot altogether who was another),

Since I obtained the company of the good;

There was no enemy, no alien, I made peace with every one.

[Guru v. Kānara.]

All beings are His, He belongs to all beings.

Whom can we revile [or say he is low]? If there were another [we might do so].

[Guru iii. Āsa.]

Pause for one moment on the thought that if there is but one self in all, where is there room for hatred? If there be but one Hari in all, where is the room for contempt? If there were more than One, if there were not One without a second, then might man be different from man and might quarrel with his brother; but if the same God abides in every heart, if the same Self animates every vehicle, where is the room for hatred or contempt? There is but One in all.

O Nānak, repeat Soham, Haṃsa; by this repetition the three worlds are absorbed in Him.

[Guru i. Var Mārū.]

Call them not pure who wash their bodies and sit,

O Nānak! Those alone are pure in whose heart He dwells.

[Guru i. Var Āsa.]

Those who practised contentment, they meditated on the true One.

They placed not their foot into evil, they did good deeds and earned virtue.

[Guru i. Āsa.]

He is Sannyāsi who serves the true Guru and removes the self from within;

Desires neither convering, nor food, takes what comes [to him] without thinking [or unasked].

[Guru i. Mārū Rāga.]

Few attain Guru's favour and are centred in the fourth state.

[Guru iii. Majh.]

Of the things to be renounced, the most to be renounced are lust, hatred and avarice.

Hear thou! meditating on Hari's name do charity to all.

Without practising virtue, devotion is not possible.

[Guru i. Japa.]

In thy own home and palace fine innate bliss; (thus) thou again shalt not return.

(Guru v. Gauri.)

O mind! practise such sannyās (renunciation): consider all abodes as forest, remaining unaffected, at heart; keep the matted locks of self-control, do the ablution of yoga, grow nails of niyama (five observances).

Make [Divine] knowledge thy Guru, and teach thyself.

Besmear [yourself with] the ashes of the Name;

Let the love [good] of thy body [consist in] eating little, little sleep, compassion, forgiveness.

Practise good disposition, contentment, transcend the three Gunas.

Do not let lust, anger, pride, avarice, obstinacy, deluded clinging (conquer you).

Then will you behold the reality (essence) of the Self and you will attain to the Supreme Spirit.

[Guru x. Shabd Hazare.]

Delay not in good; delay in evil.

[Guru v.]

Countless are the slanderers [that] burden themselves [with the sin of calumny].

If thou seekest thy own good, then do good, and let them call thee lowly.

[Guru i. Āsa.]

Weighed in the balance, he who bends down is precious.

[Guru i. Suhi]

I am not good; none else is bad.

[Guru i. Suhi.]

If one becomes a slave of slaves, and casts out the self, then he finds Hari.

[Guru iii.]

As a fish cannot live without water,

As a cuckoo cannot be satisfied without the raindrop,

As a deer [pierced, touched or enamoured by the sound [of a song] runs towards it,

As a black bee, thirsting for the scent of a flower, finding it, gets himself imprisoned,

So the saints love God and are satisfied by seeing [Him]

[Guru v. Jaitsari]

There are none who do not wrangle and oppose;

Show them to me and I will praise them.

[Guru i. Mārā.]

The devotees and worldly men seldom agree.

[Guru i. Majh.]

By the Guru's favour, practice Rāja Yoga.

There are few who annihilate duality (sense of separation) and having destroyed it practice Rāja Yoga.

[Guru v. Gauri.]

He to whose eyes the collyrium of [Divine] Knowledge has been applied, he beholds all [as] splendour.

In the darkness of ignorance he sees not, and wanders again and again (in rebirth).

[Guru v. Sorāth.]

I sought Him in the ten quarters, I found Him in the house;

I met Him, when the true Guru brought me face to face with Him.

[Guru i. Omkār.]

The delusion of whose breast (heart) is gone,

Hindu and Musalmān are the same before him.

[Guru x.]

One has become a shriven Sannyāsi, and another a Yogi, a Brahmachāri, a Yati, is considered; a Hindu, a Turk (Musalman), a Rafazi, Imāmshafi. But understand thou humanity is one. The Maker, the Compassionate, is the same, that Nourisher, and the Kind One is the same; fall not into the error and delusion of the difference of duality, One is to be served; the Gurudeva of all is one; one is the Nature and know thou the Light to be one. The temple and the mosque are the same, Pūja and Nimāz [muslim prayer] are one, all men are one, but many in manifestation; so

Gods and demons are one, Yakshas and Gandharvas. Hindus and Turks are due to the different nature of the garbs of various lands. The eyes, the ears, the body, the make is one, a combination of earth, air, fire, water; the signless Allah is the same; Purānas and Qurān are the same; one is the nature and one is the make.

As from one fire a crore of sparks arise, and becoming separate merge again into the [same] fire; as from one [help of] dust many particles fill (the sky) and these particles again disappear in the same dust; as in one river many ripples are formed, but these ripples of water are called but water; so from the Universal Form conscious and unconscious being have manifested, but they shall lose themselves into That from which they have come.

[Guru x. Kavitu.]

Surely there is nothing in all these to which the heart of every one of us cannot answer, which the heart of every one of us cannot echo, only longing that we had the same passion and devotion and only longing that our devotion might be as clear as his.

Such is the teaching and such is the heart of Sikhism. Is there anything in it which can serve but to bind together, to draw hearts close each to each, to bind men together in love? When you think of Guru Nānak, think of one of those great Prophets of peace, who from supreme love to God, would draw the blessed fruit of love to men; and then you will see that the Sikh brothers are helpers in the building up of the one nation out of India with no quarrel against any, with no hatred against any, with no strife to divide them from any other faith. If they are faithful to the teachings of their Guru, they should be friends and unifiers wherever they go, builders-up and constructors of the national life. We should not be far wrong if we said that in this religion of pure Bhakti, of love of God and man, we have one of the forerunners of that ancient Divine Wisdom, which, in these later days, the great Lodge has given to man; for here too is a unifier, a friend and brother, here too is a lover and a joiner of those who are rivals. When we speak the name of Guru Nānak. We speak the name of peace, and may He who watches over his own community make it one of the elements for the building of India.

REFERENCES

1. Life of Guru Nānak by Jogendra Singh in Central Hindu College Magazine, Benares.
2. *Ibid.*
3. *Ibid.*
4. I own most of these to Sirdars Umrao Singh and Harbans Singh, who selected the illustrative passages and translated them.

The verification of the references may be rendered more easy by the subjoined description of the contents of the Ādi Grantha Sāhab, taken from the *History of the Sikhs,* by J.D Cunningham, second edition, pp. 368-71

The Ādi Granth Sāhab is divided into parts as follows: Japji, or Guru Mantra, by Guru Nānak.

Sodur Rehi Ras.	''	with additions.
Kirtan Sohila.	''	''
31 by forms of verse:		
Shri Rāga.	Todī	Tokkāri.
Majh.	Bairāri.	Kedāra.
Gauri.	Teilang.	Bhairo.
Assa.	Sodhī.	Basant.
Gujri.	Bilāwal.	Sarang.
Deva Gāndhari.	Gand.	Mulār.
Bihāgrā.	Rām Kali.	Kanrā.
Wiad Hans.	Nat Nārāyan,	Kalyān.
Sorath.	Mati Gaura.	Parbhati.
Dhanāsri.	Marū.	Jai Jaiwanti.
Jeit Sirī.		
Bhog.		
Bhog Ka Barū.		

9

THEOSOPHY, ITS MEANING AND VALUE

Friends,—It is right that I should say at the very outset of the lecture that no society and no individual, because such a society may invite me to its platform, is in any way bound by the opinions which here I may express. It would not be just to hold the Ethical Society responsible for that which I might put forward to you, for it is only offering me a free platform, and not in any way endorsing the opinions I may lay before you. Hence in what I say I speak for the Theosophical Society, and put forward things which by study I have found to by true. But I do not desire to commit to those opinions either the gentleman who is good enough to take the chair for me, or the society of which he is the president. With that preface let me turn to what I have to say.

I want, if I can, to enable you to answer question which is very often asked—"What is Theosophy?" For very different opinions are put forward with regard to that name by those who have not much looked into the subject nor endeavoured to understand it. Some people, if you ask them, will say, "Oh, it is a kind of Buddhism;" and many other suggestions may be made. I want, if I can, to tell you what it is from the standpoint of those who study it and accept it.

Now its name, to begin with, tells you really the meaning. 'The name "Theosophy"—the name evidently drawn from the

Greek—has been taken for thousands of years to express a particular view of the universe and of men; and to express, above all, man's relationship to God. The "Divine Wisdom"—whether you take it in the Greek form, or whether you go further East and take it under the name that there has been given to it, the Brahmavidya—has always implied the very opposite of the position which was defined by the late Prof. Huxley as that of the Agnostic. Sometimes it is easier to realise a position which is unfamiliar when it is contrasted with one that you may chance to know better in the West. You will remember that Prof. Huxley defined his position to all religions and to super-physical facts as that not of a denier, nor of an affirmer, but of an agnostic. Literally, of course, the word means "without knowledge" ; but it was very well understood that when the name was taken by great scientist, the particular kind of knowledge he declared himself to be without was that which has long been known in Philosophy, as the "gnosis," or the knowledge. So that when he put the "a" before it and took the term "agnostic," he intended to convey, as he there definitely stated, that the possibilities of human knowledge were bounded by investigation into the phenomena that the senses could observe, and that which the reason could deduce from the study of phenomena. He declared that man a senses for observation; he had reason for study and for understanding what he had observed; but he stated that man had no powers, no faculties, which could carry him beyond observation and reasoning thereupon. And hence he declared that the position of himself, and those who agreed with him in this, was that all subjects beyond the reach of the senses and of the reason were unknowable by man.

Now when that proclamation was made to the Western world, science had been for some time going along lines, and was continuing to follow those lines, which took it more and more into antagonism to the religions of the world. More and more it appeared to be building up a materialistic edifice. Since that time, as you know, the lines of scientific investigation have change, and it is now engaged in various researches which are practically bringing back in a scientific form much that during the last part of the 19th century had been taught to be outside scientific possibility. If I wanted, then, to put over against the position of Prof. Huxley—the position of the agnostic—that which Theosophy is, I should say it is the "gnosis," the knowledge. And that is a declaration that just as man can study the phenomenal world by observation of the senses, just as by the reason and the intelligence he can conquer the intellectual world and so extend the results of his observation, so also does man possess not only senses and intelligence but also a spiritual nature; and that by virtue of that spiritual nature he can know the spiritual world as he can know the intellectual by the reason, as he can know the phenomenal by the senses. And, therefore, Theosophy is the declaration that man can know God—not only believe, not only think about Him, not only argue about Him, not only reason about Him, but know Him. Now that is one of the oldest affirmation in the world; it lies at the root of every great religion of the past and of the present. It is the declaration that, man being a spiritual being and the spiritual nature being the profoundest part of himself, by the unfolding of that, by the knowledge, in the deepest sense, of himself, man is able to reach the knowledge of the supreme, of the universal life. It is the assertion that man, being fundamentally a spirit, can know the spiritual; and just as in the Christian religion you have the declaration from the lips of the Christ that the kingdom of God is within you. Just as in Hinduism you have the declaration that the self in man is part of the self universal—so in modern days Theosophy reproclaims the ancient affirmation; so in the face of agnosticism it raises again the banner of gnosticism, and it declares that the spiritual nature is a fundamental part of human nature, and that man in the deepest recesses of his being has a spiritual life, and not only an intellect and a possession of the senses. That is the fundamental meaning of Theosophy.

This declaration of knowledge being possible, you will at once realise that, if that, if that be true, then religion is founded upon a bedrock which nothing will be able to shake. It does not in that case rest upon any books, however sacred, nor on any authority, however venerable. It does not in that case depend upon any Church, any sect, any congregation. It rests ultimately on the experience of human consciousness, on the testimony of that consciousness to that to which it is akin. And so religion in its ultimate essence does not become a matter of authority but a matter of experience, each man being capable of reaching the experience for himself, each man being able to find within himself the testimony to spiritual realities; and no matter what may be the differences between the religions, no matter what may be the quarrels that have divided religious men, still there remains in the heart of each the final testimony—the testimony of human experience, the most universal and the most identical throughout the whole evolution of humanity. And that is the first declaration and the essence of Theosophy.

Now in addition to that, Theosophy is a body of teachings. You may say, "How are these teachings obtained?" Look back to the last fifty years of the 19th century, and you will see that there grew up during that time—out of the many investigations into the past, out of the many unburyings of ancient cities and ancient temples—there gradually grew up what was called "the science of comparative mythology." Now that science was based upon a number of facts that it was impossible to deny. Only the ignorant could deny them. It was found that wherever you searched back into the past, certain great teachings were found in every religion. When the tombs of Egypt were opened, when the mummies were unrolled, fragments of papyrus were over and over again found on the breast of the mummy within the rolls of the cloth. These were gathered together one after another, brought up from the places where these fragments had been buried for thousands upon thousands of years. By much research, by unwearying patience, men who devoted themselves to the study of ancient Egypt at last gained clues by which they were able to translate these fragments of ancient writing that had come into their hands. They learnt to translate the hieroglyphics; they managed to discover the secret of the ancient writings, the priestly writings of Egypt. And so at last, leaf after leaf, translation after, translation they gathered together a mass of information which told to the modern world what Egypt had believed in the days of her greatness; rolled back the mists of centuries, and made the Egyptian religion live once more before the eyes of men. And when they had thus gathered together what Egypt had to tell them, they carried on the same kind of work in nation after nation, unbarring city after city. They went across the Atlantic to ancient Mexico, and there they dug down till they came to the temples of the great civilisation which was ancient when the Aztecs overthrew it—they who themselves were ancient when Cortes and his Spaniards ravaged Mexico. And as they dug up those long-forgotten temples they found there the same hieroglyphics that they had learned to read in Egypt—the same symbols, the symbols containing or concealing the same teachings. And so from America as from Egypt they brought back the facts they had discovered, and they preserved them for future study. They unburied the cities of Chaldea; they read again the old Assyrian story. Then, when they had gathered ancient religion after ancient religion together, they began to study the living religions of antiquity as they had studied those that had passed away. They asked China what she had to tell of her ancient beliefs; they went to India, and translated many a book out of her mighty literature; they asked the Buddhist what he taught; and then, coming down the stream of ages, they came to the more modern faiths, and put them side by side with the ancient living and the ancient dead. And out of that there came a conclusion that it was not possible to deny—that all the great religions of the past had taught similar doctrines; that all the great religions of the past had proclaimed a similar morality; that all the great religions of the past told of divine teachers who had been the founders and teachers of great religions—and who all had given similar teachings to the world.

And when they had gathered all this together, they baptised it with a name which showed the way in which they regarded it: for they called it "comparative mythology." And then they drew a conclusion not so certain as their facts. They declared that all the religions of the world thus shown to be identical in their main features had their root in human ignorance; that we only had in the most refined and philosophical religions a refinement which had been gradually brought about with the improvement of human reason, and with the building of human civilization; but that if you ignored that refinement, that philosophizing, then you would find that primeval ignorance lay at the root of all these great religions. Thus they struck the deadliest blow which yet had been struck at religion in showing that all were alike, and in adding that which they had not proved—that all grew out of the primeval ignorance of the savage.

It was just at that time that the "Ancient Wisdom" was again proclaimed to the modern world which accepted all these facts; it stated that many more facts of a similar nature remained to be discovered; and took as true all this great basis of knowledge that had been obtained, but challenged the deduction which "Comparative Mythology" had made from it, pointed out that there was another possibility to explain the likeness of all the religions, living and dead. And that was the possibility that there had been a primary teaching of a wisdom, and that all the religions really had their root, not in human ignorance, but in divine wisdom; and that great religious teachers were members of a mighty brotherhood who taught the same truth because truth is eternal, and only gave it different forms in order to suit the need of the people to whom they came as revealers of the truth.

So these two were put over against each other, those who maintained the origin of all religions in divine wisdom, and those who asserted their origin in human ignorance. The facts the same in both; the deductions equally, for the time being, unproved. And then the question arose, "What evidence can be found for one or the other?" Looking back into the past is there anything which may guide us to a conclusion as to whether ignorance or wisdom be really the root of the similarity among all religions? And then as, in search of that which should decide the quarrel, students went backward into the past, one thing came out strongly and universally, and that was that the further you went back along the stream of the religious teaching, the purer it became, the wiser—not the more ignorant, the more savage. The great bibles of the religions were found to contain the purest morality that these religions had taught. The philosophy of the past was searched into, and it was found that to those most ancient books of the Hindus—their Vedas—they had attached those great philosophical treatises which have been the study of Orientalists in Europe and the admiration of those who have tried to study and to understand—it was found that the further back you went the nobler the teaching, the sublimer the spirituality. And that is true of all religions alike. If you want in your own faith of Christendom to inspite people to a nobler morality you do not take the data of Ethics from Herbert Spencer, you take the Sermon on the Mount, from the lips of the Christ. There it is that you find your inspiration, and not in the later discussions. And so with all the great religions of the world. Hence along this line of study the verdict went in favour of the conclusion that the unity of religions grew out of the wisdom which lay behind them, and that you cannot prove the thesis that the comparative mythologists had started with—that they were only the refinement from savage and barbarous superstitions. And so in the second sense Theosophy came to be the great body of teachings common to all religions, the teachings which you find alike in all that are not the exclusive possession of any. And those teachings are not very many in number, however great in significance. You could count them off upon your fingers, and find them in every one of the great religions of the would. Let me run them over and you will see that this is so with the exception of one on which, perchance, you might challenge me.

The first great universal teaching common to the most ancient, the longest dead, religion of the past and to the youngest religion is the proclamation of the unity of God; the one life throughout the universe, the one consciousness from which all consciousnesses are drawn, the one mighty existence from which all other existences are derived. That is the first universal teaching of all religions without exception. Even among the savages where you find them sunk in the depth of fetishism and animism, even there you find, as Lang has shown, that behind all those results of ignorance there is ever the teaching, which they say is their oldest teaching, of the one universal and all-embracing life. Even there, behind the fragments that have come down, this one central teaching is found.

Then you find as the next point of this universal teaching that in the manifestation of life, in the building up of a universe, triple are the qualities which show themselves forth—just as your own consciousness is triple in its nature, just as in yourselves you can find in miniature the reflection of that all-pervading consciousness. And so the dogma of the Trinity grew up, the popular way of putting the philosophical conception of this threefold nature of consciousness alike in God and man. And in all these ancient religions that is the second great truth that comes out, whether you take it from the mouth of the philosopher or from the mouth of the believer in the popular form of religion.

And then the third thought that comes out equally from every faith is the great hierarchy, or hierarchies, of spiritual intelligences where of humanity is one different names are given to these in different religions; and it is the labels that make the differences and the quarrels, not the great truths that these labels denote. The Hindus called them "shining ones," devas, a word often translated by the word "gods," but not accurately or rightly thus translated. Mussalmans and Christians call them angels or archangels—the names do not matter. What does matter is the conception that humanity is not the only living intelligence within this great universe, or even in our solar system; that life is found everywhere bodied out in many forms; that evolution has been going on for ages and ages; and that man is neither its highest product nor its lowest; that above him rise vast ranks of intelligences mightier than his own, just as below him also there stretch many ranks of intelligences less unfolded than his. And it is interesting to notice how many scientists of today are now recognising the fact that it is not rational to confine this idea of intelligence embodied in matter within the narrow limits of humanity on a single globe among many globes that are found in space. A man like Sir Oliver Lodge declares that there is nothing unreasonable in believing in these great ranks of hierarchies of living intelligences who are evolving in the great field of the universe, as man is evolving in his own little globe. And so the universe becomes again, as it was of old time, the home of myriads of beings, and not of man alone;

and the same so-called heresy, which was amongst those for which Bruno was burnt in Rome, the idea of a plurality of inhabited worlds, has come back again to the thoughts of man, and it is realised that man is not alone; he is only one of a vast army of spiritual and unfolding intelligences; that he has brothers above him as well as below him, rank after rank of higher and lower evolution, and himself is evolving in the midst.

And then comes the teaching which I said some of you would challenge—and yet you cannot challenge it if you look carefully into the past history of your own faith. How does consciousness evolve? We find degrees of consciousness as marked as the various types of body. We find some people born into the world with very limited intellectual capacity, very limited moral power as well as intellect. Others are born with high intelligence; Others with saintly qualities shining out from the early days of infancy. Whence all these strange differences between man and man? Why so vast a gulf of difference between the highest that our own humanity has produced, and the lowest that it is still producing? How does consciousness unfold? And the answer given to that by all the ancient religions without exception was that this consciousness of man was a continuing thing; that it began as a germ and unfolded gradually by life after life and experience piled upon experience. And that view, known under the name of reincarnation, is the one great view which dominated alike ancient religion and ancient philosophy. You find it in the writings of the Hindus and the Buddhists; you find it in the writings—less clearly marked because they are so fragmentary—amongst the Zoroastrians; you find it in the teachings of the old Hebrews; you find it in the teachings of the Greeks and the Romans. Everywhere the same teaching comes out to you alike from religion and philosophy. And you find the teaching in the earlier centuries of the Christian Church; you find a great Christian teacher like Origin declaring that every man receives a body according to his deserts and his former actions; and you may trace that doctrine sometimes in the form of the preexistence of the soul, sometimes in the form of repeated resurrections of the body, right down from those early days of

Christianity until it was made a heresy by a Council of the Church in the sixth century. And even then it does not disappear; even then it is handed on by sect after sect. The Albigenses held it although persecuted by Rome. One sect after another through the middle Ages holds up this same teaching which came from the East. You find it peeping out frequently in the writings of the most learned of the faith of the prophet Muhammed. You find it in the Middle Ages expressed under cover often of allegory and symbol, but still definitely enough to be seen. You find it reappearing above the surface again in the time of Charles II among the clergy of the English Church. You find it reappearing again in Germany in the writings of their greatest philosophers. Goethe taught it; Fichte, Schelling, Lessing, they all put forward this explanation of the growth and development of human consciousness. You find it in your own poet Wordsworth, seeing by the insight of the poet that which other eyes are often blind to, when he declared that—

> Our birth is but a sleep and a forgetting.
>
> The soul that rises with us, our life's star,
>
> Hath had elsewhere its setting, and cometh from afar.

And so, in one after another, in Browning, Rossetti, and others, in ever-accumulating testimony, in Christendom the old truth has made its way again and has now become popular among the most thoughtful and educated of our own people. You may remember how Hume the sceptic declared that it was the only theory of immortality upon which a philosopher could look; and you may remember that in our own times one of our own philosophical writers, Professor McTaggart, has declared the same thing; and after going through various theories of immortality has declared that the most natural is that of reincarnation. And so we cannot really put Christianity outside of all the religions that have given this explanation of Divine Justice and human evolution. In Christianity, as well as elsewhere, we find the teaching, and it has again become popular in our own times among our own thinkers. Even a man like Huxley, agnostic though he was, declared that there was nothing in the analogy of nature against it and very much to support it. So that even there we find no hostility, although no definite acceptance of the idea. And this is the one teaching that I said you might challenge out of all those that universal religion has given. But that challenge grows feebler and feebler as the history of Christian doctrine becomes more accurately known. Out of that you will see at once must spring up the idea that man, passing out of the body, continues a living consciousness, passing through experiences in worlds on the other side of death, there working up all that he has gathered during his life here, changing thought into power, experience into faculty, and bringing back that transmuted thought as capacity, as the dower with which he is born to a new experience of earthly life.

The more you study this teaching the more will it recommend itself to your intelligence, the more will it explain to you the riddle of the world; the more will it render human life intelligible and full of hope, nay, full of certainty of higher and higher evolution, for then the differences between us in mind and in morals become differences of experience and not differences inherent in our nature. The lowest criminal is but a savage such as we were in lives gone by; the loftiest, divinest man is only fuller charged with experience than we are and we shall climb to the place of the genius and the saint as we have grown out of the lower conditions of mankind. And so it is a teaching of hope as well as one which comes to us with all the weight of human experience in the past. It is the necessary corollary of the scientific teaching of the evolution of the body—the unfolding of the consciousness side by side with the improving of the body, a consciousness to unfold more in ages yet to come until every man has grown into divinity, and the perfect man lives upon earth. If to these teachings we add those of the three worlds and of the universality of causation, we have completed the list of fundamental doctrines.

And so Theosophy in the secondary sense means all this teaching. Universally accepted, forming the backbone of every great religion. Hence Theosophy cannot be the enemy of any religion, but the servant and helper of each. And the great work of the Theosophist in every country is to bring out the essential verities that the religion of the country unfolds; and so to strengthen its hold on the hearts and reasons of men in order that religion may be able to justify itself at the bar of reason and prove the realities on which it rests. Hence, in becoming a Theosophist a man does not leave his own religion. He deepens it, spiritualises it, makes it more and more vital, more and more rational and intelligible. And that is the work that the Society is doing all over the world—bringing back the inner and more spiritual side; making religions realise that life is in the spirit and not in the letter. Now Theosophy does a good deal to enable religions to justify themselves in the face of the septic, for Theosophy has brought back also a scientific teaching which has never been lost in the East, but is only beginning now to be discovered in the West—the teaching that man as a spiritual intelligence is capable of reaching his own higher consciousness by a definitely scientific training, and that anyone who has the courage and strength to follow the training, and who begins with a certain capacity from the past in that direction, may reach first-hand knowledge for himself. I say "with a certain knowledge brought out of the past.' That is the condition which every science makes for those who reach its highest points of knowledge. When you have a Senior Wrangler in mathematics he is not made out of a boy who is absolutely devoid of mathematical ability. The boy must show mathematical ability first before you have the foundation upon which you can lay your training and so develop in the course of a couple of decades to a man who receives the highest honours of mathematical training. And so with every other science. All our great experts began life as children showing exceptional capacity for those lines of scientific research in which they have excelled. Go back to their childhood and in their biographies you will read how early the great men of science showed the capacity for scientific thought. And it is true of the great science—the science of the soul—that unless a person has some capacity in that direction, then in the present life he will hardly be able to gain firsthand knowledge. In other lives, yes! For the foundation must always be laid in some special life; but inborn capacity as well as training are needed for this science as well as for all others.

Now what is this science of the soul? It is the practical experience that just as you possess a physical body by which you come into touch with the physical world around you, through which your consciousness works in all its observations and reasonings, so do you possess also bodies of subtler matter in which the same consciousness—which is yourself—is able to work. And as these subtler bodies become more and more organised by study and training, the consciousness in them can come into touch with other worlds as accurately and precisely as it can come into contact with the physical by means of the physical body. Further, that it is possible for a man to separate himself consciously from his physical body and work in those subtler bodies which all men possess, and that by the means of this training we can obtain direct knowledge of those other worlds of which religion has said so much; all the great teachers of the past having claimed, remember, that they knew those things of their own personal knowledge. That science of the soul having been gradually lost religion has been left somewhat helpless when challenged to justify itself. I say that all the great religions of the past by the mouth of their founders and teachers claimed this first-hand knowledge. You may read if you like in one of the old Hindu books, "A man ought to be able to separate himself from the body as you can separate the grass stock from the sheath that is around it." And I might quote you a hundred passages like that from the philosophic treatises of the Hindus. Take again the founder of the Buddhist religion, which has become so sadly materialised. In the later days when the young Brahmana came to him the Lord Buddha, and asked him about the worlds on the other side of death, what was his answer? "If you wanted to know the way to a village you would ask the man who lived there and who knew the way to it; and so you do well to come to me and ask me, for I know those other worlds, and I know the roads that lead thereto." And I might quote to you dozens of other passages all making the same claim. Now that is a matter for personal experience, for those who would become experts in this particular science. A considerable number of Western people in the countries of Europe are studying that science now and finding by their own experience that it teaches what is true; and they are showing that in some cases by using some of the lower powers of the body, by investigations along physical lines—chemistry, electricity, and along the lines of the investigations of the physicists—showing that these subtler things can be seen and that their testimony is as natural as the testimony of the physical world around. This is not supernatural or marvellous; it is simply evolving yourselves a little more rapidly than your race is doing. Does it strike you as strange if I say to you that all of you have these subtler senses not thoroughly developed and controlled, but none the less in you? And if you ask me to prove it, my answer is simply that if you take a dozen or twenty people haphazard out of an ordinary audience of fairly educated men and women and throw them into the mesmeric trance, you will find the very large majority of them become what is technically termed clairvoyant or lucid. What is the natural deduction? Let us see what you have done. You have stopped the working of the senses you are accustomed to use. The eye of the person in the mesmeric trance is blind. If you flash an electric light into it there is no contraction of the iris. The ear is quite deaf; you can fire off a pistol beside the man, who shows no sign of hearing. But if you talk to that man ask him a question—I will give you an instance of what can be done. Ask him to tell you what is going on in a distant place, and he will be able to read a hundred miles away, although the physical eye cannot read the book you put in front of it. The case I am going to mention has a particular interest to me because it was done by my old friend, Charles Bradlaugh, who was a septic. He was a man of extraordinarily strong mesmeric power, and at one time used to make a number of experiments in mesmerism; and he used to mesmerise his own wife, and found that she became clairvoyant. One day when he had thrown her into a mesmeric trance he asked her to go to his printing office in London and tell him what was going on. She very she naturally said that his paper was being set up. That might have been thought transference, or a normal guess of what was happening. Then he asked her to look at what was being set at the moment, and she said to him: "Look at the woman who is setting up that article," and then she added, "Oh, the stupid woman, she has put that letter"—I think it was an "r"—"in upside down"; and she read the sentence. The next day's post brought to Mr. Bradlaugh the proofs set up the preceding day, and when he turned to the article of which his wife had read a part hundreds of miles away in the North, he found the letter set upside down as she had pointed out in the trance the day before that is a good example, because Mr. Bradlaugh was not what was called a religious man; he was a secularist, a materialist; but he recognised the existence of such powers as that in man. Hence his testimony becomes the more valuable not being readily given without careful investigation.

Now those powers, I say, you possess, most of you, but they are not yet so developed that they are able to work at the same time as our ordinary physical senses are working, for those senses, corresponding to coarser and grosser vibrations, drown the testimony of the finer senses which cannot make themselves herald through the vibrations of the coarser. But if you choose to go through the training that some of us have gone through you will find that you can hasten a little the normal evolution, and that those senses which are just near the surface in all cultivated people may be made active by hurrying a little that evolution to which you are all subject. That is what a number of us have done. Then it is not necessary to go into trance; then it is not necessary to close the outer senses; you can use both at the same time, and so check what you see superphysically—not supernaturally—by the observation of others who observe at the same time and who are using their waking consciousness. Thus you can discuss in your ordinary condition that which you are also observing with those keener organs of vision. These are the things which are going on around you at the present time, things which people of your own race are doing, understanding, practicing. It is that more than anything else, perhaps, which has made such tremendous changes in the ordinary thought of the time; because you find how many people are having experience of the superphysical who were ashamed to speak of it when everybody was laughing at it, who are ready to bear testimony today when the higher faculties of men are gradually showing themselves as real. The result is that you bring a new help to many religious teachings which turn upon the facts of worlds beyond our side of the grave. You can follow those who have passed through the gateway of death into the worlds where they are still alive, find them there, talk to them, know them as you knew them here on earth, not by bringing them back as the Spiritualists do, but by learning to live in the world where they are living now. And as the knowledge spreads and becomes more common many a thing that religion has hoped for will be shown to be scientifically true. That is the scientific side of the Theosophical teaching where the science of the soul and the invisible world is followed as definitely and along lines as well understood as the lines by which you train the ordinary scientist and teach him to reach the point that others have reached before.

Looking then on Theosophy in this way its value is at once obvious. You can use these higher senses for scientific investigations; you can use them, as they are being used. For medical diagnosis; you can use them along various lines of medical research, and use them without hurting either human or animal life in your investigations. As this power becomes more common that terrible road along which science in our own days has gone and is going, the road of the torture of the helpless animal, that road will be seen to be as unnecessary as it is cruel and wicked. Then we shall be using higher human faculties for study instead of trying to wring secrets out of the torture of the bodies of animals. Then medical men will begin to tread on the safer pathway of knowledge, instead of trying to invent poisons of every sort to neutralise other poisons already in the body, and so get what they call "health," which is only a diseased condition of balancing poison against poison. And as they drop those evil ways they will come back to the science of healing which is now so much cast on one side, and learn to heal along lines which work with the recuperative forces of nature, instead of trying to balance poison against poison, which is the modern way that the doctor has begun to use. And if these lines will come out as valuable even when you are dealing with human bodies what shall they do for human minds? They are beginning to make us understand the power of thought; they are beginning to teach us how by the exercise of right thought we can build up right character; how by deliberate meditating on virtue we can reproduce that virtue in ourselves, and how that power of thought is found to be the mightiest power on earth—that great creative force which belongs to the human spirit, which can be used for the noblest purposes, which can be utilised for the greater service of mankind. So you see that looking at Theosophy in this way, while I would never dream of asking you to accept it on the statement of one who has studied it even as long as I have—during the last twenty years—to find that each successive year it becomes more luminous, more helpful, and more inspiring—while I would not ask you to take it on my word, I think I have shown you enough to prove to you that it is worthy of your thoughtful consideration.

And that is all I desire to do. A lecture to do its work should not simply give information—that is better gained by each individual in his own study and by his own thinking. What a lecture should do is to stimulate people to inquire and to think and if the lecturer succeeds in doing that with even a handful of his auditory he has done his work, for no thought is worth the thinking unless it is your own and not the repetition only of someone else's. No belief is worth holding unless you have proved it yourselves and know exactly why you believe and how you have reached that point of knowledge. And a lecturer should be a signpost simply along the road that leads to knowledge, pointing out where knowledge has been found, pointing out where further knowledge may be gained. Such a signpost I would fain be to some of you tonight, telling you partly what I have learnt, but most of what I have said I have verified by my own personal investigations, by my own study, and my own practice. For I was taught when I first entered the Theosophical Society twenty years ago, not to believe because I was told, not to believe because others had experienced, but to study and experiment for myself and then speak out my belief in that which I myself knew to be true. It may be that among you are some whose minds are oppressed by the burden of the want of understanding of the world and of human life, who suffer because it is unintelligible—for the worst suffering in life is not to be found in poverty and disease and physical misery, but in the mental perplexity and bewilderment that makes the world unintelligible to us. I have found this teaching makes the world intelligible; I have found it solve the great problems of life; and therefore I bring it to you. For after all we are all seekers after truth, and if in plunging into that great ocean anyone of us has found an oyster containing a pearl, then in rising after the dive into the ocean we can show the pearl that we have found in order that others may also dive, may also seek, may also find. And so to you I come this evening to tell you of livings into that ocean that others as well as I myself have made. We have found there precious pearls that have enriched our lives; and so we say to you: "Plunge into that great ocean and have no fear; your intellect will guide you, your courage will sustain you, your strength will enable you to find; and if, like us, you come up from that dive into the ocean, your hands full of the pearls of truth you have discovered, then scatter those pearls abroad among men in order that they also may be stimulated to seek and to find."

And no greater service I believe can be done by one human spirit to another than to speak of the truth found so as to stimulate others to the finding, trying to win others to seek, rather than trying to impose upon them that which one knows oneself to be true.

—*Annie Besant*

10

CHRISTIANITY IN SOUTH INDIA

The history of Christianity in South India in general and in Madras in particular goes as far back as the first century A.D. Tradition has it that Saint Thomas visited South India about 50 A.D. He landed at Cranganore on the West Coast, and after a brief stay at Cochin came to the Coromandel Coast. It is believed that the Apostle preached his faith to the natives of India both on the West Coast of the Peninsula and on the Coromandel Coast, and made converts of them. Thus the earliest: Christian settlements in India are to be traced in parts of what is now the city of Madras and in parts of the Malayala country.

The Syrian Church

Confining ourselves to Malabar for the moment we find the Syrian Church to be a very ancient institution, as ancient as the visit of Saint Thomas to this region Marco Polo, the Venetian traveller, who came to India towards the end of the thirteenth century, refers to the place as sacred to the Apostle, and tells us that both Christians and Saracens frequented it (the Church of St. Thomas in Malabar) in pilgrimage. The Saint was known Avarian or Holy Man among the Saracens. Several miracles are narrated in the name of the Apostle, and how even the earth on which the chapel stands brought hope and relief to the suffering and diseased humanity. We have on record a series of foreign visitors during the thirteenth and fourteenth centuries. About 1291 Friar John of Monte Corvino of the Order of Minor Friars, came to India and stayed in the Church of St. Thomas for 13 months. He records in a letter that the baptized about one hundred persons in that locality. In this he was assisted by Friar Nicholas of Pistoria, of the Order of Preachers, who died there and was buried in that church. From a bull of Pope John XXII, dated 5th April 1330, addressed to the Christians of Quilon and to be delivered to them by Friar Jordanus, and from the two letters of Jordanus himself (Hakluyt Society Series), it is seen that there was a settlement of Christians (called Nascarini) in that part of Malabar. Here the Pope invites the Nascarini to abjure their schism and enter the unity of the Catholic Church. Jordanus refers in his letters the scope for conversion in India. In 1348-49 John De Marignolli, a Papal Legate, visited Quilon, famous for its pepper. He stayed there for 14 months and was paid a hundred gold *fan* every months. He places on record that the Christians of that place owned those pepper gardens and were besides masters of the public steel yard. (Yule, *Cathay and the Way Thither,* Vol. III.) But with the arrival of the Portuguese in the sixteenth century who began to assert dominion over their faith, confusion entered into the peaceful abodes of the Syrians. Effort was made to bring them into subjection to the Roman See. But the Syrians resisted this. 'The respect which they had for the Cross was better to them than the favour of the Virgin, and the long catalogue of Saints which adorned the Romist calendar.' But still the Jesuits continued their activities. Some of the Syrian Metropolitans were imprisoned and transported to Lisbon and Rome. Notwithstanding all the oppression, the old families of Syrian Christians continued their ancient faith. When Sir Thomas Munro visited them, he wrote to the British Government in their favour and obtained places of trust and emolument for them under the Government of Travancore. The missionaries of the Church Serenity were located among them. Ever since they have made great progress both in learning and religious feeling.

On the Coromandel Coast

Turning to the Coromandel Coast, tradition associates San Thome or old Mylapore with the burial place of the Apostle St. Thomas who is said to have suffered martyrdom at St. Thomas

Mount. The Arab geographers and travellers of the ninth and tenth centuries called this place Betumah or Town or Church of Thomas. We also hear that an envoy of Alfred the Great from England visited this place about 883 A.D. Then we learn of Persian merchants who were known as Nestorian Christians and who built a chapel over the tomb of St. Thomas. Marco Polo the Venetian traveller who visited the Coromandal Coast about the end of the thirteenth century refers to the prosperity of these Nestorian Christians.

San Thome became still more famous when the Portuguese occupied it about 1522. St. Francis Xavier who visited it some time after found a primitive form of Christianity prevalent among the fishermen of the place. Him they regarded as a Patron Saint. Here was built a small church, the most ancient European building on the coast of Madras. In 1606 the Pope created a separate Bishopric for San Thome, and consequently the church became a Cathedral Church.

St. Thomas Mount is also associated with the revered name of St. Thomas. Here was discovered the famous Bleeding Cross—a Stone Cross which contains an Old Pehlevi inscription, perhaps of the seventh or eighth century, and some spots resembling blood stains—in 1547 by the Portuguese. They built a church and placed the Stone Cross in the wall behind the Altar. The church was dedicated to Our Lady of Expectation. Still more interesting is a picture of the Holy Virgin and Child discovered nearby and now in the church and believed to be one of the seven portraits drawn by St. Luke and brought by St. Thomas to India.

Little Mount is another place of interest connected with St. Thomas at Saidapet (Chinnamalai). It is said that the Apostle hid himself in a cave—which is still pointed out—and afraid of his persecutors, he effected his escape to the Mount through a hole in it. But the persecutors followed him to the Mount and speared him to death. Here in 1551, the Portuguese constructed a church near a spring of fresh water which the Apostle created by hitting the stone with his staff and this is said to posses healing properties. The church is dedicated to Our Lady of Health.

The Luz Church is an ancient as the churches above mentioned, perhaps a little more ancient. It contains an inscription stating that it was build in 1516, and dedicated to Our lady of Light (De Nossa Senhora Da Luz). The story goes that mariners who were tossed off San Thome shore saw a light. They repaired towards this guiding light, and built a church on that site.

The Tranquebar Mission

Before we examine the history of the church in Madras during the time of the East India Company and after, we can say a few words about one or two missions which played in active part in the formation of Christianity in South India.

In 1620 Tranquebar was acquired by the Danish East India Company. But long before there was a Portuguese settlement at Negapatam. About 1570 the Italian traveller, Caesar Frederick who visited Negapatam observed that the Christian religion had taken a firm footing by then and the Nayak Rajas were tolerant. By 1612 Negapatam was an active centre for the Goanese Catholic missionaries. About this time was built the church at Velanganni, six miles south of Negapatam. It continues to attract pilgrims even today for its festivals. By 1660 the Dutch seized Negapatnam from the Portuguese who founded a church at Tranquebar. About 1726 a chapel was built in the suburb. Not much information is available for more than a century. About 1846 the Jesuits of Madura founded St. Joseph's College at Negapatam which became transplanted to Trichinopoly, the present much flurishing institution.

The Dances

The first Protestant mission in India was established at Tranquebar in 1706 by two young German pastors Henirich Plutuochan (also Plutscho) and Bartholamus ziegenbalg, who were out under the auspices of the King of Denmark. They learnt Tamil and preached to the natives in their own tongue. In 1710 the Society for Promoting Christian Knowledge encouraged them. A printing press from London enabled them to publish Tamil translation of the Scriptures. In August 1717 His Majesty George

I wrote a letter of encouragement to the missions and lent his patronage. From Transquebar the missionary activity spread to Cuddalore, Madras and Calcutta along the coast, and in the interior to Tanjore, Trichinopoly and Palamcottah. From 1753 missionaries frequented the capital town, Tanjore. It is said that the assistance of these Lutheran missionaries—Danish and German—was sought by the Governor and his Council at Madras for political and religious reasons. These missions also received financial assistance from the British Society for promoting Christianity. Among them was the German Schwartz who founded the mission at Trichinopoly. He joined the English missionary society S.P.C.K. in 1768. Sir Thomas Rumbold sent him on a mission of peace to Hyder Ali in 1779. He continued his missionary work as a chaplain.

In the meantime the Tranquebar mission was decaying and by 1820 it no more pursued the evangelistic activity. However, the Leipzig Lutheran Missions received it in 1841, and from that time Tranquebar continues to be their headquarters. They have built churches in different places and established schools throughout the Presidency.

The Madura Mission

A word may be said about the Madura mission. This was founded by an Italian Jesuit, Fr. Robert de Nobili (1606). A century later Fr. Francis Laynez and Fr. Venance Bouchet of the Madura Mission went to Rome to plead the cause of their missions. These were met by Fr. Beschi. In 1710 Fr. Francis Laynez returned as Bishop of Sosopolis and Coadjutor of Mylapore. Also came Fr. Bouchet and Fr. C.J. Beschi at the same time. After a few days at Goa, Fr. Beschi was attached to the Malabar Province. In 1711 he entered the Madura Mission and after years of fruitful work diet in 1747.

The early Missionaries took to the ways of living and customs of the country, especially of the Brahmans even in the mode of dress. They took even Tamil names. Through their influence the Catholic population steadily increased. On its model were founded the Mysore Mission in 1650 and Carnatic Mission in 1702. The

Madura Mission comprised in tis limits, besides Madura, what now forms the diocese of Kumbakonam, parts of diocese of Mylapore and Coimbatore and of the Archdiocese of Pondicherry. A handful of Missionaries, about ten in number, were managing this for a number of years in the first half of the eighteenth century. The Missionaries belonging to the kingdom of Tanjore were persecuted during the time of Shahji (1682-1711) and Sarboji his successor. The same fate overtook them in Trichinopoly and Ramned in the first half of the eighteenth century. Still they managed to carry on their propaganda until they obtained a firm holding.

The Madras Church

Turning once again to the church in Madras, it is interesting to investigate the name Madras. Among the different versions regarding the origin of the name, one is that the site where Francis Day, founder of Madras, settled was originally a village of fishermen, the headman of which was a Christian named Madaresan, after whose name the new settlement came to be known. A second version is that prior to the settlement of the English merchants, there was in that place a church of St. Mary (Madre De Deus) probably founded by the Portuguese of San Thome and that the settlement was named after St. Mary. Recently Very Rev. Mgr. Teixeira, Bishop of Mylapore, suggested on the basis of a tombstone inscription that the name Madras probably was after Madra, a Portuguese family of the village. There seems to be much force in this theory as the name Madraspatam existed before 1639 as the firman to Captain Day would demonstrate.

The Fort

In 1675 when Sir William Langhorn was at the head of the government of Fort St. George, a Roman Catholic Church, Church of St. Andrew, was built in the Fort for the use of the Portuguese and other Catholic inhabitants of the new settlement. Father Ephraim, a French Capuchin Friar was their first resist. But this church was demolished for military purposes during the time of Lallys siege. The Capuchins then erected a new church in Muthialpettah, now the Roman Catholic Cathedral in Armenian

Street. In 1678 was laid the foundation of St. Mary's Church in the Fort. Till then a room in the Factory House served as a chapel for Protestants. The new church, a result of voluntary donations of the English merchants, was finished in 1680. St. Mary's Church can well claim to be the first building connected with the National Church of England. It contains Registers and inscriptions which throw light on the growth and history of Madras. A congregation was organised on the model of an English parish with a vestry with the Governor as President. The vesty built up a fund and managed schools till 1805. In 1715 a charity school was established and later were founded male and female orphan asylums.

During Sir Archibald Campbell's governship (1786-89) the Rev. Andrew Bell became the first Superintendent of the Male Orphan Asylum established then. He founded a school at St. Andrews known as the Madras College. The Male Orphan Asylum was a development of the charity school under the control of the vestry of St. Mary's in the Fort. Subsequently a press was attached to the school and orphans were trained there. This was the nucleus of the Madras Male Asylum Almanac, now issued as the Lawrence Asylum Press Almanc. Thanks to the efforts of Lady Campbell, and private donations, a Female Orphan Asylum was founded in 1787. After a century of useful work it was merged, in the early years of this century, with the Lawrence Asylum at Ootacamund and with the Civil Orphan Asylum at Madras.

The Armenians in Madras

The Armenians who were the first Christian nation in Asia flourished in Madras as traders in the 17th and 18th centuries. They were among the permanent settlers in Madras in 1666. The first Armenian Church at Madras was erected in 1712 in Esplanade. Both this and the Latin Church were demolished by the British authorities as being inconvenient to the Fort. So in 1772 was built the present Armenian Church in Armenian Street dedicated to Holy Virgin Mary. A generous Armenian merchant Khojah Petrus undertook in 1726 to erect 160 stone steps from the foot that the top of the hill St. Thome interspersed with resting places for the convenience of pilgrims to see the Church at the summit of the mount. He died in Madras in 1751 and his body was interred in the Vepery Church. A son of Agah Shameer another merchant prince who died in Madras in 1797 and buried in the Armenian Churchyard, started in 1772, the first Armenian press in India. By 1781 the Armenians grew in numbers and had to find newer settlements. One party went to Negapatam and the other to Musulipatam. At the latter place they erected a church. A few families remained in Madras but gradually dwindled in numbers and significance.

Madras in the Nineteenth Century

The nineteenth century witnessed many missionary activities. There was an increase in the number of chaplains due to increase in number of English troops. A new church in the choultry plain (suburbs of Tiruvatesvarampet, Royapettah, Nungambakkam, Teynampet) was built under the supervision of De Havilland, and it was named St. George's Church (now known as St. George's Cathedral). It contains memorials of Dr. James Anderson, Surgeon and Physician General, Madras; of Bishop Heber, drowned at Trichinopoly in 1826; of the Venerable John Mousbey, the first Archdeacon of Madras; of Dr. Daniel Corrie, the first Anglican Bishop of Madras; of Bishop Caldwell and of others.

But in 1805 Madras was occupied as a station of the London Missionary Society. Mr. Loveless, the first Agent was a pious and simple man. In 1810 a chapel was built for the mission in Black Town. Two free schools, one for boys and the other for girls were established. The arrival of Mr. Knill in 1816 added new strength to the mission. He was succeeded by Mr. Traveller who exerted much among the inhabitants of Purasawakkam. In 1827 the Madras District Committee was formed. The mission was divided into two districts—Eastern and Western. Schools and preaching stations were founded. In 1831 a native church was erected in Purasawakkam.

In the meantime two missionary bodies had settled in the city. These were the Church Missionary Society and the Wesleyan

Missionary Society. The disabilities connected with the missionaries leaving England for India were removed by the Charter Act of 1813. As a result of this Act, the Church Missionary Society opened their missions in Cochin and Travancore, at Mayavaram and Madras and other places. The Wesleyan Society had their branches in Madras, Royapettah and Bangalore, at Negapatam and Melnuttam. Besides converting the natives to their faith, these societies took more and more to educational activities.

A passing mention may be made of the activity of the Madras Bible Society. The translations of the Scriptures that had been attempted in the native tongues had their own imperfections, and were found far from satisfactory. So the Madras Bible Committee appointed special Committees to give these translations in Tamil, Telugu, Canarese and Malayalam a searching examination, and pains were taken to make these translations as perfect as possible. It is only after all the tests were satisfied that they were prescribed to be taught in schools and other institutions. The Scotchmen of Madras also had a share in the missionary activity. They constructed St. Andrews Kirk in the Poonamallee Road in 1818-21 with aid from the Government, and it was opened for service in 1821. About that time other Churches—the Wesleyan Chapel in Broadway and St. Mathias Church At Vepery—were founded. Thus the nineteenth century was a period of expansion and growth of the Church in South India and especially in the city of Madras.

—V.R. Ramachandra Dikshitar

11

POLITICS AND RELIGION

In much the same way as the opening of India to Western cultural influence stimulated the renascence of Hinduism, so the imposition of foreign rule inevitably evoked powerful indigenous reactions in the political sphere. The militant xenophobia which had found expression in scattered attempts at die-hard resistance to British conquest, and in the unorganized uprising of 1857-58, finally crystallized in the late nineteenth century in the group of zealous nationalists known as the Extremists. This group possessed two weapons which were unavailable to previous opponents of British rule. Firstly, they shared with their Moderate rivals the use of a common "national" language, English, and through it enjoyed the opportunities for political agitation provided by the press, the schools, and the Indian National Congress. Secondly, they were able to draw on the newly formulated ideals of renascent Hinduism and to create a potent ideology out of the marriage between these ideals and the imported concepts of patriotism and national unity.

Being impatient to throw off the foreign yoke, the Extremists concentrated on building up mass support for the nationalist movement. To create this support and to unify the Westernized elite with the illiterate peasantry they appealed to three principal ties common to both the educated and the uneducated—language, history, and religion. Casting off the use of English wherever possible, they wrote and spoke in the regional languages understood by the common people. As a means of heightening patriotic fervor they fostered pride in a glorious past, when Hindu kings and warriors ruled the land. Most effective of all because it had the broadest appeal was the use of religious symbolism and terminology to instill in all Hindus a fervent devotion to the Motherland.

In contrast to the Moderates, the Extremists regarded such tasks as social reform and Hindu-Muslim cooperation as merely side issues draining energies from the political struggle and weakening Hindu solidarity. At times their anger at Muslim collaboration with the British spurred them to engaged openly in anti-Muslim activity, heedless of the fact that in so doing they were ruining the chances of creating an independent but undivided India. The 1905 Partition of Bengal into Hindu and Muslim majority areas drove a further wedge between the two religious communities, for it encouraged prominent Muslims to enter into a tacit alliance with the British against Hindu ambitions (the Muslim League was founded in 1906, and its demand for separate electorate was granted in 1909). The danger that the more numerous and better-educated Hindu community would pre-empt the positions of power and influence in self-governing India gave many Muslims a pressing reason to convert to friendship their traditional hostility to the British.

Both Moderates and Extremists insisted that divided Bengal be reunited, but the latter urged that radical measures be taken to coerce the ruling power. In essence, their program was much like the one Gāndhi introduced fifteen years later, being based on the principle of reducing Indian dependence on the British in every possible way. Its principal aims were the boycott of foreign goods, the use of Indian-made articles (or Swadeshi—"one's own country"), the strengthening of an indigenous system of education, and in time the creation of a parallel government of, by, and for the Indian people.

Such a bold stand, coupled with the religious ideology that motivated it, captured the imagination of younger men more readily than did the cautious policies of the Moderates, and the following of the Extremists increased rapidly in numbers after 1905. Their abortive attempt to gain control of the Congress led to a schism in that body at the 1907 session. For the next decade most of the Extremist leaders were either in jail, in exile, or in retirement, but the continuance of terrorist activity—climaxing in an attempt on the Viceroy's life in 1912—showed that their memory was still honoured in their absence. The rescinding of the Partition of Bengal in 1911 and the altered situation produced by the First World War made it possible for the Moderates and the Extremists to patch up their quarrel in 1916. The death of the Extremists' greatest leader, Tilak, in 1920 marked the end of an era, for in that same year the Congress came under Gāndhi's uniquely effective control.

Although the heyday of the Extremists was short-lived, their chief contribution to modern Indian thought—the creation of Hindu nationalism through the union of religious and political ideals—is likely to endure for some time to come. It is entirely possible that as the influence of English culture (by which all of them were deeply affected, but against which all reacted in one way or another) diminishes in independent India, a more virulent and violent form of this nationalism may yet emerge.

Bankim Chandra Chatterjee: Nationalist Author

Gokhale's saying, "What Bengal thinks today, all India thinks tomorrow." Is nowhere more applicable than in the case of the Bengali writer Bankim Chandra Chatterjee, Bankim, although he took no part in politics, first employed the triple appeal of language, history, and religion which enabled Hindu nationalism to win such widespread support in the opening decade of the twentieth century. His historical novels in Bengali reminded his readers that their glorious past should inspire them to achieve an equally glorious future, and demonstrated the power of the pen as an instrument for stirring up patriotic emotions in times when overt political action was impossible.

Bankim was born near Calcutta in 1838, the son of a brāhman landlord and local deputy collector of revenue. A brilliant student, he passed through the anglicized educational system with distinction and was in 1858 one of two in Calcutta University's first graduating class. He was immediately offered a position as deputy magistrate in the Bengal civil service, and for all but one year held this same rank until his retirement in 1891—a mute comment on the opportunities for advancement given to Indians in government service. Fortunately he found an outlet for his natural talent in another direction, and throughout his career as an official used his spare time to write stories and novels which captured the imagination of literate Bengal, Bankim employed a new prose style which combined the virtues of Sanskritized Bengali and the vigor of the common speech, an for the first time since the introduction of English education made it respectable for Bengalis to write in their own mother tongue.

Nationalism in all parts of the world has often been associated with attachment to a common language and its accompanying literary heritage. Bankim could thus be credited with quickening Bengali, as distinct from an all-Indian, nationalism. But this distinction was rendered largely superfluous after 1995, when the agitation against the Partition of Bengal took on a nation-wide character. By the same token, the poem *Bande Mataram (Hail to the Mother)* which first appeared in one of his novels soon became the *Marseillaise* of the nationalist movement throughout the country.

Bankim's original concept, "the Mother" of *Bande Mātaram,* referred at the same time to the land of Bengal and to the female aspect of the Hindu deity. From this fusion of the hitherto separate objects of patriotic and religious devotion sprang the central concept of modern Hindu nationalism. The concept of the divine Motherland, equating as it did love of country with love of God, made an instinctive appeal to the devout Hindu peasantry, for whom the secular reformism and Westernized nationalism of the Moderate leaders remained beyond comprehension.

For all the strength of dedication and mass appeal it generated, Hindu nationalism acted as a regressive force both in hindering social reform and in exacerbating the latent hostility between Hindus and Muslims. Bankim's novels faithfully reflect these two shortcomings, for with rare exceptions they picture well-meanings reformers as fools and Muslims as knaves. Nevertheless, his magic blend of religious sentiment, glorification of the Hindu past, and a beautiful style assured Bankim of lasting popularity among Bengalis, and exerted a far-reaching influence on the rise of extremist Hindu nationalism throughout India.

Bankim Chandra Chatterjee

The Language of the Masses

In a letter to the editor of a new English-language periodical, Bankim explained why he, too, was founding a review—in Bengali. His concluding remarks illustrate the linguistic complexity of India as a whole, and remain almost as true today as when they were written.

[From "Letter from Bankim Chandra Chatterjee," in *Bengal: Past and Present,* Vol. VIII, Part 2 (April-June, 1914), pp. 273-74]

I wish you every success in your project. I have myself projected a Bengali magazine with the object of making it the medium of communication and sympathy between the educated and the uneducated classes. You rightly say that the English for good or evil has become our vernacular; and this tends daily to widen the gulf between the higher and the lower ranks of Bengali society. This I think is not exactly what it ought to be; I think that we ought to *disanglicize* ourselves, so to speak, to a certain extent, and to speak to the masses in the language which they understand. I therefore project a Bengali magazine. But this is only half the work we have to do. No purely vernacular organ can completely represent the Bengali culture of the day. Just as we ought to address ourselves to the masses of our own race and country, we have also to make ourselves intelligible to the other Indian races, and to the governing race. There is no hope for India until the Bengali and the Panjabi understand and influence each other, and can bring their joint influence to bear upon the Englishman. This can be done only through the medium of the English, and I gladly welcome your projected periodical.

Hail to the Mother

In *Ānandamath* (*The Abbey of Bliss*), his most famous novel, Bankim took as his theme the Sannyāsī Rebellion in Bengal of the 1770s, attributing to these raiding ascetics a sort of religious nationalism whose focus was God in the form of the Mother. He neatly avoided the charge of disloyalty to British rule by making the Muslims (still the titular rulers of Bengal) the villains of the piece. In this excerpt, Bhavānanda, one of the sannyāsīs, reveals to a new disciple the group's mission and the *mystique* which sustains it.

[From *Abbey of Bliss,* pp. 31-37; *Bande Mātaram* translation in Ghose, *Collected Poems and Plays,* II, 227-28]

In that smiling moonlit night, the two silently walked across the plain, Mahendra [the disciple] was silent, sad, careless, and a little curious.

Bhavananda suddenly changed his looks. He was no more the steady and mild anchorite, nor wore any more the warlike hero's face—the face of the slayer of a captain of forces. Not even was there in his mien the proud disdain with which he had scolded Mahendra even now. It seemed as if his heart was filled with joy at the beauteous sight of the earth, lulled in peace and beaming under the silvery moon, and of the glory in her wilds and woods and hills and streams, and grew cherry like the ocean smiling with the rise of the moon. Bhavananda grew chatty, cheerful, cordial, and very eager to talk. He made many an attempt to open a conversation with his companion but Mahendra would not speak. Having no option left, he then began to sing to himself:

Mother, I bow to thee!
Rich with thy hurrying streams,
Bright with thy orchard gleams,
Cool with thy winds of delight,
Dark fields waving, Mother of might,
Mother free.

Mahendra was a little puzzled to hear the song; he could not grasp anything. Who could be the mother, he thought,

Rich with thy hurrying streams,
Bright with orchard gleams.
Cool with thy winds of delight,
Dark fields waving, Mother of might,
Mother free.

He asked, "Who is the mother?" Bhavananda did not answer but sang on:

Glory of moonlight dreams
Over the branches and lordly streams,
Clad in thy blossoming trees,
Mother, giver of ease,
Laughing low and sweet!
Mother, I kiss thy feet,
Speaker sweet and low!
Mother, to thee I bow.

"It is the country and no mortal mother,' cried Mahendra. "We own no other mother," retorted Bhavananda; "they say, the mother and the land of birth are higher than heaven.' We think the land of birth to be no other than our mother herself. We have no mother, no father, no brother, no wife, no child, no hearth or home, we have only got the mother—

Rich with hurrying streams,
Bright with orchard gleams.

Mahendra now understood the song and asked Bhavananda to sing again.He sang:

Mother, I bow to thee!
Rich with thy hurrying streams,
Bright with thy orchard gleams,

Cool with thy winds of delight,
Dark fields waving, Mother of might,
Mother free.
Glory of moonlight dreams
Over thy branches and lordly streams,
Clad in thy blossoming trees,
Mother, giver of ease,
Laughing low and sweet!
Mother, I "kiss thy feet,
Speaker sweet and low!
Mother, to thee I bow.
Who hath said thou art weak in thy lands,
When the swords flash out in twice seventy million hands
And seventy million voices roar[1]
Thy dreadful name from shore to shore?
With many strengths who are mighty and stored,
To thee I call, Mother and Lord!
"Thou who savest, arise and save!
To her I cry who ever her foemen drave
Back from plain and sea
And shook herself free.
Thou art wisdom, thou art law,
Thou our heart, our soul, our breath,
Thou the love divine, the awe
In our hearts that conquers death,
Thine the strength that nerves the arm,
Thine the beauty, thine the charm,
Every image made divine
In our temples is but thine.

Thou art Durga[2], Lady and Queen,
With her hands that strike and her swords of sheen,
Thou art Lakshmi[3] lotus-throned,
And the Muse a hundred-toned.
Pure and Perfect without peer,
Mother, lend thine ear.
Rich with thy hurrying streams,
Bright with thy orchard gleams,
Dark of hue, O candid-fair
In thy soul, with jewelled hair
And thy glorious smile divine,
Loveliest of all earthly lands,
Showering wealth from well-stored hands!
Mother, mother mine!
Mother sweet, I bow to thee
Mother great and free!

Mahendra saw that the outlaw was weeping as he sang. He then asked in wonder, "Who may you be, please?"

Bhavananda answered, "We are the Children."

"Children! Whose children are you?"

"Our mother's."

"Well, but does a child worship its mother with the proceeds of robbery?"

"We do nothing of the sort."

"Presently you looted a cart."

"Was that robbery? Whom did we rob?"

"Why, of course the king!"

"The king! What right has he to take this money?"

"It is the royal portion which goes to the king."

"How do you call him a king who does not rule his kingdom?"

"I fear you will be blown up before the sepoy's cannons one of these days."

"We have seen plenty of sepoys; even today we have had some."

"You haven't yet known them aright, you will know them one day however."

"What then? One never dies more than once."

"But why should you willingly invite death?"

"Mahendra Sinha, I thought you to be man amongst men, but I now see there is little to choose between you and the rest of your lot—you are only the sworn consumer of milk and butter. Just think of the snake. It creeps on the ground; I cannot think of any creature lower and meaner than it; but put your foot on its neck and it will spread its fangs to bite you. But can nothing disturb *your* equanimity? Look round and see, look at Magadha, Mithila, Kasi, Kanchi,[4] Delhi, Kashmir—where do you find such misery as here? Where else do the people eat grass for want of better food? Where do they eat thorns and white-ants' earth and wild creepers? Where do men think of eating dogs and jackals and even carcasses? Where else can you find men getting so anxious about the money in their coffers, the *salgram*[5] in their temples, the females in the Zenana,[6] and the child in the mother's womb? Yes, here they even rip open the womb! In every country the bond that binds a sovereign to his subjects is the protection that he gives; but our Mussulman king—how does he protect us? Our religion is gone; so is our caste, our honour and the sacredness of our family even! Our lives even are now to be sacrificed. Unless we drive these tipsy longbeards away, a Hindu can no longer hope to save his religion."

"Well, but how can you drive them away?"

"We will beat them."

"Alone, will you? With a slap, I presume."

The outlaw sang:

Who hath said thou art weak in thy lands,
When the swords flash out in twice seventy million hands

And seventy million voices roar
Thy dreadful name from shore to shore?

M: "But I see you are alone."

Bh: "Why, only now you saw two hundred of us."

M: "Are they all children?"

Bh: "They are, all of them."

"How many more are there?"

"Thousands of them; we will have more by and by."

"Suppose you get ten or twenty thousands. Could you hope to depose the Mussulman king with them?"

"How many soldiers had the English at Plassey?"

"Tut! to compare the English with the Bengali!"

"Why not? Physical strength does not count for much; the bullet won't be running faster, I ween, if I am stronger."

"Then why this great difference between the English and the Mussulman?"

"Because an Englishman would die sooner than fly; the Mussulman will fly with the first breath of fire and look about for *sherbet.*[7] Secondly, the English have determination: what they want to do they will see done. The Mussulman soldiers come to die for pay, and even that they don't always get. Lastly there is courage. A cannon ball falls only on one spot and cannot kill two hundred men together. Yet, when such a ball falls before the Mussulmans, they fly away in a body, while no Englishman would even fly before a shower of balls."

"Have you these qualities?"

"No, but you don't pluck them like ripe fruits from trees; they come by practice."

"What is your practice?"

"Don't you see we are all anchorites? Our renunciation is for the sake of this practice alone. When our mission is done or the practice is completed, we shall go back to our homes. We too have wives and children."

"You have left them all? How could you break the ties of family life?"

"A Child must not lie! I will not brag in vain to you. No body can ever cut the bond. He who says that he never cares for the family bonds either did never love or merely brags. We don't get rid of the bonds but simply keep our pledge. Will you enter our order?"

"Till I hear of my wife and child, I can say nothing."

"Come and you will see them."

So saying they began to walk along. Bhavananda sang the song "Hail Mother" again. Mahendra had a good voice and had some proficiency in music which he loved; so he joined Bhavananda in his song. He found that it really brought tears to the eye. "If I have not got to renounce my wife and daughter," said he, "you may initiate me into your order."

"He who takes this vow," said Bhavananda, "has to give up his wife and children. If you take it, you need not see your wife and daughter. They will be well kept, but till the mission is fulfilled, you are not to see their face[s]."

"I don't care to take your vow," blurted our Mahendra.

Mahendra does take the vow, but is later reunited with his wife and daughter.

Why the British Came to Rule India

In the final chapter of *The Abbey of Bliss,* after the sannyāsīs have routed both the Muslims and the British, Bankim has a supernatural figure explain to their leader Satyānanda, that the British have been forced to rule in India in order that Hinduism might regain its pristine power.

[From *Ānandamath,* Part IV, Chapter 8. Tr. by T.W. Clark]

S: Come, I'm ready. But, my lord, clear up this doubt in my mind. Why at the very moment in which I have removed all barriers from before our eternal Faith, do you order me to cease?

He: You task is accomplished. The Muslim power is destroyed. There is nothing else for you to do. No good can come of needless slaughter.

S: The Muslim power has indeed been destroyed, but the dominion of the Hindus has not yet been established. The British still hold Calcutta.

He: Hindu dominion will not be established now. If you remain at your work, men will be killed to no purpose. Therefore come.

S: (greatly pained) My lord, if Hindu dominion is not going to be established, who will rule? Will the Muslim kings return?

He: No. The English will rule.

S: (turning tearfully to the image of her who symbolized the land of his birth) Alas, my Mother! I have failed to set you free. Once again you will fall into the hands of infidels. Forgive your son. Alas, my Mother! Why did I not die on the battlefield?

He: Grieve not. You have won wealth; but it was by violence and robbery, for your mind was deluded. No pure fruit can grow on a sinful tree. You will never set your country free in that way. What is going to happen now is for the best. If the English do not rule, there is no hope of a revival of our eternal Faith. I tell you what the wise know. True religion is not to be found in the worship of 33 crores of gods; that is a vulgar, debased religion, which has obscured that which is true. True Hinduism consists in knowledge not in action. Knowledge is of two kinds, physical and spiritual. Spiritual knowledge is the essential part of Hinduism. If however physical knowledge does not come first, spiritual knowledge will never comprehend the subtle spirit within. Now physical knowledge has long since disappeared from our land, and so true religion has gone too. If you wish to restore true religion, you must first teach this physical knowledge. Such knowledge is unknown in this country because there is no one to teach it. So we must learn it from foreigners. The English are wise in this knowledge, and they are good teachers. Therefore we must make the English rule. Once the people of India have acquired knowledge of the physical world from the English, they will be able to comprehend the nature of the spiritual. There will then be no obstacle to the true Faith. True religion will then shine forth again of itself. Until that happens, and until Hindus are wise and virtuous and strong, the English power will remain unbroken. Under the English our people will be happy; and there will be no impediment to our teaching our faith. So, wise one, stop fighting against the English and follow me.

S: My lord, if it was your intention to set up a British government, and if at this time a British government is good for the country, then why did you make use of me to fight this cruel war?

He: At the present moment the English are traders. Their minds are set on amassing wealth. They have no desire to take up the responsibilities of government. But as a result of the rebellion of the Children, they will have to; because they will get no money if they do not. The rebellion took place to make the English ascend the throne. Come with me now. Know and you will understand.

S: My lord, I do not desire knowledge. It cannot help me, I have vowed a vow and I must keep it. Bless me, and let me not be shaken in my devotion to my Mother.

He: Your vow a fulfilled. You have brought fortune to your Mother. You have set up a British government. Give up your fighting. Let the people take to their plows. Let the earth be rich with harvest and the people rich with wealth.

S: (weeping hot tears) I will make my Mother rich with harvest in the blood of her foes.

He: Who is the foe? There are no foes now. The English are friends as well as rulers. And no one can defeat them in battle.

S: If that is so, I will kill myself before the image of my Mother.

He: In ignorance? Come and know. There is a temple of the Mother in the Himalayas. I will show you her image there.

So saying, He took Satyānanda by the hand. What incomparable beauty! In the dim light, in the deep recesses of Vishnu's temple, two human forms radiant with light stood before a mighty four-armed figure.

One held the other by the hand. Who held the hand; and whose was the hand he held? Knowledge was holding Devotion by the hand; Faith that of Action; Self-sacrifice that of Glory; Heavenly Joy that of Earthly Peace. Satyānanda was the Earthly Peace; He was Heavenly Joy. Satyānanda was Glory; He was Self-sacrifice.

And Self-sacrifice led away Glory.

Bāl Gangādhar Tilak: "Father of Indian Unrest"

Impressed by his grandfather's recollections of the days before British rule reached Mahārāshtra, and of the Mutiny and Rebellion of 1857-58, it is not surprising that Bāl Gangādhar Tilak (1856-1920) should have grown up questioning the right of the British to govern his land. Like Rānade and Gokhale (with whom he fought a running political duel for many years) Tilak was descended from the Chitpavan brāhman caste, but unlike them he maintained an uncompromising hostility to foreign domination.

In addition to the Marāthā history he imbibed at his grandfather's knee, Tilak learned Sanskrit and English from his father, a schoolteacher and deputy inspector of education in a small town on India's western seacoast. When he was ten, the family moved to Poona, but at sixteen Tilak was an orphan. A self-reliant but weak-bodied youth, he devoted a year to building up his physique with exercises. After receiving his B.A., he took a Bachelor of Laws degree, but refused to enter government service, the usual haven of educated Indians in those days. Instead, with a few like-minded friends he started a school and two newspapers in order to spread Western knowledge among the people of their native region of Mahārāshtra. After helping to found the Deccan Education Society and Fergusson College, Tilak opposed the reform program of Agarkar and Gokhale and resigned from the group in 1890.

Tilak now purchased from the group the Marāthī weekly *Kesari* (The Lion), which he had named and helped to edit, and its English counterpart, the *Mahrata.*[8] Henceforth he poured his energies into educating the people of his province through the columns of these newspapers. His Marāthī style was particularly effective and made a direct appeal to the villagers who would gather to have it read to them. Tilak also promoted in his papers the celebration of two new annual festivals—one dedicated to the Hindu god Ganesh, the other honouring the Marāthā hero Shivaji. His purpose in organizing these festivals was to develop in the Marāthā people a sense of pride in their common history and religion; however, the Muslim community could not ignore the fact that one of them was made to coincide with their own festival of Muharram, and the other extolled the Mughal empire's fiercest enemy. As eaters of beef, Muslims were further alarmed at the anti-cowkilling agitation which had been started by Dayānanda, and which Tilak continued to sponsor.

Tilak's success in arousing popular enthusiasm through these activities began to worry the government after the assassination of two British officials in Poona in 1897. Tilak was accused of fanning hatred for the officials with his *Kesari* articles, and was sentenced to jail for eighteen months. Imprisonment only whetted his fighting spirit, and the Bengal agitation of 1995 found him in the front lines of the fray. "Militancy—not mendicancy" was the slogan the Extremist faction used to disparage the Moderates, and his cry "Freedom is my birthright and I will have it" swept the country. When the Extremists failed to wrest control of the Congress from the Moderates at the 1907 session, Tilak defied the chairman (who refused to recognise him); whereupon the meeting degenerated into a riot in which shoes and chairs flew through the air.

Shortly afterward Tilak was again arrested and tried for countenancing political assassination in his speeches and writings. He was sentenced to six years' rigorous confinement in Mandalay, Upper Burma. Books helped him to pass the time, and he returned to his Sanskrit studies. Earlier he had written two books arguing that the Vedas were over six thousand years old. His *magnum opus,* written in prison, was his lengthy commentary on the *Bhagavad Gītā*.

Tilak's interpretation of the *Gītā,* emphasizing as it does the importance of action in this world, gives us the key to his own character and to the influence he has had on political thought in twentieth-century India. He stressed that Hinduism's most popular sacred poem preached political as well as religious activity, and hinted that violence in a righteous cause was morally justifiable. His followers, however, cut themselves loose from the known but foreign standards to which the Moderates remained attached and drifted into the uncharted depths of revolutionary violence and terrorism. Tilak himself never used such methods, but when others used them he maintained a silence which implied assent. The "Father of Indian unrest," as the British journalist Valentine Chirol called him, was not the man to reprimand his own offspring.

By the time of his death in 1920 Tilak had tempered his opposition to British rule sufficiently to favour contesting the election provided for under the Montagu-Chelmsford Reforms of 1919, in contrast to the younger Gāndhi, who wished to boycott them. But Tilak's example of fearless defiance was remembered by those who came after him, and the title of Lokamānya—"Honored by the People"—is still used as a reminder of his efforts to transform the nationalist cause from an upper-class into a truly popular movement.

Bāl Gangādhar Tilak

The Tenets of the New Party

At the end of the Congress session of 1906, it was clear that the gap between the moderates and the Extremists had been bridged only temporarily by the meditation of Dādābhāi Naoroji. At this juncture Tilak delivered an address summarizing the aims and methods of the new party of which he was the leader.

[From *Bal Gangadhar Tilak: His Writings and Speeches,* pp. 55-57, 61, 63-67]

Calcutta, 2nd January, 1907

Two new words have recently come into existence with regard to our politics, and they are *Moderates* and *Extremists*. These words have a specific relation to time, and they, therefore, will change with time. The Extremists of today will be Moderates tomorrow, just as the Moderates of today were Extremists yesterday. When the National Congress was first started and Mr. Dādābhāi's views, which now go for Moderates, were given to the public, he was styled an Extremist, so that you will see that the term Extremist is an expression of progress. We are extremists today and our sons will call themselves Extremists and us Moderates. Every new party begins as Extremists and ends as Moderates. The sphere of practical politics is not unlimited. We cannot say what will or will not happen 1,000 years hence—perhaps during that long period, the whole of the while race will be swept away in another glacial period. We must, therefore, study the present and work out a program to meet the present condition.

It is impossible to go into details within the time at my disposal. One thing is granted, namely, that this government does not suit us. As has been said by an eminent statesman—the government of one country by another can never be a successful, and therefore, a permanent government. There is no difference of opinion about this fundamental proposition between the old and new schools. One fact is that this alien government has ruined the country. In the beginning, all of us were taken by surprise. We were almost dazed. We thought that everything that the rulers did was for our good and that this English government has descended from the clouds to save us from the invasions of Tamerlane and Chingis Khan, and, as they say, not only from foreign invasions but from internecine warfare, or the internal or external invasions, as they call it. We felt happy for a time, but it soon came to light but the peace which was established in this country did this, as Mr. Dādābhāi has said in one place—that we were prevented from going at each other's throats, so that a foreigner might go at the throat of us all. *Pax Britannica* has been established in this country in order that a foreign government may exploit the country. That this is the effect of this *Pax Britannica* is being gradually realized in these days. It was an unhappy circumstance that it was not realized sooner. We believed in the benevolent intentions of the government, but in politics there is no benevolence. Benevolence is used to sugar-coat the declarations of self-interest and we were in those days deceived by the apparent benevolent intentions under which rampant self-interest was concealed. That was our state then. But soon a change came over us. English education, growing poverty, and better familiarity with our rulers, opened our eyes and our leaders; especially, the venerable leader who presided over the recent Congress was the first to tell us that the drain from the country was ruining it, and if the drain was to continue, there was some great disaster awaiting us. So terribly convinced was he of this that he went over from here to England and spent twentyfive years of his life in trying to convince the English people of the injustice that is being done to us. He worked very hard. He had conversations and interviews with secretaries of state, with members of Parliament—and with what result?

He had come here at the age of eighty-two to tell us that he is bitterly disappointed. Mr. Gokhale, I know, is not disappointed. He is a friend of mine and I believe that this is his honest conviction. Mr. Gokhale is not disappointed but is ready to wait another eighty years till he is disappointed like Mr. Dādābhāi. . . .

You can now understand the difference between the old and the new parties. Appeals to the bureaucracy are hopeless. On this point both the new and old parties are agreed. The old party believes in appealing to the British nation and we do not. That being our position, it logically follows we must have some other method. There is another alternative. We are not going to sit down quiet. We shall have some other method by which to achieve what we want. We are not disappointed, we are not pessimists. It is the hope of achieving the goal by our own efforts that has brought into existence this new party.

There is no empire lost by a free grant of concession by the rulers to the ruled. History does not record any such event. Empires are lost by luxury, by being too much bureaucratic or overconfident or from other reasons. But an empire has never come to an end by the rulers conceding power to the ruled. . . .

We have come forward with a scheme which if you accept [it], shall better enable you to remedy this state of things than the scheme of the old school. Your industries are ruined utterly, ruined by foreign rule; your wealth is going out of the country and you are reduced to the lowest level which no human being can occupy. In this state of things, is there any other remedy by which you can help yourself? The remedy is not petitioning but boycott. We say prepare your forces, organize your power, and then go to work so that they cannot refuse you what you demand. A story in *Mahabharata* tells that Sri Krishna was sent to effect a compromise, but the Pandavas and Kauravas were both organizing their forces to meet the contingency of failure of the compromise. This is politics. Are you prepared in this way to fight if your demand is refused? If you are, be sure you will not be refused; but if you are not, nothing can be more certain than that your demand will be refused, and perhaps, forever. We are not armed, and there is no necessity for arms either. We have a stronger weapon, a political weapon, is boycott. We have received one fact, that the whole of this administration, which is carried on by a handful of Englishmen, is carried on with our assistance. We are all in subordinate service. This whole government is carried on with our assistance and they try to keep us in ignorance of our power of cooperation between ourselves by which that which is in our own hands at present can be claimed by us and administered by us. The point is to have the entire control in our hands. I want to have the key of my house, and not merely one stranger turned out of it. Self-government is our goal; we want a control over our administrative machinery. We don't want to become clerks and remain [clerks]. At present, we are clerks and willing instruments of our own oppression in the hands of an alien government, and that government in ruling over us not by its innate strength but by keeping us in ignorance and blindness to the perception of this fact. Professor Seely[9] shares this view. Every Englishman knows that they are a mere handful in this country and it is the business of every one of them to be fool you in believing that you are weak and they are strong. This is politics. We have been deceived by such policy so long. What the new party wants you to do is to realize the fact that your future rests entirely in your own hands. If you mean to be free, you can be free; if you do not mean to be free, you will fall and be for ever fallen. So many of you need not like arms; but if you have not the power of active resistance, have you not the power of self-denial and self-abstinence in such a way as not to assist this foreign government to rule over you? This is boycott and this is what is meant when we say, boycott is a political weapon. We shall not give them assistance to collect revenue and keep peace. We shall not assist them in fighting beyond the frontiers or outside India with Indian blood and money. We shall not assist them in carrying on the administration of justice. We shall have our own courts, and when time comes we shall not pay taxes. Can you do that by your united efforts? If you can, you are free from tomorrow. Some gentlemen who spoke this evening referred to half bread as against the whole bread. I say I want the whole bread and that immediately. But if I can not get the whole, don't think that I have no patience.

I will take the half they give me and then try for the remainder. This is the line of thought and action in which you must train yourself. We have not raised this cry from a mere impulse. It is a reasoned impulse. Try to understand that reason and try to strengthen that impulse by your logical convictions. I do not ask you to blindly follow us. Think over the whole problem for yourselves. If you accept our advice, we feel sure we can achieve our salvation thereby. This is the advice of the new party. Perhaps we have not obtained a full recognition of our principles. Old prejudices die very hard. Neither of us wanted to wreck the Congress, so we compromised, and were satisfied that our principles were recognized, and only to a certain extent. That does not mean that we have accepted the whole situation. We may have a step in advance next year, so that within a few years our principles will be recognized, and recognized to such an extent that the generations who come after us may consider us Moderates. This is the way in which a nation progresses, and this is the lesson you have to learn from the struggle now going on. This is a lesson of progress, a lesson of helping yourself as much as possible, and if you really perceive the force of it, if you are convinced by these arguments, then and then only is it possible for you to effect your salvation from the alien rule under which you labour at his moment.

There are many other points but it is impossible to exhaust them all in an hour's speech. If you carry any wrong impression come and get your doubts solved. We are prepared to answer every objection, solve every doubt, and prove every statement. We want your cooperation; without your help we cannot do anything single-handed. We beg of you, we appeal to you, to think over the question, to see the situation, and realize it, and after realizing it to come to our assistance, and by our joint assistance to help in the salvation of the country.

The Message of the Bhagavad Gītā

Differing from the nondualistic interpretation of the *Gītā* as pointing the path to renunciation of the world, Tilak held that it preached a life of desireless action *in* the world. In the conclusion to his *Mystic Import of the Bhagavad Gītā* he links this message with the revival of India's political fortunes.

[From Tilak, *Srimad Bhagavadgītā Rahasya,* II, 712-13]

The religion of the *Gītā*, which is a combination of spiritual knowledge, devotion, and action, which is in all respects undauntable and comprehensive, and is further perfectly equable,- that is, which does not maintain any distinction, but gives release to everyone in the same measure, and at the same time shows proper forbearance towards other religions, is thus seen to be the sweetest and immortal fruit of the tree of the Vedic religion. In the Vedic religion, higher importance was given in the beginning principally to the sacrifice of wealth or of animals, that is to say, principally to action in the shape of ritual; but, when the knowledge expounded in the Upanishads taught later on that this ritualistic religion of the Shrutis was inferior, Sānkhya philosophy came into existence out of it. But as this knowledge was unintelligible towards abandonment of action, it was not possible for ordinary people to be satisfied merely by the religion of the Upanishads, or by the unification of the Upanishads and the Sānkhya philosophy in the Smritis. Therefore, the *Gītā* religion fuses the knowledge of the Brahman contained in the Upanishads, which is cognoscible only to the intelligence, with the "king of mysticisms" (*rāja-guhya*) of the worship of the perceptible which is accessible to love, and consistently with the ancient tradition of ritualistic religion, it proclaims to everybody, though nominally to Arjuna, that, "[to] perform lifelong your several worldly duties according to your respective positions in life, desirelessly, for the universal good, with a self-identifying vision, and enthusiastically, and thereby perpetually worship the deity in the shape of the Paramātman (the Highest Ātman), which is eternal, and which uniformly pervades the body of all created things as also the cosmos; because, therein lies your happiness in this world and in the next"; and on that account, the mutual conflict between action, spiritual knowledge (jnāna), and love (devotion) is done away with, and the single *Gītā* religion, which preaches that the whole of one's life should be turned into a sacrifice (yajna), contains the essence of the entire Vedic religion. When hundreds of energetic noble souls and active persons were busy with the benefit of all created things, because they looked upon that as their duty, as a result of their having realized this eternal religion, this country was blessed with the favour of the Parameshvara.[9] and reached the height not only of knowledge but also of prosperity; and it need not be said in so many words, that when this ancient religion, which is beneficial in this life and in the next, lost following in our country, it (our country) reached its present fallen state. I, therefore, now pray to the Parameshvara, at the end of this book, that there should come to birth again in this our country such noble and pure men as will worship the Parameshvara according to this equable and brilliant religion of the *Gītā* which harmonizes devotion, spiritual knowledge, and energism. . . .

Aurobindo Ghose: Mystic Patriot

The agitation against the Partition of Bengal drew into public life one of the most fascinating figures modern India has produced—a completely Westernized intellectual who became a fanatic nationalist and ended his days an accomplished yogi. Aurobindo Ghose (1872-1950)—or Sri Aurobindo, as he is known to his followers—spent only four years in active politics, but in that brief span his passionate devotion to the national cause won him reknown as an Extremist leader second only to Tilak in nation-wide popularity.

Aurobindo's father, an English-educated Bengali doctor, was so determined to give his son a completely European education that he sent him to a convent school at five and to England at seven. Isolated from all Indian influences, Aurobindo studied in England until he was twenty. Leaving Cambridge University, he returned to India in 1893 to enter the civil service of the progressive princely state of Baroda. Sensing himself "denationalized" by his foreign education, he turned his attention to Indian culture and politics. He was inspired by the writings of Rāmakrishna, Vivekānanda, and the novels of Bankim Chandra Chatterjee, and after studying Sanskrit was able to appreciate in the original the Upanishads and the *Gītā*.

His fascination with Hindu culture, when combined with the sense of patriotism he had imbibed along with the rest of his English education, naturally led Aurobindo to sympathize with the Extremist politicians. Despite the fact that he was unusually shy, during the agitation against the Partition of Bengal he gave up his post as vice-principal of Baroda College and threw himself into the maelstrom of Bengal politics. His articles in the English-language weekly *Bande Mataram* made him famous, especially after the government tried and failed to prove seditious their deftly phrased innuendos. In 1907 Aurobindo led a large Bengali delegation to the crucial Congress session at Tilak's request, and served as Lokamanya's right-hand man during the stormy days of the split between the Moderate and the Extremists.

Shortly afterward Aurobindo consulted a Hindu holy man who advised him to void his mind of all thought so as to be able to receive supermental inspiration. He followed this advice faithfully, and when he found himself jailed as a suspected member of a bombing plot, he heard the voice of Vivekānanda guiding him in his practice of yoga, and saw all men as incarnations of God. After his release Aurobindo gradually withdrew from political life, and in 1910 abandoned Bengal—and his wife—for the French settlement of Pondichéry, where he spent his remaining forty years doing spiritual exercises and writing. All efforts to bring him back into the political arena proved ineffectual.

Brief as his political career was, Aurobindo defined the essence of religious nationalism in a manner which for sheer passion has never been surpassed. Because of his prolonged absence from India, Aurobindo came to idealize both his native land and its ancestral faith and to identify one with the other in a way no previous thinker had dared to do. The very fervour of his faith in "India" helped his Hindu countrymen to transcend the many differences of caste, language, and custom which had hindered the development among them of allegiance to one nation.

Autobindo was free of the region-centered nationalism which limited the effectiveness of a Bengali like Bankim or a Mahārāshtrian like Tilak. Along with Bankim and Tilak, however, he failed to perceive that the greater the zeal of the Hindu nationalists became, the more difficult grew the task of uniting both Hindus and Muslims in loyalty to a single non-British government.

Aurobindo Ghose

The Doctrine of Passive Resistance

In a series of articles under this heading penned in April, 1907, Aurobindo outlined the Extremists' program of national self-reliance. Both the negative and the positive aspects of this program were later utilized by Gāndhi.

[From Ghose, *The Doctrine of Passive Resistance*, pp. 73-74, 77-79]

We desire to put an end to petitioning until such a strength is created in the country that a petition will only be a courteous form of demand. We wish to kill utterly the pernicious delusion that a foreign and adverse interest can be trusted to develop us to its own detriment, and entirely to do away with the foolish and ignoble hankering after help from our natural adversaries. Our attitude to bureaucratic concession is that of Laocoon: "We fear the Greeks even when they bring us gifts." Our policy is self-development and defensive resistance. But we would extend the policy of self-development to every department of national life; not only Swadeshi and National Education, but national defense, national arbitration courts, sanitation, insurance against famine or relief of famine—whatever our hands find to do or urgently needs doing, we must attempt ourselves and no longer look to the alien to do it for us. And we would universalize and extend the policy of defensive resistance until it ran parallel on every line with our self-development. We would not only buy our own goods, but boycott British goods; not only have our own schools, but boycott government institutions; not only organize our league of defense, but have nothing to do with the bureaucratic executive except when we cannot avoid it. At present even in Bengal where boycott is universally accepted, it is confined to the boycott of British goods and is aimed at the British merchant and only indirectly at the British bureaucrat. We would aim it directly both at the British merchant and at the British bureaucrat who stands behind and makes possible exploitation by the merchant. . . .

The double policy of self-development and defensive resistance is the common standing-ground of the new spirit all over India. Some may not wish to go beyond its limits, others may look outside it; but so far all are agreed. For ourselves we avow that we advocate passive resistance without wishing to make a dogma of it. In a subject nationality, to win liberty for one's country is the first duty of all, by whatever means, at whatever, sacrifice; and this duty must override all other considerations. The work of national emancipation is a great and holy yajna[10] of which boycott, Swadeshi, national education, and every other activity, great and small, are only major or minor parts. Liberty is the fruit we seek from the sacrifice and the Motherland the goddess to whom we offer it; into the seven leaping tongues of the fire of the yajna we must offer all that we are and all that we have, feeding the fire even with our blood and lives and happiness of our nearest and dearest; for the Motherland is a goddess who loves not a maimed and imperfect sacrifice, and freedom was never won from the gods by a grudging giver. But every great yajna has its Rakshasas[11] who strive to battle the sacrifice, to bespatter it with their own dirt, or by guile or violence put out the flame. Passive resistance is an attempt to meet such disturbers by peaceful and self-contained *Brahmatej*;[12] but even the greatest Rishis of old could not, when the Rakshasas were fierce and determined, keep up the sacrifice without calling in the bow of the Kshatriya. We should have the bow of the Kshatriya ready for use, though in the background. Politics is especially the business of the Kshatriya, and without Kshatriya strength at its back, all political struggle is unavailing.

Vedantism accepts no distinction of true of false religions, but considers only what will lead more or less surely, more or less quickly to moksha, spiritual emancipation and the realization of the Divinity within. Our attitude is a political Vedantism. India, free, one and indivisible, is the divine realization to which we move, emancipation our aim; to that end each nation must practice the political creed which is the most suited to its temperament and circumstances; for that is the best for it which leads most surely and completely to national liberty and national self-realization. But whatever leads only to continued subjection must be spewed out as mere vileness and impurity. Passive resistance may be the final method of salvation in our case or it may be only the preparation for the final sadhana.[13] In either case, the sooner we put it into full and perfect practice, the nearer we shall be to national liberty.

Nationalism Is the Work of God

Addressing a Bombay audience soon after the Moderate-Extremist split, Aurobindo made his mind a blank and spoke as the spirit moved him. The result was a startling declaration of the religious significance of Indian nationalism.

[From Ghose, *Speeches,* pp. 7-9]

There is a creed in India today which calls itself Nationalism, a creed which has come to you from Bengal. This is a creed which many of you have accepted when you called yourselves Nationalists. Have you realized, have you yet realized what that means? Have you realized what it is that you have taken in hand? Or is it that you have merely accepted it in the pride of a superior intellectual conviction? You all yourselves Nationalists. What is Nationalism? Nationalism is not a mere political program; Nationalism is a religion that has come from God; Nationalism is a creed which you shall have to live. Let no man dare to call himself a Nationalist if he does so merely with a sort of intellectual pride, thinking that he is more patriotic, thinking that he is something higher than those who do not call themselves by that name. If you are going to be a nationalist, if you are going to assent to this religion of Nationalism, you must do it in the religious spirit. You must remember that you are the instruments of God. What is this that has happened in Bengal? You call yourselves Nationalists, but when this happens to you, what will you do? This thing is happening daily in Bengal, because, in Bengal, Nationalism has come to the people as a religion, and it has been accepted as a religion. But certain forces which are against that religion are trying to crush its rising strength. It always happens when a new religion is preached, when God is going to be born in the people, that such forces rise with all their weapons in their hands to crush the religion. In Bengal too a new religion, a religion divine and sattwic[14] has been preached, and this religion they are trying with all the weapons at their command to crush. By what strength are we in Bengal able to survive? Nationalism is not going to be crushed. Nationalism survives in the strength of God and it is not possible to crush it, whatever weapons are brought against it.

Nationalism is immortal; Nationalism cannot die; because it is no human thing, it is God who is working in Bengal. God cannot be killed, God cannot be sent to jail. When these things happen among you, I say to you solemnly, what will you do? Will you do as they do in Bengal? [Cries of "Yes."] Don't lightly say "yes." It is a solemn thing; and suppose that God puts you this question, how will you answer it? Have you got a real faith? Or is it merely a political aspiration? Is it merely a larger kind of selfishness? Or is it merely that you wish to be free to oppress others, as you are being oppressed? Do you hold your political creed from a higher source? Is it God that is born in you? Have you realized that you are merely the instruments of God, that your bodies are not your own? You are merely instruments of God for the work of the Almighty. Have you realized that? If you have realized that, then you are truly Nationalists; then alone will you be able to restore this great nation. In Bengal it has been realized clearly by some, more clearly by others, but it has been realized and you on this side of the country must also realize it. Then there will be a blessing on our work, and this great nation will rise again and become once more what it was in the days of its spiritual greatness.

India's Mission: The Resurrection of Hinduism

In a memorable speech to the Society for the Protection of Religion after his release from prison in 1908, Aurobindo relayed to his countrymen the messages which had mystically come to him during his confinement. He was first of all to dedicate himself to God's work. Secondly, through her national revival, India was to spread the universal truth of Hinduism throughout the world.

[From Ghose, *Speeches,* pp. 76-80]

The second message came and it said: "Something has been shown to you in this year of seclusion, something about which you had you doubts and it is the truth of the Hindu religion. It is this religion that I am raising up before the world, it is this that I have perfected and developed through the rishis, saints, and avatars, and now it is going forth to do my work among the nations. I am raising up this nation to send forth my word. This is the Sanatan

Dharma, this is the eternal religion which you did not really know before, but which I have now revealed to you. The agnostic and the sceptic in you have been answered, for I have given you proofs within and without you, physical and subjective, which have satisfied you. When you go forth, speak to your nation always this word, that it is for the Sanatan Dharma that they arise, it is for the world and not for themselves that they arise. I am giving them freedom for the service of the world. When therefore it is said that India shall rise, it is the Sanatan Dharma that shall rise. When it is said that India shall be great, it is the Sanatan Dharma that shall be great. When it is said that India shall expand and extend itself, it is the Sanatan Dharma that shall expand and extend itself over the world. It is for the dharma and by the dharma that India exists. To magnify the religious means to magnify the country. I have shown you that I am everywhere and in all men and in all things, that I am in this movement and I am not only working in those who are striving for the country but I am working also in those who oppose them and stand in their paths. I am working in everybody and whatever men may think or do they can do nothing but help on my purpose. They also are doing my work, they are not my enemies but my instruments. In all your actions you are moving forward without knowing which way you move. You mean to do one thing and you do another. You aim at a result and your efforts subserve one that is different or contrary. It is Shakti[15] that has gone forth and entered into the people. Since long ago I have been preparing this uprising and now the time has come and it is I who will lead it to its fulfilment."

This then is what I have to say to you. The name of your society is "Society for the Protection of Religion," Well, the protection of the religion, the protection and upraising before the world of the Hindu religion, that is the work before us. But what is the Hindu religion? What is this religion which we call Sanatan, eternal? It is the Hindu religion only because the Hindu nation has kept it, because in this Peninsula it grew up in the seclusion of the sea and the Himalayas, because in this sacred and ancient land it was given as a charge to the Aryan race to preserve through the ages. But it is not circumscribed by the confines of a single country, it does not belong peculiarly and forever to a bounded part of the world. That which we call the Hindu religion is really the eternal religion, because it is the universal religion which embraces all others. If a religion is not universal, it cannot be eternal. A narrow religion, a sectarian religion, an exclusive religion can live only for a limited time and a limited purpose. This is the one religion that can triumph over materialism by including and anticipating the discoveries of science and the speculations of philosophy. It is the one religion which impresses on mankind the closeness of God to us and embraces in its compass all the possible means by which man can approach God. It is the one religion which insists every moment on the truth which all religions acknolwledge that He is in all men and all things and that in Him we move and have our being. It is the one religion which enables us not only to understand and believe this truth but to realize it with every part of our being. It is the one religion which shows the world what the world is, that it is the Lila of Vasudeva.[16] It is the one religion which shows us how we can best play our part in that Lila, its subtlest laws and its noblest rules. It is the one religion which does not separate life in any smallest detail from religion, which knows what immortality is and has utterly removed from us the reality of death.

This is the word that has been put into my mouth to speak to you today. What I intended to speak has been put away from me, and beyond what is given to me I have nothing to say. It is only the word that is put into me that I can speak to you. That word is now finished. Is poke once before with this force in me and I said then that this movement is not a political movement and that nationalism is not politics but a religion, a creed, a faith. I say it again today, but I put it in another way. I say no longer that nationalism is a creed, a religion, a faith; I say that it is the Sanatan Dharma which for us is nationalism. This Hindu nation was born with the Sanatan Dharma, with it is moves and with it grows. When the Sanatan Dharma declines, then the nation declines, and if the Sanatan Dharma were capable of perishing, with the Sanatan Dharma it would perish. The Sanatam Dharma, that is nationalism. This is the message that I have to speak to you.

Brahmabāndhab Upādhyāy: Hindu Catholic Nationalist

A Hindu sannyāsī, a Roman Catholic, a fiery nationalist—all three descriptions apply equally well to the Bengali brāhman Brahmabāndhab Upādhyāy (1861-1907).

Brahmabāndhab grew up in a village near Calcutta, the third and youngest son of an inspector of police. His mother had died before he was a year old; one of his uncles, Kāli Charan Banerjee, later a prominent Protestant minister, used to visit that family frequently and teach the boy reading and writing.

Brahmabāndhab was an avid student of Sanskrit literature, and had read the *Mahābhārata* and *Rāmāyana* many times before entering his teens. The novels of Bankim Chandra Chatterjee excited his fertile imagination, and Surendranāth Banerjee's speeches inspired him to dedicate himself to patriotic service. At seventeen he ran away from college to "learn the art of fighting and drive out the English."[17] Unable to enlist in the Mahārāja of Gwalior's army, after a period of wandering he returned disillusioned to Calcutta and became a teacher in a boys' school.

Calcutta in the early 1880s was the scene of an unusual religious ferment. Brahmabāndhab fell under the influence of Keshub Chunder Sen, and through him met Rāmakrishna, with whom he was less deeply impressed. He also became a good friend of Narendranāth Datta, the future Vivekānanda. In 1887 he joined the Brāhmo Samāj and soon emigrated with a few friends to found a school for the teaching of Sanskrit and moral character in the province of Sind, in western India.

Four years later, after much reading and prayer, his restless spirit embraced Christianity, first as a Protestant, and then as a Roman Catholic. He nevertheless continued to consider himself as every inch a Hindu, and from 1894 until his death followed strictly the celibate and dietary regimen of a Hindu sannyāsī. Throughout this period he tried to reconcile Hindu philosophy with Christian theology, but his efforts to this end were regarded with some anxiety by the Catholic hierarchy, which twice forbade him to write on the subject.

In 1901 Brahmabāndhab joined Rabindranāth Tagore in setting up a rural school on classical lines at Shāntiniketan. In 1902 he made a trip to Rome and England, feeling that by lecturing on Indian thought at Oxford and Cambridge he was carrying on the work begun by Vivekānanda.

A new phase in his life began in 1905, when his weekly Calcutta newspaper *Sandhyā* (*Twilight*) became a sort of headquarters for the great anti-Partition agitation. Although less important as a political figure than they, he worked with Aurobindo, Tilak, Bepin Chandra Pāl and other Extremist leaders. In 1907 the government arrested and tried him for seditious journalism, for he had written some passionately anti-British editorials in his paper. During the trial he underwent a minor operation and died of lockjaw from a resulting infection.

The life of Brahmabāndhab Upādhyāy illustrates once more the fact that for Hindu nationalists the religious and political spheres of action were virtually inseparable. Moreover, his success in adopting the Christian faith while retaining his status as a brāhman testifies to the great freedom of thought which Hindu society permits to its members. It is also possible to conclude from his experience that it Christianity is to with future converts in Asia it will depend increasingly on the sort of religious synthesis Brahmabāndhab tried to create.

Brahmabāndhab Upādhyāy

Hinduism's Contribution to Christianity

In an article of 1897 Brahmabāndhab stated his aim of explaining Christian doctrine in terms of Hindu concepts. The influence of Keshab Chunder Sen is perceptible in this passage.

[From Animananda, *The Blade,* pp. 67-68]

Christianity has again after a long period-come in contact with a philosophy which, though it may contain more errors—because the Hindu mind is synthetic and speculative—still unquestionably soars higher than her Western sister. Shall we, Catholics of India, now . . . .[let Hindu make] it their weapon against Christianity or shall we look upon it in the same way as St. Thomas looked upon the Aristotelian system? We are of [the] opinion that attempts should be made to win over Hindu philosophy to the service of Christianity as Greek philosophy was won over in the Middle Ages.

We have no definite idea as regards the *modus operandi* of making Hindu philosophy the handmaid of Christianity. The task is difficult and beset with many dangers. But we have a conviction and it is growing day by day that the Catholic Church will find it hard to conquer India unless she makes Hindu philosophy hew wood and draw water for her. The more we mediate on the cogitations of Hindu philosophy concerning the Supreme Being, on its marvellous but fruitless effort to penetrate into His inner nature . . . the more light is thrown upon the ever-mysterious Christian doctrine of the One God., one yet multiple, absolute yet related within Himself, discovering in it a new fitness to appease the noblest carvings of man and satisfy the demands of the loftiest intellect. . . .

The development of the Christian religion has not come to an end. It will grow, blossom, and fructify till the end of the time, Indian soil is humid and its humidity will make the ever-new Christian revelation put forth newer harmonies and newer beauties revealing more clearly the invincible integrity of the Universal Faith deposited in the Church by the Apostles of Jesus Christ. The Hindu mind and heart, coming under the dominion of the One, Holy, Apostolic and Catholic Church, will sing a *new* canticle which will fill the earth with sweetness from end to end.

Hindu Catholicism

Pride in Hindu upbringing, Brahmabāndhab asserted, is totally compatible with Catholic faith, which is universal.

[From Animananda, *The Blade,* pp. 71-73]

By birth we are Hindus and shall remain *Hindu* till death. But as *dvija* (twice-born) by virtue of our sacramental rebirth, we are *Catholic,* we are members of an indefectible communion embracing all ages and climes.

In customs and manners, in observing caste and social distinctions, in eating and drinking, in our life and living, we are genuine Hindus; but in our faith we are neither Hindus nor European, nor American, nor Chinese, but all inclusive. Our faith fills the whole world and is not confined to any country or race; our faith is universal and consequently includes all truths.

Our thought and thinking is emphatically Hindu. We are more speculative than practical, more given to synthesis than analysis, more contemplative than active. It is extremely difficult for us to learn how to think like the Greeks of old or the scholastics of the Middle Ages. Our brains are molded in the philosohic cast of our ancient country.

We are proud of the stability of the Hindu race. Many a mighty race did rise and fall, but we continue to exist, though we had to buffet many a religious deluge and weahter many a political storm. We believe in the future greatness of our race and in this belief we shall live and die.

The more strictly we practice our universal faith, the better do we grow as Hindus. All that is noblest and best in the Hindu character, is developed in us by the genial inspiration of the perfect Narahari (God-man) [Jesus Christ], our pattern and guide. The more we love Him, the more we love our country, the prouder we become of our past glory.

Do we really believe in Hinduism? The question must be understood before it can be answered. Hinduism has no definite creed. Kapila and Vyasa[18] were opposed to each other and yet both of them are considered to be rishis. The Hindu Vedantists of the school of *Ramanuja* look down upon the Hindu Vedantists of the school of *Sankara* as blasphemers; the *Vaishnava* doctrines differ as widely as the poles from the Shaiva doctrine; even the gods have been made to fight one another in the Puranas. The test of being a Hindu cannot therefore lie in religious opinions.

However we are fully imbued with the *spirit* of Hinduism. We hold with the Vedantists that there is one eternal Essence from which proceed all things. We believe with the *Vaishnavas* in the necessity of incarnation and in the doctrine that man cannot be saved without grace. We agree in spirit with Hindu lawgivers in regard to their teaching that sacramental rites (Sankaras) are vehicles of sanctification. With wondering reverence do we look upon their idea of establishing a sacerdotal hierarchy vested with the highest authority in religious and social matters.

In short, we are Hindus so far as our physical and mental constitution is concerned, but in regard to our immortal souls we are Catholic. We are Hindu Catholics.

Independence for India

Love of India and scorn of the foreigner are expressed in these excerpts from the *Sandhyā* of the anti-Partition days.

[From Animananda, *The Blade,* pp. 136, 137]

I swear by the moon and the sun that I have heard in my heart of hearts this message of freedom. As the tree in winter gets a new life with the touch of the breeze of spring, as you feel joy at the return of love, as the heart of a hero dances to the call of the trumpet of war, so a feeling has throbbed in my heart.

But independence will mean both freedom from our slave complex and freedom from gerrymandering politics.

With the spread of English rule and culture, India lost her own ideal of civilization. Our educated classes think as they have been taught by their Firinghi[19] masters. Our minds have been conquered. We have become slaves. The faith in our own culture and the love for things Indian are gone. India will ready Swaraj the day she will again have a faith in herself, Rāmakrishna had gone in that line. So did Bamkin. So did Vivekānanda. The whole mass of our people must now be made to appreciate things Indian and to return to our ancient way. That is Swadesh as opposed to Bidesh.[20] [p. 136]

I see the fort of *Swaraj* built in various places. There shall be no connection with the foreigner. These forts will be purified by the incense of sacrifice, resounding with the cry of victory, filled to overflowing with corn and grain.

Foreigners will not enter there. There we shall be our own masters, from the Thakurghar[21] to the cowshed. All our laws will be observed there, our own Varna-Asram. Let the Englishman be like the *Chaukidar* or *Jamadar*[22] like the watching dog at the door: "If the dog enters your kitchen you break the cooking pot and chase him out." Outside this, our own jurisdiction, we shall observe the laws of the Firinghi for fear of assault and we shall pay the taxes. But if he were to trespass on our God given rights, woe betide him? We shall give thrashing for thrashing. [p. 137]

"First Let the Mother Be Free. . . ."

The sedition charge for which Brahmabāndhab was tried in 1907 rested primarily on this editorial, which extols India as the Mother in the same way as did the sannyāsīs of Bankim's *Abbey of Bliss*.

[From Animananda, *The Blade*, pp. 170-71]

We have said over and over again that we are not Swadeshi only so far as salt and sugar are concerned. Our aspirations are higher than the Himalayas. Our pain is as intense as if we had a volcano in us. What we want is the emancipation of India. Our aim is that India may be free, that the stranger may be driven from our homes, that the continuity of the learning, the civilization and the system of the rishis may be preserved. We have often heard the voice from heaven: Selfish men! We have not entered the lists to play the mudi [grocer].

First free the Mother from her bondage, then seek your own deliverance. The fire of desire has been kindled within our bosom. We do not know whence. Heaven we do not want. Deliverance we seek not. O Mother! let us be born again and again in India till your chains fall off. First let the Mother be free, and then shall come our own release from the worldly bonds. This is no mere child's play. O Feringhi [*sic*], here I am with my neck outstretched—offer it up as a sacrifice. You will see, I shall again be born in the land of Bengal and shall cause much more serious confusion. Can you intimidate us? Our power is more than human. It is divine. We have heard the voice telling us that the period of India's suffering is about to close, that the day of her deliverance is near at hand. It is because we have heard the voice that we have left our forest-home and came to town. Your overweening pride is due to our possessing a few cannon and guns. Just see to what plight you are reduced. You imagine that by causing a *Kabulyat*[23] of loyalty to be written, you will drive us to a corner. But the signatories of that document are nonentities. We have all the advantages of the ancient greatness of India on our side. We are immortal. If you are wise, you should help towards the attainment of deliverance by India. Otherwise, come, let us descend into the arena of war. We hereby summon you to battle. See what a mighty contest presently begins all over the country. The sons of the Mother are preparing themselves. All the arms—fiery (Agneya), watery (Varuna), airy (Vayabya)—in her vaults, are being polished. Hark, the flapping of the fourfold arms of the Mother? Are we afraid of your cannon and guns? Arm brothers, arm! The day of deliverance is near. We have heard the voice and we cannot fail to see the chains of India removed before we die. It is now too late to recede.

REFERENCES

1. When used as a national anthem, this figure was changed to 300 million.
2. The Goddess Mother, much-worshipped in Bengal.
3. The Goddess of Wealth.
4. Names of ancient Indian elites and kingdoms, used here in lieu of modern palce-names.
5. Family idol.
6. The rooms of a house in which women are secluded.
7. A chilled sweet drink.
8. The old spelling for Marāthā.
9. Refers to Sir John Robert Seeley, author of *The Expansion of England* (London, 1895).

10. The Highest God.
11. Ritual sacrifice.
12. Demons.
13. Divine power.
14. Spiritual discipline leading to attainment of the highest good.
15. Pure, holy.
16. Divine creative power.
18. The play or sport of God.
17. Quoted in B. Animananda, *The Blade,* p. 14.
19. The founders of the Sānkhya and Vedanta systems respectively.
20. Foreigner.
21. "One's own country" as opposed to "a foreign country."
22. Doorkeeper or guard.
23. Lord's house.
24. Certificate.

12

THE SCIENTIFIC APPROACH TO RELIGION

The study of the scientific approach to religion forms an integral part of the wider study of the scientific approach to all human knowledge and experience. This is a modern phenomenon arising from what has come to be known as modern science. The impact of this modern scientific approach has been revolutionary in its scope and pervasive in its results. Originating as a passion for truth and a spirit of free inquiry and critical investigation in a few centres of Western Europe just over four centuries ago, and gathering force and momentum in its onward march, the modern scientific spirit and approach have, within the brief span of four centuries, not only advanced human knowledge and enlightenment enormously but have also transformed profoundly man and his environment, the temper of his thought and outlook as much as the pattern of his life and tion.

Modern Science and the Spirit of Free Inquiry

What is that in this scientific spirit and approach which has produced such revolutionary results? I have said earlier that at the root of these revolutionary achievements lie two values, namely, a passion for truth and a spirit of free inquiry and critical investigation. Today we take these things for granted. But the situation was completely different four centuries ago. The ancient Greeks had cultivated this passion and this spirit assiduously and had advanced contemporary human knowledge, particularly in the field of the social sciences. After the eclipse of the short-lived but glorious Greek culture and civilization, Rome carried on the tradition in the same field in a small way in thought and in a big way in practice. But with the destruction of the Roman civilization at the hands of barbarian invaders at the beginning of the fifth century A.D., the light of scientific quest and knowledge went out in the western world; darkness set in and continued for over eight hundred years.

But one light flickered during this dreary period, namely, the light of religion, which was lit up and tended with rare devotion by a succession of great Christian mystics whose scientific approach to religion was, however, more often thwarted than aided by the prevailing church organization which became increasingly entangled, as centuries rolled on, invested interests in the form of finished and final dogmas in the intellectual field and wealth and power in the physical field. To religious or political power so organized and entrenched, reason with its doubt and questioning cannot but be anathema, not only in the field of religion but also in the field of physical science and all positive knowledge. Love of truth and its search have its enemy in all forms of finished and final dogma. Man's love of truth and search for knowledge lay under a heavy weight of unquestioning acceptance of authority and tradition not only of the contemporary church and state but also of ancient writers and their books. Those bright spirits who dared to try to lift this weight, paid the penalty in torture and death. From the point of view of human cultural history, nothing could be more dismal and dark.

The Dawn of The Modern Science

But soon the signs of a new dawn appeared on the horizon; this proceeded from two sources: firstly, European students returning from the Moorish centres of higher learning in Spain fostered by that Arab culture and civilization which had assimilated ancient Greek and ancient Indian learning and held the torch of reason bright during the period covered by the dark ages in Europe; and secondly, Greek scholars coming to Western Europe with the treasures of their ancient learning in the wake of the capture of Constantinople by the advancing Turks, and helping Western Europe to effect a revival of Greek culture and knowledge.

By about the end of the fifteenth century, Western Europe had begun to experience, in a perceptive way, what in history is called a renaissance. A wind of change began to blow through the mental life of Western Europeans whose youthful vitality and bubbling energies soon converted the gentle initial upsurge into a powerful force of all-round human transformation everywhere through the slow and steady perfecting of the scientific spirit and method in its pure and applied forms.

The history of modern science records a typical episode which well illustrates the impact of this wind of change then blowing gently over Western Europe during the latter half of the fifteenth century. A group of scholars of the Oxford University was assembled in its library hall and engaged in solving what to the participants was a momentous problem in zoology, namely, how many teeth a horse has. They followed the method of the centuries-old tradition for solving such problem, namely, reference to ancient authorities. The scholars vied with each other in taking ancient books out of the library and consulting their authors. The author most consulted was Aristotle whose authority, already binding, but still more reinforced by the patronage of the Medieval Church, was unquestioned and supreme When the scholars were warmly engaged in the debate quoting authorities to uphold one's position or refute that of one's opponent, one young scholar quietly left the hall and, in a few minutes, came back, to the horror of all those present, leading a live horse; and stationing it in the centre of the hall, he calmly addressed his fellow-scholars: gentlemen, you want to know how many teeth a horse has. Here is a live horse; please open its mouth and count its teeth, and thus ascertain the truth for yourself. The rest of the scholars were thoroughly shocked by the foolhardy audacity of the young scholar and condemned him for believing and asking them to believe that a horse could have more or less teeth than what Aristotle and other authorities had provided for it in their books.

But that young scholar, who had been affected by the prevailing scientific wind, was like the stone, in the words of the Bibld, that the builders rejected but became the coping stone of the new edifice.

The Scientific Method

This is the new magnificent edifice of modern science whose bricks are facts and not opinions and whose blueprint was provided in the newly defined inductive method, what Bacon termed the *novum organon.* It summoned man to study the book of nature ever held out before him and, to this end, to discipline his mind in attitudes and methods which will enable it to read that book effectively. This is the scientific spirit, method, and approach which has succeeded in wringing secrets after secrets from nature with amazing rapidity and profusion; it has converted his knowledge into power creating, in the process, an entirely new culture and civilization of world wide dimensions.

It is necessary to understand the driving force behind these extraordinary achievements. That driving force is the human mind disciplined in the spirit and methods of science. What is the nature of this discipline? To quote the scientist Karl Pearson (*Grammar of Science,* 1900 Edition, p. 6):

"The classification of facts, the recognition of their sequence and relative significance is the function of science, and the habit of forming a judgment upon these facts unbiased by personal feeling is characteristic of what may be termed the scientific frame of mind."

The mind that seeks facts, that questions facts and questions with a serious intent and purpose, that tests and verifies the answers it gets, has a dynamic quality about it which enables it to forge ahead in any field of inquiry or endeavour.

Science and Religion: The Western Approach

Modern western history is fascinating precisely because it reveals the human mind forging ahead under this scientific discipline in the diverse fields of the physical sciences. It was assumed in the last century, in the wake of the revolutionary advances of the physical sciences, that any knowledge outside the fields of the physical sciences could not be called scientific. It might be termed private belief or faith but could not be given the status of verified truth which is science. The official approach of the West to religion was of the former type; religion was the product of a final revelation to be accepted in faith and not to be questioned by human reason, it dealt with the supernatural whereas science dealt with the natural, with reason as its instrument. The approach of the West to both science and religion gave rise to a whole host of dichotomies and irreconcilable contradictions such as natural versus supernatural, science versus religion, reason versus faith, and secular versus sacred. Western religion, on its part, carried these contradictions further into the field of inter-Christian and Christian-non-Christian relations as well.

This parallel running of religion and science can at best be a short-term tactical device based on social expediency. This was the position at the end of the nineteenth century which saw the failure of religion to suppress emerging science during the previous three centuries, the final trimuph of modern science, and the relegation of religion itself to the position of being a dangerous error, to begin with, and a harmless illusion, in the end.

It was unfortunate that the organization of ignorance and prejudice against science came from the side of religion. But let it not be missed that this was only a Western experience; it was, as I said earlier, a product of the official Western approach to both science and religion. The approach of the great mystics of the West to religion, however, as of all mystics anywhere, was scientific in being experimental and experiential. But their approach and their voice were stifled by the dogmatic spirit and approach upheld by the organized churches with the result that the West could not and did not develop a scientific tradition in the field the religion. That explains its recurring experiences of intolerance, hostility, and conflict not only between religion and science but also between Christian and non-Christian faiths and between the various denominations of Christianity itself.

Western approach to science in the last century, on the other hand, tended to equate science with physical science and set up a permanent wall of separation between the world of facts and the world of values, denigrating the latter and impoverishing human life in a fundamental way in the process.

Even though twentieth century science, in spite of its revolutionary advance has found, officially speaking, no valid basis for religion, several individual scientists, some of them eminent, acknowledge the limitations of their science to comprehend. Reality and accept as valid the approach of religion, as also of art, to Reality in their own special ways.

Science and Religion: The Indian Approach

It is in this context, against this background, that the Indian approach to religion becomes significant. From the time of the Upanisads to our own times, India has sought in religion, not a finished dogma to believe in, but a method and a means to pierce the veil that hides the ever-present meaning and mystery of existence. The Upanisads glowingly register this passion of the Indian mind to seek and find truth through a penetrating study of experience. In the appreciative words of Robert Ernest Hume (*The Thirteen Principal Upanisads,* p. 30, footnote):

> "The earnestness of the search for truth is one of the delightful and commendable features of the Upanisads."

In the Upanisads we get an intelligible body of verified and verifiable spiritual insights which have stood the test of time. Subsequent advance in the field of the physical sciences, including the revolutionary advances of the modern age, have not only not affected their truth-value but have, on the contrary, only helped to reveal their rational basis and enhance their spiritual appeal. This is no wonder for those who know the Indian approach to religion, because these insights are the products of an equally scientific investigation into a different field of experience, namely, the non-physical, the world of man's inner life.

In the words of Eddington (*Science and the Unseen World,* p. 54):

'You will understand the true spirit neither of science nor of religion unless seeking is placed in the front.'

Dogmatism and cocksureness which stifle the spirit of free inquiry are as much enemies of true science as of true religion. There are not wanting scientists even in this century who would, taking a narrow view of the scope and function of science, prefer to go the dogmatic way and cry halt to advancing knowledge and the unifying of experience. That way spells danger to science now as it has spelt danger to religion before. A greater devotion to the spirit of free inquiry and a broader conception of the aim and temper of science is our only safeguard against such pitfall.

Pointing out to the existence of a science of religion which is overlaid with the weight of dogmatic religion, Vivekananda says in his lecture on 'Religion and Science' (*Complete Works,* Vol. VI, Sixth Edition, p. 81):

'Experience is the only source of knowledge. In the world, religion is the only science where is no surety, because it is not taught as a science of experience. This should not be. There is always, however, a small group of men who teach religion from experience. They are called mystics, and these mystics in every religion speak the same tongue and teach the same truth. This is the real science of religion. As mathematics in every part of the world does not differ, so the mystics do not differ. They are all similarly constituted and similarly situated. Their experience is the same; and this becomes law.'

Explaining the close inter-relation between physical sciences and the science of religion, Vivekananda says (*ibid.;* Vol. II, Ninth Edition, p. 432):

'There are two words the microcosm and the macrocosm, the internal and the external. We get truth from both these by means of experience. The truth gathered from internal experience is psychology, metaphysics, and religion; from external experience, the physical sciences. Now a perfect truth should be in harmony with experience in both these worlds. The microcosm must bear testimony to the macrocosm; physical truth must have its counterpart in the internal world, and internal world must have its verification outside.'

The 'Within' and the 'Without' of Nature

This inner aspect of man, and, through him, of the universe, is slowly dawning on the horizon of modern scientific thought. Highlighting some of the revolutionary trends in twentieth-century biology, the eminent paleontologist, the late Pierre Teilhard de Chardin asks (*The Phenomenon of Man*, 1959, p. 52):

'Up to now has science ever troubled to look at the world other than from without?

And he proceeds (*ibid.*, p. 55):

'In the eyes of the physicist, nothing exists legitimately, at least up to now, except the *without* of things. The same intellectual attitude is still permissible in the bacteriologist, whose cultures (apart from substantial difficulties) are treated as laboratory reagents. But it is still more difficult in the realm of plants. It tends to become a gamble in the case of a biologist studying the behaviour of insects or coelenterates. It seems merely futile with regard to the vertebrates.

Finally, it breaks down completely with man, in whom the existence of a *within* can no longer be evaded, because it is the object of a direct intuition and the substance of all knowledge.'

And Chardin concludes (ibid., p. 56):

'It is impossible to deny that, deep within ourselves, an "interior" appears at the heart of beings, as it were seen through a rent. This is enough to ensure that, in one degree or another, this, "interior" should obtrude itself as existing everywhere in nature from all time. Since the stuff of the universe has an inner aspect at one point of itself, there is necessarily a *double aspect to its structure,* that is to say, in every region of space and time—in the same way, for instance, as it is granular: *Coextensive with their Without,* there is a Within to things.'

Vedanta: The Synthesis of the 'Within' And the Without'

The study of this within of nature through an inquiry into the within of man, who is the unique product of nature's evolution, is religion according to Indian thought. The synthesis of the knowledge of the 'without' which the physical sciences give and of the 'within' which religion gives, is what India achieved in her Vedānta. This she calls *Brahmavidyā* or philosophy, Brahman standing for the totality of Reality, physical and non-physical. *Brahmavidyā* is *sarvavidyāpratisthā*—'philosophy is the basis and support of all knowledge, says the *Mundaka Upanisad* (l. i. l); *ksetraksetrajnayorjnānam yattat jnanam matam mama*— 'the knowledge of the *ksetra,* the object (the 'known' or the 'without' of things), and of the *ksetrajna,* the subject (the 'knower' or the 'within' of things), is *jnāna,* wisdom (or philosophy), according to Me', says Krishna in the Gita (XIII.2).

The Scientific Approach to Religion

What is the scientific validity of religion so defined: Nineteenth century science, just emerged victorious from its conflict with dogmatic religion, and tying itself down to its own dogma of materialism, rendered itself incapable of assessing or appreciating scientifically the subject of religion. That century was the century of conflict and division as the present century bids fair to become the century of reconciliation and union as a result of the revolutionary advances in science and a sincere effort on the part of both science and religion to reassess itself and to understand the other. The humility of twentieth-century science presents a sharp and welcome contrast to cocksureness of its nineteenth-century counterpart. It has realized that the spirit of rational inquiry, with its passion for facts and testing and verification of conclusions, on which it has thrived, may find expression in fields beyond its own narrow departments, and that it is this spirit, unbiased by personal likes and dislikes, that makes a study scientific and not the mere subject-matter of that study. To quote the great biologist J.A. Thomson (*Introduction to Science* Home University Library Edition, p. 58):

'Science is not wrapped up with particular body of facts; it is characterized as an intellectual attitude. It is not tied down to any particular methods of inquiry ; it is simply sincere critical thought which admits conclusions only when these are based on evidence. We may get a good lesson in scientific method from a business man meeting some new practical problem, from a lawyer sifting evidence, or from a statesman framing a constructive bill.'

This has been the Indian approach to religion. It was the neglect of this approach that made religion in the West, down the centuries, less and less equipped to meet the challenge of advancing knowledge. Referring to this unique characteristic of the Indian approach as enshrined in its Vedānta, Romain Rolland says (*The Life of Vivekananda and the Universal Gospel,* Third Impression, 1947, p. 196):

'The true Vedāntic spirit does not start out with a system of preconceived ideas. It possesses absolute liberty and unrivalled courage among religions with regard to the facts to be observed and the diverse hypotheses it has laid down for their co-ordination. Never having been hampered by a priestly order, each man has been entirely free to search wherever he pleased for the spiritual explanation of the universe.'

Speaking on the subject of 'Reason and Religion' in a lecture in England in 1896, Swami Vivekananda sums up the results of this neglect of the scientific approach to religion on modern man (*Complete* Works, Vol. I, Eleventh Edition, p. 366):

'The foundations have all been undermined; and the modern man, whatever he may say in public, knows in the privacy of his heart that he can no more "believe". Believing certain things because an organized body of priests tells him to believe, believing because it is written in certain books, believing because his people like him to believe, the modern man knows to be impossible for him. There are, of course, a number of people who seem to acquiesce in the so-called popular faith but we also know for certain that they do not think. Their idea of belief may be better translated as "not-thinking-carelessness" This fight cannot last much longer without breaking to pieces all the buildings of religion.'

And pleading for a rational approach to religion with a view to easing the contemporary conflict between the two great disciplines of science and religion which need each other to lead man to total fulfilment, he continues (*Ibid.*):

'Is religion to justify itself by the discoveries of reason, through which every other science justifies itself? Are the same methods of investigation, which we apply to sciences and knowledge outside, to be applied to the science of religion? In my opinion this must be so, and I am also of opinion that the sooner it is done the better. If a religion is destroyed by such investigation, it was then all the time useless, unworthy superstition; and the sooner it goes the better. I am thoroughly convinced that its destruction would be the best thing that could happen. All that is dross will be taken off, no doubt, but the essential parts of religion will emerge triumphant out of this investigation. Not only will it be made scientific—as scientific, at least, as any of the conclusions of physics or chemistry—but will have greater strength, because physics or chemistry has not internal mandate to vouch for its truth, which religion has.'

The Fruit of the Scientific Approach to Religion

The scientific spirit and approach find expression in any department of scientific study in the gathering of relevant facts, their rational interpretation, and facing the final challenge of verification. And this has been the Indian approach to religion from the time of the Upanisads; according to this approach the *practice* of religion is a cease less quest after the facts of man's inner life at the innermost depth of which it finds the truth of God, which it defines as infinite existence, infinite knowledge, and infinite bliss, the *Sat-Cit-Ananda Brahman;* it comes across, at the intermediate depths, all higher values which find expression in man's ethical, moral, and aesthetic experiences. A dispassionate study of these facts constitutes the science of religion, the science and art of the spiritual life.

Explaining this Indian approach to religion and the cause of the misunderstanding between science and religion, Swami Vivekananda says (*Complete Works,* Vol. VI, Sixth Edition, p. 81):

'Religion deals with the truths of the metaphysical world just as chemistry and the other natural sciences deal with the truth of the physical world. The book one must read to learn chemistry is the book of (external) nature. The book from which to learn religion is your own mind and heart. The sage is often ignorant of physical science because he reads the wrong book—the book within; and the scientist is too often ignorant of religion because he, too, reads the wrong book—the book without.'

Modern Science and The Mystery of Man

In modern science external nature has yielded her jealously kept secrets, one after another, to the disciplined mind of one of her own evolutionary products, namely, man. But that disciplined mind today admits its utter incapacity to pierce the heart of nature's mystery. For that mystery is overshadowed by a profounder mystery, namely, man himself. In the words of Lincoln Barnett (*The Universe and Dr. Einstein,* Mentor Edition, pp. 126-27):

'In the evolution of scientific thought, one fact has become impressively clear: there is no mystery of the physical world which does not point to a mystery beyond itself. All highroads of the intellect, all byways of theory and conjecture, lead ultimately to an abyss that human ingenuity can never span. For man is enchained by the very condition of his being, his finiteness and involvement in nature. The further he extends his horizons, the more vividly he recognizes the fact that, as the physicist Niels Böhr puts it, "We are both spectators and actors in the great drama of existence." *Man is thus his own greatest mystery.* (italics not author's). He does not understand the vast veiled universe into which he has been cast for the reason that he does not understand himself. He comprehends but little of his organic processes and even less of his unique capacity to perceive the world around him, to reason and to dream. Least of all does he understand his noblest and most mysterious faculty: *the ability to transcend himself and perceive himself in the act of perception.'* (italics not author's).

Vedanta and the Mystery of Man

Here is the meeting-point of science and religion as revealed in Indian thought. For religion, as expounded in Vedanta, takes up the investigation of the mystery of existence where the physical sciences, the study of the 'without' of things, leave off. And it is the object science of religion to unravel that mystery of man's 'noblest and most mysterious faculty, to which Lincoln Barnett refers, and to confer spiritual freedom on man who, in the words of Barnest , is enchained by the very condition of his being, his finiteness and involvement in nature', by discovering the infinite dimension of his finite personality. God *enchained* is man and man *unchained* is God, says Sri Ramakrishna. The technique of this inquiry into the 'within' and its unique fruits of freedom from finitude and fear are expounded in a brief but profound utterance of one of the Upanisads (*Katha Upanisad,* IV. I):

Parānci khāni vyatṛnat svayaṁbhuḥ

tasmāt parāṅpaśyati nāntarātman;

Kaścit dhīraḥ pratyagātmanam aikṣat

āvṛttacakṣuh amṛlatvamicchan—.

'The self-existent One created the sense-organs (including the mind) with the defect of an outgoing disposition; therefore, beings perceive (perishable things) outside but not the (immortal) Atman (Self) within. A certain wise and heroic seeker, desiring to achieve immortality, realized the inner Self by turning his senses (including the mind) inward.'

The fruit of this technique, followed with scientific thoroughness and detachment by the sages of the Upanisads, and revalidated by a succession of spiritual experimenters from Buddha to Sri Ramakrishna, is glowingly revealed in one of the immortal verses of all the Upanisads which Vivekananda quoted with telling effect in his address at the Parliament of Religions at Chicago in September 1893 (*Complete Works,* Vol. I, Eleventh Edition, p. 11):

Śṛṇvantu viśve amṛtasya putrāh

āye dhāmāni divyāni tasthuḥ;

Vedāhmetaṁ puruṣām mahāntam

ādityavarṇam tamasaḥ parastāt.

Tameva viditvā atimṛtyumeti

nānyaḥ panthā vidyate ayanāyā—.

'Hear ye all, children of immortal bliss! aye, even those who reside in the celestial regions!

I have *realized* the infinite dimension of the human personality, luminous as the sun, beyond all darkness.

By knowing Him alone shall man transcend (finitude and) perpetual death; there is no other way to the goal (of fulfilment)'

The Synthesis of Science and Religion

In ancient Vedanta, internal nature has yielded its secrets to the spiritually disciplined mind of man, enabling him to unravel the mystery of even that external nature which baffles all modern physical science, and to proclaim the unity of the external and the internal, of the 'without' and the 'within' of things, in the spiritual unity of Brahman or Atman.

Vedanta has provided the science of religion with an international and intelligent framework of terms and concepts which help the various religions of the world to understand themselves, to understand each other, and to understand the physical sciences. This is precisely the service that modern science has rendered to all physical or positivistic knowledge.

The combination of these two—Vedanta or to scientific approach to the 'within' of nature, and Modern Science, the scientific approach to the 'without' of nature—constitutes the complete education for fulfilment for all humanity today. Echoing this conviction in the concluding portion of his *Autobiography,* astro-physicist R.A Millikan says:

'It seems to me that the two great pillars upon which all human well-being and human progress rest are fist, the spirit of religion and second, the spirit of science—or knowledge. Neither can attain its largest effectiveness without support from the other. To promote the latter, we have universities and research institutions. But the supreme opportunity for everyone with no exception lies in the first.'

—Swami Ranganathananda (Belur Math)

13

THE RELIGION OF THE NEW CIVILISATION

Friends

In my first lecture I pointed out two very opposite dangers which threatened respectively America and Europe. In Europe we had the excess, the terrible excess, of poverty; in America, what may sound strange to you, the excess of wealth. Both of these act as a practical cancer to civilisation, the one by reducing large numbers of the people to a constant struggle to exist-I do not say to live, but to exist; the other bringing satiety which leads to a constant attempt to find new excitement, of living on the surface of things, of seeking satisfaction in ever greater and greater excitement, even the excitement of crime.

Today I am to deal with the first of the three great departments of human life which affect every human being; and however much you may subdivide them they remain. I think, fundamentally three in number. The first of those, as I have put their order, in Religion. The work of religion, I shall submit to you, is to change our attitude and object in life, to seek unselfish, rather than selfish, ideals, and unselfishness ever widening out into larger and larger circles, until at last it shall embrace in one mighty Brotherhood everything that lives. Then, after that, what we may call in a sense the most important of all—Education. That evolves and moulds our capacities, brings out the seeds of human power and faculty, and enables them to grow and to develop. That is necessary in order that by knowledge we may begin to understand; when to knowledge we add love, that turns it into wisdom. Education should be of a nature which shall help everyone who comes into the world to develop his faculties to the very best advantage For out of education comes the Culture of the individual and of the Nation; and Culture is the application of what we have learned in education to human life and the growth of humanity. Then in the third place I have put Economics—Religion in the New Civilisation, Economics in the New Civilisation.

Now Economics is the necessary basis that lies at the very root, the very foundation, of Society. It means the science of the right production and the right distribution of the various articles that form the material side in life. It means, in addition to that, full opportunities for everyone to lead a really human life. For by human life I do not mean simply abundance of all that satisfies the physical body. I do not mean by human life all that gives physical pleasure, physical luxury, the possession of much, and far more than is necessary for the physical life. But I do mean by human life, the development of those higher faculties in man which find happiness, not in the things that perish in the using, but that increase and grow with the using and the sharing; the treasures of the human mind as you find them in literature, the treasures of human emotion as you find them in art in all its many phases—I mean those greater and relatively permanent enjoyments which refine, which cultivate, which develop the higher side of our nature, and help to make man what he ought to be if he is to reach perfection the natural end of evolution.

And the first of those departments is the one with which I am to deal to-night—Religion in the New Civilisation. Naturally, then, we ought to begin with a clear understanding of what we mean by Religion. Do we mean by it only the various religions of the world, each of them with its own particular value to those who follow it, but each of them necessarily partial and changing with the changes of the generations of men? I should define Religion as that inner urge that we find in the human being to realise that life which is the life of God in man, the God within the man. cramped and cramped and cabined by His material surroundings reaching out, as it were, to the God outside Him, universally enveloping Him as well as entering Him, called often in Philosophy. God Immanent in the first case, Transcendent in the second case.

If it be true that there is but one Life, that that one Life is the all-enveloping Power, outside which nothing can exist, then it is fairly clear that that life abiding in the heart of a rational and emotional being, a being also of activities whereby he is affecting the material world around him, that that God within must necessarily be for ever striving to reunite Himself, as it were, with the God around. And so, wherever you find the human race, except for brief periods which soon slay themselves by their own excesses, we find this seeking after God, this urge, as I have called it, of the God within to satisfy Himself by reunion with the God around Him, the God in His fellow-creatures, as well as the transcendent Life that includes all things.

That to me is what I mean by Religion, this inner urge to know the greater Self. And the religions of the world might fairly be regarded as the answers of God without to this urge within the members of the human race—temporary answers, differing in much of their detail, but ever with the same Love without, seeking the Love within.

So we find that with each great human type, a separate religion appears, and we can trace them down through the ages, one in their essence but each with its own symbology, each with its own dominant virtue, adding to that great garland of symbology and of virtues which we find when we realise the inner oneness and the outer differences of the religions of our world. For we can see in the great Mother-Race that Unity is the one dominant idea, the "One, without a second". Then we can find that that idea is repeated in Egypt by the Sun, in Persia by Fire, in Greece by Harmony, music, sound. We can find in each as well that that note exists in man as well as in the world around him, and that each religion has its own specific dominant virtue, adding to the growing possibilities of the human race.

Seeing that Unity amid diversity, seeing these gradual additions to the religious wealth of the world, the next thing is to pierce that diversity and find the inner Unity of all these different faiths. As we look at them from the standpoint, then it is that we begin to realise that all these religions are only differing answers from the one Religion. We see in each of these the Unity which it shares with everyone of its fellow-faiths. And the first point in that Unity is the Immanence and Transcendence of God. Then we find, following upon that, the Perfectibility of Humanity, as the goal of these divine lives in all the world. Then we see that if perfection is to be the goal, life after life must follow, ever growing in greatness, in radiance, and in strength. And so, in every great religion, we find that third common truth of Reincarnation. Then in order that these lives may be orderly and successful, we find that the life period is distributed through three worlds, the physical, the intermediate, and the heavenly; and that in the physical, man gathers experience—experience of good and evil—experience of every type and kind of life; that he gathers up that experience and carries it with him through the gateway of death. Then in the intermediate world we find that some of the experience has sorrow at its heart, because it is against the order of the universe and the beauty of the universe; that that bears its natural fruit of dissatisfaction and craving; dissatisfaction because in that subtler world the body, having disintegrated, the carvings of the body can find no satisfaction there; and then a gradual withdrawal from such experience as "evil," and the storing of that withdrawal as part of the conscience of the future.

And then there is the passing on of those who have gathered experiences in the physical world and have separated them into good and evil in the intermediate world, to a long productive Heaven-world, where all the useful experience is woven into character, where the germs of faculties grow and are ready to bud into flower, where every noble aspiration helps to form a capacity to achieve, every high thought a faculty of the mind that shall be re-embodied in the physical world, every longing to help and to succour becomes that love which last, which death cannot touch or injure, creates a deeper passion, a stronger emotion, a more compelling enthusiasm; so that after every leaving of that native land of ours, the Heaven-world, we come back from that long sojourn, back from that long weaving of experience into power, we come back again to the physical world with the germs of the faculties we have created out of experience within us to be developed by a short life-period in the physical world. And so there is the turning over and over again of the wheel of births and deaths. That great doctrine, that great gospel of hope for every man, the certainty of perfection, no matter how he tries and tails and struggles, that has been part of the heart of every great religion, obscured for a few centuries only in the life of Christendom for a very definite reason. The special work that had to be carried on in Christendom was to bring out creative activity, was to teach great lessons of activity as service, through that sub-race especially to which this work was confided.

Now we find that the knowledge of Reincarnation lessens—and it is only fair to recognise that it lessens—to some extent the value of each separate human life. For people may sometimes think: "Well, if I do not do a thing in this life, I can do it in another. If I do not conquer and make this particular faculty now, I have a long future before me in which I can sow and cultivate it." It does to a certain extent limit the value of each separate human life. And since in the religion that was to rule in Christendom the concrete mind was to be highly developed, the activities to which it gave birth were to be fully utilised, each life was to be full of energy, of effort, in order that that individuality might be developed, as it only could be developed by struggle and by effort, for a short time only, this great truth of Reincarnation was veiled from ordinary sight, although it never quite perished out of Europe. For, even when denounced as a heresy by the dominant Church, some of the heretical sects preserved it and handed on the tradition to the future. Every now and then the truth comes out, as when in one of the great Musalman doctors of the Middle Ages you find this doctrine embodied. He wrote:

I died out of the mineral and became a plant;
I died out of the plant and became an animal;
I died out of the animal and became a man.

Then he asks triumphantly:

When did I ever grow less by dying?

Then it again woke in the poets and the philosophers of Europe, especially of Germany. It came across the sea to the poets of England, as to Wordsworth, where again you find its reappearance. And today from every side you can hear the statement of this idea of a continuing soul passing from life to life, growing, increasing, working for perfection; as was said by one professor, "it is the only rational theory of immortality"; it is recognised as the one great gospel of hope, that however low we may be at the moment, we shall at last attain that perfection which the Christ commanded when He told His followers: "Be ye therefore perfect, even as your Father in Heaven is perfect. " You know every one of you well enough that in this one brief life we cannot gain perfection. You know that with our vagrant thoughts, our unruly emotions, our activities so often stained with selfishness and greed, that we cannot gain Divine perfection before we pass out of this life, although the Christ whom Christendom worships as God, commands that His followers should reach that point. Only through Reincarnation can you obey Him. Only through Reincarnation can you prove His command to be possible of fulfilment.

And these great basic truths are the truths that all religions have, and they all lead us up from the Unity of life to the Brotherhood of all that lives; that is the end which they seek to substitute for selfish striving, for individual gain at the loss of others, the Fatherhood of the one Life, the Brotherhood of all that lives; that is the attitude of all religions to the world. These basic truths are the foundation of their Unity.

And so we have—what has been called in America at the same time that the Theosophical Society was proclaiming that

Unity in Asia—so we have the thought which is expressed by the words "The Fellowship of Faiths"; the Fellowship is proved by their Unity of origin, their sufficiency at different stages of human progress, for those to whom they were given.

And that Fellowship of Faiths will be a central characteristic of the New Civilisation. That means that religious quarrels will find their ending, that religious wars will be looked upon as the worst of crimes, that instead of fear and distrust and even hatred between the members of these different Faiths, all shall recognise the Fellowship, that they shall be as many jewels in a single diadem, many pearls in a great necklace round the neck of humanity.

And in the New Civilisation, this Fellowship will develop and grow—not suddenly, there are no such sudden leaps in Nature, but there will be a steady growth in that direction, and you can see the beginning of that around you at the present day. Not very long before I left America I read in a Boston paper that the various Protestants of Boston City—for Boston is, of course, of the New England type of religion—that the various Protestants of this city met together in order to point out the excellences of the Roman Catholic religion. Surely a remarkable gathering, that these two forms, which have been fighting for centuries, should by their representatives in a New England city, the inheritance of the Puritans, that these should meet together, not to criticise, not to quarrel, not to denounce, not to hate, but to explain the value of a Faith, a form of which they did not hold, and a Faith also which does not respond to such an action unhappily at present, as it claims that it is the unique form of Christianity. Such a meeting is surely a sign of progress towards the Fellowship. And when we find other meetings, wherein the Hebrew Rabbi and the Christian Minister joined together similarly in their recognition of the one God and of His Worship ; when meeting after meeting is taking place in which so-called different religions are joining hands; when we read that in one of the great religious cities in India—Madura in the south—Musalmāns and Hindus met together in common public meeting and showed their Brotherhood by worshipping together and by exchanging tokens of love and trust, those two Faiths that often fight in Indian cities, those two Faiths that draw against each other, not only the weapons of the mind, but physical weapons by which they destroy each other's bodies, when they can meet in friendship in one of the most religious cities of India, surely the Fellowship of Faiths should not be so far off. And that is one of the things after which all who believe in Religion ought to strive, not to obliterate all differences, but for the recognition of their value. For that is one of the lessons that the very earnest religionist sometimes finds it difficult to learn, that differences should not be used as reasons for discord, causes of disharmony, but rather as enrichment of concord, just as notes, dissonant if played alone, in combination may form part of the most splendid chords in music. Beethoven, the great master of chords, thus used apparent dissonances, reconciled them and made those magnificent chords which perhaps more than anything else rendered his name immortal amongst the masters of that great art. We learn along that line of thought that wherever we find difference of opinion we should welcome it rather than dislike it, utilise it to learn some new aspect of the many-sided truth, utilise it so as to see from our brother's angle of vision as well as from our own. How little would you know of the shape of any globe, if all of you stood on one side and saw that alone! But the man who is facing north learns something from the man who is facing south, and he of the east from him of the west. Every different angle shows the unity of the apparently diverse truths. And in the Fellowship of Faiths we learn the value of our brother's religion by those differences, as well as by the great truths in which it is in accord with our own.

Passing from that, we may ask: What will be the next great feature of Religion in the New Civilisation? Knowledge, I think, rather than faith. Of that there are already signs. For that new race of which I have so often spoken is, as you know, developing a quality of Intuition, that which Bergson pointed out as more allied to instinct, inherited experience, than to the reasoning faculty in man. And you should take the inherited experience as the experience inherited from one life after another, until that inherited experience shows itself as the life-product which we call instinct, which does not need experience before it causes action, which does not need reasoning before it acts ; that is a life-preserving instinct in its lower forms ; it is a truth-revealing intuition as it shows itself beyond the reasoning faculty and intellect in man.

Now it is that particular faculty which is showing itself in the children of the new sub-race. And as we look forward into the future and the New Civilisation, which is to learn through centuries, remember, to build this up gradually, we begin to realise that the effect of this intuition in religion will be to transform religion from faith to knowledge. For intuition is a recognition of truth at sight, a recognition of truth that comes from the inner life and not from that life working through the external instruments of matter. The veil of subtle matter is only the garment of the soul, as intuition is developed ; and that may be developed, as you probably all know, in advance of its appearance in the ordinary evolution of man.

I spoke to you, I think, last year on that great Science which is called the Science of Yoga, the Union of the human Spirit with the Divine Life, self-consciously attained. That is won by using the laws of the mind as we know them, just as a gardener desiring to produce finer flowers uses the laws of natural growth in the vegetable kingdom, eliminating those that are against his aim, and using untrammelled those that produce the result that he desires in the flower which he sees in idea before he is able to produce it in vegetable matter. So it is we may work with mind as he works with the vegetable kingdom. We may develop from the resources of our own higher nature, drawing down by the laws in which we live, those higher powers that we desire to make available in the world, in which our great work is the spiritualising of matter and the making of matter the obedient servant and instrument of Spirit. So, if we choose, by hard work—and certainly by a good deal of what may be looked on as self-denial, save that nothing should be called by that name which leads us to the object which we will to achieve—we find it is possible to develop this intuition ahead of our race, and so to attain the knowledge of the eternal verities before that knowledge is reached by the average evolution, which only works slowly by the many workings and antagonism in

Nature; whereas evolution can work more rapidly when the antagonism in Nature; whereas evolution can work more rapidly when the antagonisms are eliminated and the powers we desire to develop are given their full scope. And in this Science of Yoga, there are, as you know, two distinct paths that were very well explained by Dr. Van der Leeuw during our late Convention, the path of the Mystic and the path of the Occultist. They both seek the same goal and they both seek to bring human consciousness to the Real and the Eternal—two names really only for one great truth. The Mystic finds it by plunging down into the depths of his own nature, putting aside everything that is passing, everything that is transient, everything that is temporary, using that phrase that Mr. Jinarājadāsa used a little time ago, the Sanskrit phrase, "Neti, neti—not this, not this," and so putting aside everything of the changing mind—'not this, not this" all the thoughts that flow or drift through the mind or are created by it—"not this, not this." Naught that changes is Eternal; naught that is transient is Real.

And so he who follows the Mystic path puts aside all these changing things, and they become to him indifferent. He does not seek pleasure, if it is not there. He does not reject it, if it is there. He takes the things as they come and go, the contacts of matter impermanent, with that higher indifference which rejects naught and desires naught, to which nothing is alien. And so, putting aside the transitory, one thing after another, that which is in the cravings of the body, that which is in the satisfactions of the emotions, that which is in the thoughts of the mind, he goes down into the depths of his own nature and finds at its very centre the Life of God. A solitary path, for none may help him in it. A path often misunderstood, because as he treads it he seems strange and self-contradictory. And when he finds his goal, silence is all that he can show to the outer world. Philosophy can explain itself, metaphysic can explain itself, all that the mind constructs by the mind can be understood. But that Supreme which is the Reality, that Supreme which is the Eternal, from that it is written the intellect sinks back silent, and in that silence the great truth is found. And so Mysticism can never be really taught to the end.

There are many things that can be done, many ways of thinking that can be learned, but when the God without reveals Himself to the God within, in that Union silence is the natural, the inevitable atmosphere. And so it is written in one of the Hebrew Scriptures that the day shall come when no man shall say to his brother: "Know the Lord," for all shall know Him from the least to the greatest—direct knowledge gained by each for himself.

The path of the Occultist differs very much from that, though it leads to the same goal. For men's temperaments are so different. The Occultist seeks to learn and to amass knowledge, so that by gaining knowledge all the powers of Nature may come within his grasp. So for the Occultist it is possible that he may take the left-hand path rather than the right. His road branches off into those two ways; the path of the Mystic is but one. For if there be in the Occultist the desire to possess, if he does not purge himself of all desire to possess, if he does not purge himself of all desire for aught but service, if he does not from his very heart tear out the root of selfishness and seek only the larger hope, the God in all, then his path is a path of terrible danger, and many are the wrecks, says H.P. Blavatsky, that strew that path.

But if he has learned that greatest of all lessons, the longing to serve the larger Life; if he only desires power that he may help the weak; righteousness that he may help the unrighteous; purity that he may help the impure; everything in order that he may give of himself to help his brother, then his path will climb the high mountain peak, and he will become one of the great helpers of the world. Along that path as well as along the Mystic feet have trodden of our own humanity. And in the New Civilisation as it grows and bads, there will be many Mystics and many Occultists in advance of their race. For wisdom is wanted to build the material fabric of that Civilisation as well as that union with the Divine which sheds the radiance of Divinity on the paths which are trodden by men. So we shall find in that New Civilisation the same great truths which are the heart of every religion, but we shall also find faith more and more replaced by knowledge, as I said. And so the evolution of the people shall be quickened and the darkness of ignorance shall pass more and more away from our world.

The condition of this growth is, I just said, Service. And the way to learn to love Service, to learn to find in it the one satisfaction that makes life worth living, is to strive to share with others the things that you already have. All that is best in you of knowledge, of art, of culture, of all these thins which make a great Civilisation, Religion will lead you to share them abundantly, until all have part of the gains that may have been made by the one. For what is that fine verse of one who was a great Occultist, the Apostle S. Paul, when he spoke of the poverty of the Christ; "Though He were rich, yet for our sakes. He became poor"? And the reason is given: in order that "by His poverty, we might be made rich". Gradually we learn as we strive to live the Christ-life, which is the life of the Spirit striving upwards towards his liberation, we learn that all the really precious things we have are the things that we can share with our fellow-men if they lack them. For to grow into "the full stature of the Christ," to become a Saviour of the world, means that you keep nothing back for yourself, but share all you have of precious and of rare with those that are around you. It means that you are continually pouring out all that you possess, and that when you have poured it out, there flows from above, from the inexhaustible reservoir of God Himself, into your empty hands there pours down the power of the God-head. And that is the aim of the Occultist, that he may spread that power over the whole of the world, that in silence and in secret he may send out thoughts, thoughts that are powers, in order that the Civilisation in which he lives may be saved from its dangers and helped to all that is good. For even in this stage of our world that can be done to some extent. This ought not to be a wonderful thing to you, nor a thing incredible, when you see how the ordinary scientist has found out that these powers largely exist, and that he can utilise the subtler powers that have been discovered in order to spread human thought and human knowledge.

Moreover, owing to the cyclic law by which the Rays come into power in due succession, the Ray known as the seventh—during the dominance of which there is a more widely spread communication between the physical and the subtler worlds than has existed for ages—is now coming into power once again. Later this, by the use of due and appropriate ceremonial, whether in the various religions, or in such ceremonies as have come down from the Ancient Mysteries of Egypt and Chaldea, of which fragments are found in different Masonic Rites, the inhabitants of the subtler worlds can co-operate with human beings, and both again by such co-operation increased power to aid and quicken evolution. In the religions, the Beings variously known as Angels, Devas, Shining Ones, are drawn to the ceremonies and take effective part in them, making them more potent for the helping of the human beings who perform them: and also taking from the human beings vibratory forces belonging to the physical world that the human beings naturally use, and that the inhabitants of the subtler worlds cannot themselves generate. This co-operation between angels and human beings is thus profitable to both, and you may remember that it is specially mentioned in the *Bhagavad-Gita* as bringing great good to the inhabitants of the different worlds of denser and subtler matter.

Most religions in their rituals appeal to the Angels or Devas, to join with the human worshippers, and it is obviously wrong to use invocations us a mere formality, not expecting that any response will be made by the Beings who are invoked. I have myself often observed how ready is the response, and how the atmosphere is changed when a real invocation with expectation of the due reply is made.

As more and more children are born into the world who are clairvoyant, the centre in the head which is developing and is the organ for clairvoyant vision will come more and more into use. Later still, the Angels will be more ready to densify their subtle bodies, and become thus visible to ordinary sight. Then the "Fellowship of Angels and Men" will again become a generally recognised part of human life, and their radiant happiness and beauty will shed their benignant influence on our earth.

Even now you can do much by the deliberate use of your thought-power. For what is your thought-power? It is a power that in your own brain can be measured by a galvanometer. And as you have more strength, as you have more power under your control, your galvanometer needle swings more strongly. And what you call thought becomes a galvanic current in your brain—for all these forces are linked together. The worlds are not separated really from one another, but interpenetrate each other, and all the finer forms of matter interpenetrate the coarser, as you may send gas through water, or water through a porous solid substance. Why, then, think it strange or incredible that human thought, trained and developed to a knowledge of the powers which that thought can command, can be used to improve the civilisation of the world, to get rid of its evils, and to strengthen all that is good?

And when many join together in combination to use that thought-power, when many congregating together work along the same lines in order that the power may be well directed, when the human will, which is our highest and divinest power, directs the way in which that current shall travel, do you wonder then that great changes may be made even by comparatively a few people using the power? That is the power used by the Inner Government of the world, subject to conditions. For all Nature's laws have to be obeyed. Knowledge is learned by obedience and not by disobedience to law. But if there were many of us, friends, who had the courage and the knowledge to tread this difficult path of the Occultist, then we might change the face of Europe and save it from the dangers that menace it toady. I do not know that there is time enough to do it. I do not know that there are enough of us, so we must put our strength together to accomplish as much of the purpose as we can; but in the New Civilisation which is dawning, in the New Civilisation that is beginning to appear, although still veiled and incomplete, in the Civilisation the power of thought will be acknowledged and the outer Civilisation will be shaped by the thoughts of the noblest and the best. And in order that we may share in laying its foundations, in order that our knowledge may not remain without its fruit, in order that we may learn something of what the future may be, and use our dawning powers to hasten its coming, shall not be found in this great land of Britain who will put, not only their country, but the world before their individual gain and interest, some who will throw away the transient and work in the Eternal, and in that way become helpers, a benediction to the world? That is the thought I will leave with you as the outcome of our thinking of the new Religion in the New Civilisation. The new Religion will be a religion of sacrifice prompted by love and guided by knowledge. The new Religion will have as one of its motroes the pyrase voiced by my friend William Stead and myself for a smaller effort: "The union of all who love in the service of all who suffer." That is one of the ideals that we shall strive to realise. For that we seek the powers by which we may help our race. And those who seek honestly shall find; those who give the fourfold knock, the knock of the Cross of Sacrifice on the closed door, to them that door will be opened; and by the foundations of the New Civilisation will be laid.

—Annie Besant